Broken *yet* Beloved

Broken
yet
Beloved

A
Pastoral
Theology
of the Cross

Sharon G. Thornton

CHALICE
PRESS
ST. LOUIS, MISSOURI

Cover art: "Imago Pietatis" by Giovanni Bellini, Alinaria/Art Resource, N.Y.
Cover design: Ross Sherman
Interior design: Elizabeth Wright
Art direction: Michael Domínguez

Visit Chalice Press on the World Wide Web at
www.chalicepress.com

10 9 8 7 6 5 4 3 2   06 07 08 09 10 11

Library of Congress Cataloging–in–Publication Data

Thornton, Sharon G.
    Broken yet beloved : a pastoral theology of the Cross / Sharon G. Thornton.
        p.   cm.
    Includes bibliographical references.
    ISBN-13: 978-0-827202-32-0
    ISBN-10: 0-827202-32-6 (alk. paper)
    1. Pastoral counseling. 2. Church and social problems. 3. Pastoral theology. 4. Suffering–Religious aspects–Christianity.   I. Title.
BV4012.2 .T53   2002
253.5–dc21   2001006456

Printed in the United States of America

Dedicated to
the San Francisco Network Ministries
Glenda Hope
The memory of Scott Hope
The men, women, and children of the Tenderloin

Contents

Acknowledgments

A book represents a community of people, and this one is no exception. The ideas presented here were first tested in a small writing group at Pacific School of Religion in Berkeley, California, with Jeffrey Kuan, Mary Donovan Turner, and Joseph Driskill. Jane Maynard and Jean Heriot read drafts of the first chapters, as did Susan Harlow and Randy Walker. My colleague at Andover Newton Theological School, Brita Gill Austern, read the entire manuscript and offered insightful comments and tremendous support. Margaret Benefiel offered companionship and a quiet place for writing at her home in Glouster, Massachusetts. Rosalie Romano listened to my first thoughts and encouraged me to put pen to paper.

I am grateful to the students who entered into conversation with me on many of the themes that comprise this book, particularly Janet Gear, who shares my respect and admiration for Dorothee Soelle. I am indebted to the various communities I have been privileged to serve that have deepened my commitment to the wedding of pastoral care and social justice, especially Christ Church of Chicago (United Church of Christ) and the San Francisco Network Ministries to whom this work is dedicated. My spouse, Fumitaka Matsuoka, is an ongoing source of joy and inspiration. He is my chief critic and "in-house" consultant. My children, Douglas Todd Cole, his spouse Marcie Sims, Traci Cole, and her spouse David Haygood, have given their support in countless ways. Jon L. Berquist has been a fabulous editor, patient and wise in his suggestions. This work is a better product because of his careful attention to form and details.

In the end all books have limitations, and this one is no exception. I accept full responsibility and offer these pages as an invitation for ongoing dialogue. Where there are ideas worth developing, let them continue to grow. Where there are thoughts worth discarding, let them go.

Introduction

Brokenness is not just that which is to be fixed but also the very path toward wholeness.[1]

GARY GUNDERSON

This is a book about suffering. "[We] are born to trouble just as sparks fly upward" (Job 5:7) and cannot escape it. Suffering seems to be our birthright, a part of what it means to be a human being. As the author of Job proves, the reality of suffering tests and pierces the depths of our souls and is unavoidable. At the same time, not all suffering is inevitable, and some suffering need never be at all, particularly the wounds we collectively inflict on people over time in our society both intentionally and through our indifference to one another. These "historical injuries" to people who experience things such as interracial animosity, gender discrimination, and class division, as well as those injuries imposed by wars and genocide, challenge us the most, and until recently have been addressed the least by pastoral theologians. This is a book about suffering, particularly historically imposed suffering.

Suffering takes so many different forms, not the least of which is the failure of a dream. The American Dream to build a society that succeeds where others have not has failed many of its citizens. The "Life, liberty and the pursuit of happiness" dream of our founders has become an empty dream and even a nightmare for a growing number of people. The belief

---

[1]Gary Gunderson, *Deeply Woven Roots: Improving the Quality of Life in Your Community* (Minneapolis: Fortress Press, 1997), 123.

1

in the ability to prosper through hard work, and a trust in something vaguely defined as "progress," is experienced as pain for a large number of people who work and still do not prosper. In truth and in practice, progress means profit. And the ability to profit in a market economy is seen as a sign of virtue and the measure of success. When some cannot compete, they are seen as failures, personally and socially. They become the ones who struggle to survive on the margins of society, ignored and despised. They become invisible and silent, their voices largely absent from our theories and practices of care and our communities of faith. Many of these injuries are brought about by forces of economic and societal injustice and are seen as objectives of the prophetic ministry of the church, but until recently they have not been the focus of pastoral care. This is a book about suffering, including the suffering brought on by of the loss of a dream, and our place in it.

Robert McAfee Brown had historical suffering in mind when he said, "When we hear the cry, 'I'm hurting' we must take it seriously."[2] He wrote these words a little more than thirty years ago when he introduced liberation theology to North America. They are still relevant today. He wrote to signal that for theology to have any real authority and meaning, it must begin with the cry of suffering in our midst. His words were meant to unsettle us, so we would stop, listen, and see with more compassion than ever before all the people who are suffering and whose anguish is not assuaged. When we hear the cry "I am hurting," we are to listen with a deep and focused attention, especially to those who have become broken not simply by chance. We are to listen precisely because their cries critique the ways we live our faith and do theology when our eyes and ears are diverted elsewhere–anywhere but the circumstances of their despair.

But even when we look away, the cries of those who have been exploited or abandoned will not be silenced, except by death–and even in death the "stones will cry out" (Hab. 2:11) The stones will "hold their place." They will trip us when we walk past without noticing. Or as Dorothee Soelle says, "The victims of earlier times are with us and their unheard cries are still waiting for an answer."[3] There is no place to hide–for long– from the voices calling out from their suffering and affliction. Their voices, the stones beneath their feet, the winds that carry their memories, provide the only starting place, as Brown suggests, for a pastoral theology that is credible today. If pastoral theologians are to speak convincingly at the beginning of this twenty-first century, we must attend to the cries of the suffering in our midst in new and critical ways.

---

[2]Robert McAfee Brown, "Liberation Theology: Paralyzing Threat or Creative Challenge" in *Mission Trends No. 4: Liberation Theologies*, ed. Gerald H. Anderson and Thomas F. Stransky, C.S.P. (New York: Paulist Press; Grand Rapids: Eerdmans, 1979), 20.

[3]Dorothee Soelle, *Choosing Life* (Philadelphia: Fortress Press, 1981), 58.

This is a book about suffering, but it is also a book about hope. And strangely, one of the theological places for discovering authentic hope is the cross. The cross names suffering for what it is and can be a means for radically critiquing all attempts to camouflage, minimize, or distort the truth of its reality. The cross names reality and unmasks false optimism in all its forms. It is a timely faith perspective for pastoral theology and one that can offer a response to the cry "I'm hurting" by taking it seriously.

The recent reemergence of the cross in political theologies of Europe, the liberation theologies of Latin American, South African, and Asian countries, and the liberation and political theologies emerging in North America are challenging any and all dominant theologies of glory–progress, optimism, success–in whatever form they take. Theologies that bend their trust toward a growing economy, the melding of church and social structures that burden and strangle large portions of God's creation, and triumphal ideologies that justify the systems that keep oppressive social structures in place must be dismantled. Even theologies that elevate human will and potential to an exaggerated level must go. The cross, interpreted politically, challenges us to cast our work in a different mold. It calls us not to glory but to a harder way, one that dares to name the historical conditions in which we live. As such, the cross is critical to a pastoral theology as it seeks to participate in the vision of a new reality, a creation marked by just communities of compassion and meaning open to the dawning realm of God–a healed world, to which the cross points. This work draws on the growing body of political theologies of the cross to inform an alternative pastoral paradigm that can bring compassion and justice together in order to address the cries of suffering people today.

The first chapter introduces my initial exploration of historical suffering for pastoral care and my discovery of a political theology of the cross for addressing it. Chapters 2 and 3 give a brief overview of the liberal paradigm that has governed the development of modern pastoral theology and care, and its limitations. Chapters 4 and 5 introduce an alternative faith posture based on a political reading of the cross. Representative biblical, historical, and contemporary expressions are offered. Chapter 6 is a transitional chapter that begins to show some of the implication of theology of the cross for pastoral theology by reintroducing the language of love to our theory and practice. Chapters 7 and 8 continue an alternative approach to pastoral theology by reinterpreting the classical pastoral functions–guiding, healing, sustaining, and reconciling–from the perspective of the political cross as solidarity, empowerment, and the work of justice toward more compassionate and humane communities. Chapter 9 offers a concrete example of a community of faith, the San Francisco Network Ministries, that practices an alternative pastoral care from the perspective of the political cross. Here the traditional metaphor of the shepherd is augmented by a communal understanding of the body of Christ as the suffering righteous

One, where care and justice go hand in hand. Chapter 10 outlines practices of care based on a communal understanding of the way of the cross.

This work contributes to the current conversations in pastoral theology that are addressing social and cultural issues for theory and practice. Like others, I am proposing that pastoral theology utilize the tools of social and political analysis to shed new light on the conditions and contours of human suffering that have been historically ordered. Making the connections between personal suffering and political structures visible means they can no longer remain hidden and obscured, capable of being reduced to individual problems alone. Bringing the reality of historical injuries to the center of our work today is not only necessary but also indispensable for healing in our communities.

However, I want to be clear that this book does not attempt to answer the age-old question, "Why does a good God permit suffering?" nor does it offer to explain the fact of human affliction. The aim of this work is more modest. It seeks to respond to the cry of modern women, men, and children by offering a perspective from which we can attempt to see more clearly the depth and scope of their questions for our time and place. It is my belief that bringing these questions into the foreground of pastoral theology, from a faith perspective of the political cross to inform human reason, will shed more light on the conditions that cause and perpetuate suffering. It is hoped that this will inch us a little closer to a true foundation of hope for our aching and yearning world. As we work together to eliminate the causes of suffering where we can and stand vigil with people when nothing else can be done, we will find ways to communicate clearly, "You are broken and yet beloved."

To this end, this work is not simply a theology to be applied to pastoral situations. It is not a functional theology in this sense at all. Rather, it is an overture to enter a theology that seeks to participate in and be faithful to "God's transfiguration of human existence."[4] It is to this end that I begin with the confession that the most profound expression of this hope for transformation is the political cross of Christ. Here, the pain of God interprets human suffering. Here, in the truth of the cross, where the cry of the tortured and suffering righteous One rent the temple veil, is where hope for justice and healing in the divine-human community begins.

---

[4]Arthur C. McGill, *Suffering: A Test of Theological Method* (Philadelphia: Westminster Press, 1982), 122. McGill points out that the very act of theology is involved with this process in the world. He stresses that it is a mistake to conceive of "thinking about God's love" as something that needs to be made practical and relevant, as though the very struggle were of some secondary nature.

CHAPTER
ONE

Broken, Not by Chance

When we hear the cry, "I'm hurting," we must take it seriously.[1]

ROBERT MCAFEE BROWN

Early in my ministry I worked as a chaplain in the emergency room of the community hospital in the city where I was living. It was an urban hospital located in the heart of town, supplied with all the latest medical equipment that modern technology had to offer at the time. It had become an emblem of hope for local residents who were without much to look forward to in their rapidly changing community. The fire department's emergency crews stopped there first when there was a life-or-death situation. The police brought in those who needed medical attention before they were booked or put in jail. It was a powerful and visible beacon on the landscape that drew the problems of the city to itself like a magnet.

The hospital functioned with an unofficial open-door policy. Since these were the days before managed health care, no one was turned away because of inability to pay for services. Many who lived in the area ended up using the emergency room as a drop-in clinic, where they could bring their various ailments as well as their daily troubles. These were folks who had very

[1]Robert McAfee Brown, "Liberation Theology: Paralyzing Threat or Creative Challenge," in *Mission Trends No. 4: Liberation Theologies,* ed. Gerald H. Anderson and Thomas F. Stransky, C.S.P. (New York: Paulist Press; Grand Rapids: Eerdmans, 1979), 20.

limited resources, and only a few had private doctors or medical insurance. Most were just hanging on to their lives by their fingernails. Over time some of them became known as "regulars," because they seemed to arrive at the emergency room on an almost predictable schedule. They were ones who were routinely transferred to the psychiatric unit after their initial examinations.

My experiences of attending to these people and watching them struggle to keep body and soul together had a profound effect on me. Their pain was intense. It reached beyond my understanding and ran deeper than my ability to provide relief. I also found the forms of pastoral care I had been taught and the theories that informed them woefully inadequate for addressing their particular needs.

The models of pastoral care I was trained in described the chaplain's role as a "ministry of presence." I learned to appreciate this presence as best expressed through my ability to show empathy for the life situations of the people I met. This meant I would demonstrate my emotional availability by listening to and accepting the feelings of those who were willing to tell me about their lives. I learned to respond in nonjudgmental ways and encourage people to express in words, tears, or shouts whatever it was they were experiencing. This, I believed, most of the time, would lead them to new insights about themselves that could lead to their healing.

Yet as I got to know the people who kept coming back to the hospital, I began to wonder about the adequacy of this orientation for responding to their hurts and ills. Many of the men and women who were admitted to the psychiatric unit were street people. They were the ones who held out their paper cups to moviegoers at the entrance of the local theater. They were those who aimlessly roamed the sidewalks whispering, "Spare change?" as they looked for temporary places to lay their heads. A disproportionate number of these people were African American or Hispanic. Many were women. Too many were children. Without exception, all were poor. When they walked through the emergency room doors, many of them were incoherent, talking to no one in particular and everyone at once. To the last one they were in need of a shower or a bath. It was not uncommon that a woman had been physically abused, and often she had been raped, perhaps repeatedly. I began to ask new questions about the meaning of suffering and the purpose of pastoral care as I became aware of all the different forces that combined to ravage these men, women, and children.

After I had been working at the hospital for a while, I began to notice a recurring pattern. Once these folks were admitted to the psychiatric unit, it wasn't long before many of them began to look and sound very different from what they did when they first came to the emergency room. It took a couple of weeks, sometimes longer, sometimes less. But within a relatively short period of time many of them seemed like anyone that you might meet in the local grocery store or standing in line to use the ATM machine.

Perhaps the human attention, the talking and listening and the experience of "feeling heard" bolstered a sense of well-being and self-confidence for these men and women–for a while. But I began to wonder how much of the change that seemed to occur within such a short stay in the hospital was really stimulated by the drug and talk therapy they received and how much was actually due to having a safe environment and a daily routine. In the hospital they at least had a clean bed to sleep in instead of a park bench, a place to bathe and wash their hair, plus three well-balanced (however tasteless) meals a day. Yet a few weeks after they were discharged, many would return in the same condition they were in when they were first admitted to the emergency room, and the whole cycle would begin again.

I began to ask myself, What does pastoral care mean when it is expressed inside the hospital through listening and empathy, while on the other side of the door a whole different set of realities is impacting the lives of these people? What does health even look like in a broken society? The feminist expression of the early 1970s, "the personal is political," began to take on a different meaning for me in this community hospital. It prompted me to ask about the social realities that influenced the personal experiences of the people I worked with here. Their struggle to survive on the streets certainly said something about the public policies and social conditions that helped put them there in the first place. And these same social realities contributed to bringing them to the hospital. This emerging political awareness became a defining turning point for me. While others have also reached this conclusion, it was in this particular setting that I first began to realize the need for pastoral care to move beyond its intra-psychic preoccupation with the individual to include the person embedded in social, cultural, and economic settings. When social and political realities make people "sick," they, too, need to be recognized and engaged as legitimate concerns for pastoral care in order to foster human wholeness and well-being.

I still appreciate the expression "the personal is political" and think it continues to carry value. But it has become so familiar and been applied so indiscriminately, and sometimes inappropriately, over the years that some caution needs to be taken when it is used today. Since this phrase was first coined, at times it has been used in ways that obscure its public intention and hence its political implication. Initially, "the personal is political" was introduced to say that personal experience is crucial for social analysis and that social analysis better enables us to see the complexity of personal experience. The difficulty arises when the political is collapsed into the personal, thus minimizing the mutual critique between personal experience and social analysis. When the political becomes overly identified or even identical with the personal, any understanding about where political activity takes place becomes truncated, and attempts to foster public and communal interactions toward a mutual construal of justice break down into efforts primarily aimed at satisfying personal needs.[2] When this happens, the capacity for critical judgment risks becoming lost in the rhetoric of self-fulfillment. Whereas pastoral theologians have tended to collapse theology into psychology, resulting in a restricted form of self-realization, our secular counterparts have been vulnerable to jettisoning the political and the personal in ways that generate a narrow vision of self-enhancement. In a culture that thrives on pop psychology and self-help books, both pastoral theologians and secular social critics need to be on guard against tendencies that foster constricted views of self and world in their respective disciplines. It is important to recognize when and where this happens as well as who benefits and who loses when it does.

Limits of Pastoral Care Literature

Until recently the literature on pastoral care offered little to help address the particular anguish of the people I was encountering in my ministry. Modern pioneers in the field such as Seward Hiltner, Wayne Oates, Carroll Wise, and others provided valuable wisdom on matters of personal growth, the meaning of wholeness, and the importance of insight. However, the historical contexts and social and economic realities that contribute to the hardship and misery of people were rarely discussed. And the political conditions that militate against wholeness were not talked about at all. These were not their questions. Their theories were conceived and practiced within academic settings among persons that were primarily white, middle class, and normally male. Not surprisingly, the special circumstances of people who are poor and marginalized were largely absent from their writings.

Furthermore, the imaginations of these pastoral theologians were kindled by the curative promises of clinical psychology, and they were eager to draw on these sources for pastoral care. Even Seward Hiltner, who recognized the importance of reclaiming theology as a rightful partner for the future of pastoral care, relied heavily on the practical wisdom and theoretical foundations of psychology. Drawn in particular to Carl Rogers, Hiltner adopted Rogers' optimistic view of human understanding and the individual person's ability to generate well-being from within him- or herself. From this perspective political, social, and other environmental influences were minimized. The limitation of personal insight was not an issue for these scholars during the mid-twentieth century, when trust in human potential for addressing the ills of hurting people was at its peak. In-depth social analysis of the multiple causes of human misery and the enormous toll on society were not seen as being within the domain of pastoral care.

---

[2]For a discussion of "mutually constructed ground of experience" see the work of anthropologists Brian Moeran and Paul Rabinow, *Reflections on Fieldwork in Morocco* (Berkeley and Los Angeles: University of California Press, 1978), 39.

Because their focus was elsewhere, the power of external forces that contribute to human brokenness were all but ignored and thus were unavailable for comprehensive examination for pastoral theology.

By the mid 1970s, Charles Gerkin and Alastair Campbell began to emerge as two counter-voices to the over-reliance on psychology and its emphasis on individual healing. They drew attention to certain dimensions of crisis in modern life that demanded additional interpretive frameworks for addressing them. They also called on pastoral care to more intentionally reclaim theology in order to address the needs of people. Yet even they paid little attention to the interrelationship between a person's experience of suffering and the societal and historical circumstances that guaranteed its continuance. This was particularly true of their earlier writings.

By the early 1980s, however, societal concerns were starting to be taken more seriously. In his groundbreaking work *The Relational Self,* published in 1982, Archie Smith, Jr., brought sociology into conversation with psychology and the Black Church experience as a way to make connections between personal problems and larger social issues. Building on Smith's work, in 1992 Larry Graham wrote *Care of Persons, Care of Worlds* using a psychosystems approach to pastoral care in order to attend to the ways social systems affect people. And in 1995 Rodney Hunter and Pamela Couture co-authored *Pastoral Care and Social Conflict,* emphasizing the importance of the social context for pastoral care and theology.[3] The works of Pamela Couture, *Blessed Are the Poor?* and her most recent book, *Seeing Children, Seeing God,* focus on the interface between public policy and pastoral care as they address the specific circumstances of women and children who are affected by the decisions we make that govern our lives.[4]

Fortunately, today there is a growing movement within the field of pastoral theology that takes the context of pastoral care seriously by recognizing people in their social and cultural settings.[5] These scholars are asking hard questions about the roles of culture, gender, race, and class. My work joins with these and others who are starting to focus on the need to view people relationally within their entire personal, social, cultural, and historical environments, realizing that healing in one area will not be

---

[3]Archie Smith, Jr., *Relational Self: Ethics and Therapy from a Black Church Perspective* (Nashville: Abingdon Press, 1982). Larry Kent Graham builds on this work in his book *Care of Persons, Care of Worlds: A Psychosystems Approach to Pastoral Care and Counseling* (Nashville: Abingdon Press, 1992). More recently Pamela D. Couture and Rodney J. Hunter edited a volume: *Pastoral Care and Social Conflict* (Nashville: Abingdon Press, 1995).

[4]Pamela D. Couture, *Blessed Are the Poor? Women's Poverty, Family Policy, and Practical Theology* (Nashville: Abingdon Press, 1991), and *Seeing Children, Seeing God* (Nashville: Abingdon Press, 2000).

[5]See representative works: Christie Cozad Neuger and James Newton Poling, eds., *The Care of Men* (Nashville: Abingdon Press, 1997); Charles Gerkin, *An Introduction to Pastoral Care* (Philadelphia: Fortress Press, 1998); Jeanne Stevenson Moessner, ed., *Through the Eyes of Women* (Philadelphia: Fortress Press, 1998); Bonnie J. Miller-McLemore and Brita L. Gill-Austern, eds., *Feminist and Womanist Pastoral Theology* (Nashville: Abingdon Press, 1999).

effective without healing in all spheres. Yet even as this orientation begins to take hold, there is still a need to keep challenging and deepening our inquiry through theological perspectives that ask the hard faith questions about human brokenness and the possibility for renewing our lives together. My present work seeks to explore a theological lens that can help reveal more fully this important landscape for pastoral theology and communities of faith, particularly as we engage contemporary experiences of social and historical injuries.

Held by a Slender Thread

As I worked in hospital settings and as I moved into other urban settings, including the local church, I became haunted by the faces and experiences of people who endured some of the most unimaginable suffering. They were the faces of people living daily with the constant pain resulting from historical injuries. They included faces of people who were, in the words of the poet Theodore Roethke, "living at odds with circumstance." They were ordinary men, women, and children who bore the marks of existentially given pain invading their lives. Many times I doubted that I had much to offer those who looked into my eyes with question marks and fear in theirs. I wondered what kept some people going, and I continue to marvel at the unexplainable tenacity of the human spirit under extraordinary conditions.

And yet I also heard something from the patients I met and parishioners I have served that is only hinted at in the pastoral care literature. It is a posture of faith that seems to surface when people are facing the extremities of life. One woman in particular became an unforgettable soul who profoundly influenced my budding pastoral theology as she shared her faith with me. She was a patient I met at a large research and teaching hospital on the campus of a major university. I will call her Mrs. Clark.

Mrs. Clark was an unsophisticated woman, rather plain and unassuming. But she was also forthright, and she spoke in a very direct manner with anyone who came into her hospital room. She didn't waste words and talked about her faith in very matter-of-fact terms. Her faith was vital and alive, as inseparable from her daily life as was her breathing, her eating, her picking up the soap to wash her hands. Her illness was not fatal; neither was it curable. She knew that she would have to live a long time, perhaps indefinitely, with many restrictions and ongoing pain. One day I asked her, "What gives you such courage, especially with the kind of joy you radiate?" She looked me straight in the eye and said to me, "Honey! If Jesus could stand the cross, I can live with this. I know my Lord lives in me and walks with me every step of the way."

I must say I was a little taken aback. Not many people call me "Honey!" And her manner of talking about her faith was very different from the way my more reserved Anglican upbringing had prepared me to express mine. Even so, I was touched by her frankness, and I paused to listen to her, really listen to her, perhaps for the first time. To my surprise, I began to hear something in what she was saying that I had not expected to hear. She was telling me about how absolutely important her faith was to her as she struggled with her illness. It may have been then, as I understood what she was actually saying to me, that I also began to hear what other patients were telling me as well. I realized that on many occasions I had been passing over significant things that were begging to be heard. Many times I thought I was attending to a patient's "real needs" by keeping away from their religious language and rephrasing it in other words. But, in truth, I was avoiding what they were saying to me. Instead, I was paying attention to comments that fit more readily into the clinical model of listening I had been trained in. I had been taught to question straightforward religious confessions because they might be signs of "denial," ploys to avoid what was really at stake, or ways to lessen the severity of a situation. Thanks to Mrs. Clark I began to question my own immediate suspicion of these expressions of faith.

Mrs. Clark invited me to hear and believe what she and others were saying when they told me that Jesus' agony on the cross was a genuine source of solace and hope to them. She helped me hear their statements as something other than fatalistic resignation. I didn't need to hear them as merely a denial of the grave situations they were facing. I started to hear that for some patients the cross had come to represent a source of courage and strength that helped them face what they were going through. Somehow, without discouraging them, the cross spoke to them about the real pain they were experiencing without pretending to make it better. The cross helped them see their suffering as something that could not easily be "gotten over," if ever resolved at all. The cross "told it like it was" and let them accept their own situations as they were. In a way, the cross allowed them to embrace their suffering without simply giving in to it as if it were their "fate." The people I met who accepted their experiences in this way were not passive; in fact, they became active participants in their care and decisions about their lives. They were realistic as they faced the difficult circumstances that were theirs, finding some ability to do so through a faith appropriation of the cross.

I remember a woman with incurable cancer who said to me, after her doctor finally told her that she would probably not live out the year, "I am incredibly sad, but now I finally have hope. At least I know what I'm dealing with." She was holding a cross, and she looked at it and said, "Finally I know what this means." By having her reality named in all its harshness, the cross came to represent for her the real possibility of hope in the midst of what could have been a situation of hopeless desperation. It represented a turning point for her at her impasse between expectancy and despair. I heard her difficult confession of faith become a source of confidence as she looked to her uncertain future with trust. Hers was a trust devoid of any trace of optimism. It was a fragile trust. But I sensed that in the midst of the heartrending reality her doctor named, the cross represented courage and seeded hope in her, helping her lean into an open future.

What is it about Jesus and the cross that speaks to people so deeply in their situations of suffering? This is not merely a clinical question; it is a theological inquiry. I have discovered this expression of faith time and again in the various settings in which I have worked. People who have been formed in the Christian faith do draw on the cross as they struggle to make meaning of the painful experiences in their lives. Not all people of faith do this, of course. And not all people who draw on the cross do so in a healthy way. But still, there is what Douglas John Hall calls a "thin tradition"[6] that threads its way through communities of faith, offering a perspective on what it means to experience ultimate limitation, failure, humiliation, torture, abandonment, and loss. This "thin tradition" of the cross, about which I will say more later, "holds" people, offering them new ways of seeing, believing, and living into a future.

Shadows of the Cross Give Horizons of Hope

In hospitals, churches, community settings, and classrooms, I have met people who identify with the suffering of Jesus, or more accurately, people who allow Jesus' suffering to identify theirs. Because of their faith, they believe that Jesus understands them precisely because of his suffering on the cross. In the cross of Jesus they seem to see the depth and the magnitude of suffering that no other source of meaning provides for them. In the cross they even discover an expression of suffering that embraces their own. A question that most intrigues me is, What moves these people from this awareness and identification with the suffering of Jesus to an experience of new life? What gives them that sense of their life being given back to them, often accompanied by gratitude and joy? Another way of saying this is, How do they move through death to resurrection? Although it has usually been patients or parishioners going through personal travail that has evoked these questions, they also apply to the companions who wait and watch with these people.

I remember a young mother whose six-year-old daughter was dying from a brain tumor. She stayed with her child, slept with her child, bathed and fed her, stroked her, and comforted her. Her total attention was focused on her child as she sang to her and rocked her hour after hour. When she finally died, the mother was understandably distraught, and it seemed as though her tears would never cease flowing. She had stayed with her daughter. She had loved her completely. And she grieved mightily. I thought

---

[6]Douglas John Hall, *Lighten Our Darkness: Toward an Indigenous Theology of the Cross* (Philadelphia: Westminster Press, 1976), 113–15. Hall used the term *thin tradition* to talk about the cross of Christ in history. He sees this as a way of proclaiming the possibility of hope without shutting out the data of despair.

about her often during the weeks and months after she left the hospital. Nearly a year later she returned to volunteer on the pediatric unit and offer support to other families.

As I think of that young mother now, she reminds me of the women at the foot of the cross when Jesus was crucified. They, too, faced the stark and hollow experience of death. They, too, had their lives torn asunder. What motivated them to stay there? Why didn't they just give up? Why didn't they hang their heads in defeat, believing their lives had been tricked by a cruel hoax, angry that their trust had been betrayed through the horrific death of their friend? How did they endure the incredible void that must have threatened to devour their last shreds of life? And then the next question, Why was it that they were the first ones who were able to witness the resurrection? Yes, I think of these friends of Jesus, and that young mother became one of them when she returned to the pediatric unit to carry out her volunteer work with other children and their families

I searched for how this faith orientation from the perspective of the cross was represented in the field of pastoral theology. I found it alluded to at times but not developed. I began to explore other forms of theology and discovered a wealth of information. For example, I found political and pastoral theologians in Europe such as Elizabeth and Jürgen Moltmann, Dorothee Soelle, and Johann Baptist Metz articulating interpretations of the cross to address the ongoing pastoral challenges to Germany in the aftermath of World War II. Contextual theologian Douglas John Hall, feminist theologian Rosemary Radford Ruether, and womanist theologian Emilie Townes reference the cross to engage various personal, social, and political needs in North America. The cross figures prominently in pioneering work of liberation theologian Gustavo Gutierrez, who brings his involvement with people living in the slum area of Lima to his pastoral writings on spiritual practices and political protest. Other South American liberation theologians such as Jon Sobrino and Leonardo Boff also develop theologies of the cross to address the pastoral needs of their communities. Alan Bozak and Desmond Tutu bring the cross to South Africa's conflicts and wounds, and Kosuke Koyama from Japan, C. S. Song from Taiwan, and Andrew Park from Korea have reintroduced the cross to address needs of people in their contexts. Andrew Park's political and theological treatment of *han* is particularly meaningful as a pastoral tool for Korean Christians.

These theologians are persuasive because they stay close to the experience of the people they are engaged with and reflect a deep commitment to their well-being. Their theologies have a stake in the lives and common struggles of their people. Some have even risked their lives as a result of their commitments. They use social and cultural analysis to offer interpretations of the cross that speak about personal suffering and also the troubles facing whole communities within their historical and political situations. Through their political and pastoral interpretations of the cross they link pastoral care with struggles for justice and human dignity. Many of these authors even suggest that those who experience injustice or endure unmerited pain are intimately related to a pain in the very heart of God.

Because many of these theologians risk their lives and know the immediacy of terror through their solidarity with people, their writings give the cross more than the polite or embarrassed "liturgical nod" it often gets from comfortable churchgoers on their way to Easter Sunday services. Instead, the cross is planted squarely in the cauldron of political unrest and personal devastation, revealing the crucified people of today. It is positioned where people name their harsh realities and rise up against the intolerable circumstances under which they live. In this way the cross becomes a source for critical theology as it interrogates the meaning of suffering for all people. It frames personal suffering and amplifies the cry for justice.

Anchored in the cross, theology now speaks about the nature of God's entry into the sphere of human history from the perspective of the crucifixion. As Walter Wink says,

> As the Crucified, Jesus thus identifies with every victim of torture, incest, or rape; with every peasant caught in the cross fire of enemy patrols; with every single one of the forty thousand children who die each day of starvation...with every mother or father who cradles the lifeless body of a courageous son or daughter; with every Alzheimer's patient slowly losing the capacity of recognition. In Jesus we see the suffering of God with and in suffering people.[7]

The basic point of this theological orientation is to reveal to us the One who meets us in the midst of our suffering and pain. It is from this perspective that the resurrection is understood in terms of a certain tenacity of life, directed toward new life marked by liberation and reconciliation. As pastoral theology attends to radical forms of suffering and the complex interrelationship between personal experience and societal and historical circumstances, the cross speaks louder than ever and challenges the adequacy of the clinical assumptions of the past for addressing contemporary needs.

From a Christian perspective, *cross-resurrection* is the central symbol of the way things are and the way things will be. It engages all of life's hopes and certainties, failures and ambiguities–and opens up everything. When interpreted from its political standpoint, this core belief offers new and challenging pastoral perspectives on the complex experiences of modern

---

[7]Walter Wink, *Engaging the Powers: Discernment and Resistance in a World of Domination* (Minneapolis: Fortress Press, 1992), 142.

life. It brings the pastoral and prophetic aspects of care together in critical ways, revealing the fundamental relationship between personal well-being, political realities, and pastoral concerns. Thus, it becomes a critical lens for viewing both personal ills and public life. It is my strong belief that bringing this particular political interpretation of the cross into conversation with pastoral theology makes it possible for the circumstances of contemporary suffering and the hope for relief to be more fully addressed.

The Personal Is Political Is Pastoral

The prophetic and political implications of faith have given rise to powerful expressions of resistance to the violation of people all over the world. In many cases these movements have also been seen as pastoral. Here in the United States, African American churches inspired the civil rights movement and offered prophetic leadership in a pastoral way to a whole nation. Many of us remember Martin Luther King, Jr., who looked deeply into our wounded nation to chastise our distorted way of living. He touched our deep longing for healing and offered us a different way. "I have a dream," he said as he named personal pain, advocated for political action, and brought a pastoral vision that still has power today. For King and others, the cross has figured prominently as a religious and political symbol to provide pastoral wisdom and hope. Today, church and community leaders continue to make connections between internalized racism and African American people's struggles with depression, addiction, and low self-esteem, and they seek pastoral as well as political measures to address these struggles. The connection between black suffering and white privilege reveals the *relational* nature involved in these political issues, indicating another pastoral application of "the personal is political." African American churches and their leaders have modeled a prophetic understanding of "the pastoral is political" by being forthright, vocal, and compassionate in forging communal ways for combating the evil and abusive forces of racism.

The women's movement here and elsewhere is another contemporary example where the personal and political have found pastoral expression in communities of faith—even as some within them struggle mightily. Some believe that the male-dominated church can change to honor the experience of women, welcome their full participation through ordination, encourage their public leadership, and respond to their needs. Others are convinced that this will never happen. A growing number of women are recognizing how the historical practices of the church are linked with the social reality of violence against women and are moving outside the institutional church to cultivate alternative spiritual practices. In response to these forces, New Testament scholar Elisabeth Schüssler Fiorenza helps ground Christian communities to resist the ecclesial and societal failures and to work toward new and just social-political relationships. According to Schüssler Fiorenza, the political and social dimensions of Jesus' ministry were critical for early followers and central to the development of their communities and early missionary movements.[8] From the beginning, the political was linked with the pastoral needs of communities. In this light, she criticizes any interpretation of the cross that does not take the political concreteness of Jesus' crucifixion into account.

The growing movement for gay, lesbian, bisexual, and transgendered persons also demonstrates places where the personal, political, and pastoral meet. The recent horrific and galvanizing image of Matthew Shepard lashed to a fence and left to die has reminded some Christians of another man nailed to a tree and left hanging until dead. Perhaps no other single event has so brought the gay and lesbian and straight communities together across lines of difference to combat homophobic forces in the church and society at large. This personal crime perpetrated against a mother's son has evoked a public outcry awakening the political nature of this atrocity. Pastoral outpourings have reminded many of us of the need for a prophetic response. However, as this emerging coalition gains political force in the wider society, conflicts still abound in various faith communities. Not all communities of faith are responding with compassion and hospitality. In light of this, some believers from both the gay and straight communities are committed to forming new churches, while others are working to revitalize and reform existing communities of faith. Still others are convinced that the church will continue to ignore or brutalize those who are "different" and therefore want no part of organized religion. All the same, forces are in motion that challenge the way we live as the political nature of personal suffering is revealed and addressed.

As long as race, class, gender, and sexual orientation are critical factors in our communities of faith, Ronald Thiemann says they are "rooted in social problems that are part of our common public life."[9] In this way the church and every aspect of its life, including pastoral care, are intimately linked to matters of public responsibility. If we agree with the historical record that says that healing is the aim of all pastoral care, we need to understand that healing must be addressed in both personal and public spheres, or else no healing in the truest sense can ever occur. As Walter Brueggemann says, "There are no personal issues that are not of a piece with the great public issues. To divide things up into prophetic and pastoral is to betray both."[10] This implies that as pastoral theology reunites with its prophetic legacy, it will become a public theology.

---

[8]Elisabeth Schüssler Fiorenza, *In Memory of Her: A Feminist Theological Reconstruction of Christian Origins* (New York: Crossroad, 1985), 188.

[9]Ronald F. Thiemann, *Constructing a Public Theology: The Church in a Pluralistic Culture* (Louisville, Ky.: Westminster/John Knox Press, 1991), 118.

[10]Walter Brueggemann, *Hopeful Imagination: Prophetic Voices in Exile* (Philadelphia: Fortress Press, 1986), 18.

The complex nature of contemporary suffering calls for this strong and clear reuniting of the pastoral and prophetic, which brings the focus back to Robert McAfee Brown's challenge to all theology: "When we hear the cry, 'I'm hurting,' we must take it seriously." A pastoral theology that begins with the anguish of this cry arising at the intersection of public and private life will find itself at the foot of the cross. There it will see the face of the One who endured excruciating personal suffering as a result of injustice and socially inflicted pain. When pastoral theology dares to look at this face, other faces and communities will be reflected back to us, and we will find ourselves engaged in many unexpected ways in the divine human web that weaves and binds us all into an incredibly complex quest for healing and new life. By attending to the personal as related to the public spheres of life, pastoral theology will be deepened and enabled to enrich the lives of people in the church and wider society.

Presence before the Cross

The implication of the political cross for North American pastoral theology means we cannot hide and cover our ears. We must listen to the cries of suffering in our own neighborhoods and hear what people are saying to us. Our listening needs to begin with the disenfranchised in our midst, giving a "preferential option," as liberation theologians claim. It needs to stay close to those who sense no end to the suffering that is theirs. This means we must listen to those who can no longer afford housing, to those who tell us that racial profiling by law enforcement officers is real, to our children who tell us that school is no longer a safe place for them to learn. This means we stay by the bedside of the one who can only groan and sigh when medical intervention no longer provides relief. When we listen, as we must, the cross will intensify the voices that have previously been muffled, ignored, or silenced outright in our culture and our textbooks. They call us back to the way of justice, compassion, and companionship firmly rooted in the Jewish and Christian traditions. They ask us to seek with them the repairing of our world and to remain faithful in the process; in these ways we can offer courage and hope in the face of adversity.

But the political cross does more than reveal the suffering of others. It challenges any of us who may be tempted to think that we are shielded from the harsh realities that many experience. It reveals that kind of thinking to be an illusion, a sham of such proportion that it denies the fullness of life and dims the possibility of a renewed future for us all.

From the perspective of the political cross, a ministry of presence begins to take on significantly broader meaning than the one-to-one model of pastoral care. Presence now becomes theologically active. It becomes an expression of communal life. It accents the interdependent nature of wholeness and well-being achieved through human solidarity. This expression of presence involves struggle and nonabandonment.

Yet can the cross be the symbol that illuminates our present age of suffering and hope? As Edward Farley reminds us, the deep symbols of our culture are in danger of no longer functioning to enliven and guide the life and meaning of our communities. Care must be taken to rethink this thin but powerful tradition in a way that captures our imagination toward something new. The cry of suffering that arises out of concrete historical and social causes begs for a reexamination of the cross that does not rely on individualistic interpretations or justify passivity and quietism. An alternative reading of the cross may help lead pastoral theology to participate more extensively in the divine human project of mending a world so desperately awaiting a healing touch.

The Cross Is a Stumbling Block

Then again, it might not be so easy to reintroduce pastoral theology to the cross. Many communities of faith may not welcome a political reading of the cross either. The cross is a powerful stumbling block just as it is a powerful source of courage and hope. Bishop Roy Sano of the United Methodist Church frequently points out the prominence of the "levitating cross" in Protestant churches in the United States. This is a cross that does not touch the ground. From on high it shines in glory as it reflects a golden radiance to worshipers. It beckons with a promise of eternal prosperity and triumph. In this form the cross is a symbol that captures most clearly the pervasive spirituality of North America—optimism. Douglas John Hall has called the United States the "officially optimistic society." Optimism promises much, but delivers little. The gilded golden cross is not the foundation of Christian hope.

Compounding our unexamined confidence in success that the gold cross represents is the mounting challenge of pluralism here in the United States. There are competing claims being made on our values, resources, and time, fueling a climate of moral opposition that is spreading through our political and ecclesial bodies across the conservative-liberal spectrum. We hear it in the public rhetoric of both our major political parties. We see it in our conflict and competition over public goods. While some people are concerned about animal rights, others care about preserving old-growth forests, and still others advocate for keeping abortion legal, and so forth. We lack overarching issues that bring us together. What some of us want is not what all of us desire. Often, then, we rely on short-term solutions for addressing complex issues: for example, promoting school vouchers to solve the systemic problems of public education. In our churches we sometimes resort to gimmicks to attract members instead of education to promote discipleship across differences. The twin icons of North American culture, individualism and privatism, permeate our conflicting aims, our churches, and our pastoral theology as well.

Optimism, moralism, privatism, individualism—these are strong deterrents to an alternative reading of our current situation. The cross, especially its political interpretation, may indeed be a powerful stumbling block if reintroduced to our churches and pastoral theology. However, without some corrective pastoral theology, our churches are in danger of not really offering an alternative to the secularly ordained progress and self-sufficiency worldview governing contemporary North American society. Although many are seeking ways to ground pastoral care in theology, what this means is still being determined. In practice, pastoral theology is still vulnerable to being collapsed into psychology. When this is the case, we continue to perpetuate the predominantly psychotherapeutic vision that still dominates North America at this beginning of the twenty-first century. As Philip Rieff has noted, the "triumph of the therapeutic" has little to offer in terms of an alternative future. "The language of science is not revelatory but analytic; for this reason, the scientist can never claim that his own terms have a prophetic vision."[11] A political interpretation of the cross can offer a corrective to this prevailing ethos in many of our churches and in the wider culture by providing an alternative posture for engaging the complexities of our current generation. It is a framework that is timely for informing pastoral theology.

Confessional Forms of Engagement

A theology of the cross is a confessional theology. According to H. Richard Niebuhr, confessional theology is a form of theology that "carries on the work of self-criticism and self-knowledge in the church."[12] A political interpretation of the cross for pastoral theology will need to take this form of self-criticism. This means pastoral theologians will need to join the lively theological conversation that is already taking place in many communities practicing the ways of life without denying the wiles of death. For members of these communities of faith, the cross is understood as revelatory, as the central Christian symbol that illuminates the conditions that give rise to human and divine suffering in particular times and specific places. Again, as Niebuhr reminds us, when the cross is understood as the center of the revelatory event, it provides Christians with a frame of reference for the meaning of life. It signifies that special occasion that provides believers an image through which all the occasions of our personal and common life become meaningful.[13] Theology from the perspective of the cross is confessional, because it is only by faith that the believer knows that the God who wills a good and just world also endures suffering in order to secure its completion.

The cross is not the end in itself; until God's broken world is restored to wholeness, it offers a compelling symbol of the deep commitment on

---

[11]Philip Rieff, *The Triumph of the Therapeutic: Uses of Faith After Freud* (New York: Harper & Row, 1966), 234.

[12]H. Richard Niebuhr, *The Meaning of Revelation* (New York: Macmillan, 1941), 13.

[13]For a more complete reading of Niebuhr's understanding of revelation, see *The Meaning of Revelation*.

the part of the One who accompanies us toward the day of wholeness and reconciliation for all. In this way the cross points beyond itself to the day of an unburdened and healed creation. It reveals the bountiful meal prepared and served to all the persons who ever walked through the doors of a community hospital or a neighborhood church, who thought they would never receive satisfaction for their hunger. The cross foreshadows a day when every tear shall be completely wiped away. Mourning shall cease, as the Psalmist promised, and all who have suffered will know joy experienced through the resurrection of Christ in all creation. The cross is indeed deeply pastoral in nature.

Confession means that faith and the theological tradition provide the appropriate interpretive framework for orienting pastoral care and theology in relationship to other forms of knowledge. It means that deep symbols will be remembered and cultivated in order to seek out places for meeting with other schools of thought and understanding. Confession provides an authentic starting place where one names his or her own "religious location." And this can be done without imposing one's faith on others. For example, I remember a powerful exchange between Robert McAfee Brown and Elie Wiesel. Brown was introducing his friend Wiesel, who was to be the speaker at a major theological conference. He began by saying, "I am a better Christian because of my friendship with Elie Wiesel, who is such a faithful Jew." When Elie Wiesel stood up to speak, he responded to his friend by saying, "And I am a more committed Jew because my friend Bob Brown is such a committed Christian." Confessions of faith are very specific. They are not general pronouncements. In fact, confession critiques all claims to universality that deny suffering through abstraction and inflict damage because they do not account for specific people. Confession stays close to the ground and remains critically engaged through participation in projects of hope that address conditions for establishing just and mutual relationships for all. It is critical because it is not naive.

And Yet Faith Falters...

The perspective of the political cross does not mean that the faith tradition itself does not have ambiguities and contradictions, or that its interpreters have not distorted it. One has only to think of the crusades or the eighteenth-century witch-hunts and the burning of women, not to mention the exploitation of the lonely by television evangelists today. The Bible itself, even certain interpretations of the cross, has been a major source of suffering for many people when it has been used to justify behavior and practices that have elevated some at the expense of others. Recent feminists, womanist scholars, and other voices from underrepresented communities attest to the sexist, racist, and homophobic attitudes and practices perpetuated by the misuse of the biblical faith and the church's traditions. These theologians now are drawing on the faith heritage with a "hermeneutic of suspicion" as they seek alternative interpretations of the gospel for the liberation and healing of all creation.

As pastoral theologians identify with the findings of some of these cutting-edge theologians and join with their objectives, new requirements are placed on us. The "hermeneutic of suspicion," or the questioning of all previously held assumptions, means that pastoral theology must allow itself to be "seen naked"–that is, revealed in all of its biases and partialities. The implications of this are far-reaching. It means that we will need to listen even more carefully and be willing to believe those who say that the way we go about our practices of care are not helpful to them. It will mean critically examining our basic theories and the contexts in which we develop them and being willing to question our methods for their limitations and any self-serving ends. Only a thorough and rigorous self-critical approach can be trusted to guide pastoral theology as it seeks to be in conversation with other disciplines and communities of interpretation. A political reading of the cross offers such a form of self-critical confession, because it, too, questions the faith tradition while testing other forms of knowledge. It does so because its starting point is the cry of the One who suffered and was crucified because of the social and political circumstances of his day.

The cry of anguish in all its depth and complexity is still the starting place of a theology grounded in the cross today. As this cry informs pastoral theology, it calls for a response that is not necessarily an answer or even an explanation. Insight by itself offers no lasting solution. A new kind of engaged response is called for that involves honoring the wisdom from the faith tradition, critical analysis, and political action. For these reasons pastoral theology cannot be a simple correlation or even a critical correlation between the faith tradition and perceived pastoral needs. The cry of suffering itself critiques such an easy identification. The political cross means first to become involved. The context for developing pastoral theology, then, is with people who are engaged in the world, willing to struggle for just and compassionate communities. These communities need to be our primary conversation partners along with other academic disciplines or graduate institutions.

As we have seen, many European American churches, through their own acculturation to secular values, contribute to diluting and trivializing the cross. Some churches get caught up in church growth as primarily a numbers game, believing that more members will assure faithful fellowships, while others practice styles of worship that aim to entertain without requiring much from their participants. On Sunday morning one of the most widely watched television broadcasts is the "Hour of Power" broadcast from the Crystal Cathedral in Los Angeles, California. The weekly preaching on positive thinking invites believers to think that the heart of the scriptural message is a variation on the theme "Every day in every way, things are getting better and better." Until we are able to provide an authentic alternative theology to these overly optimistic options, we will impede the possibility of new life for others and ourselves.

Given the decline in membership of liberal denominations and a growing factionalism in many communities of faith, the lackluster participation on the part of some of the laity, and evidence of burnout among the clergy, we must pose a pivotal question: Where are the communities of faith that give rise to a pastoral theology that takes cross and resurrection seriously in the lives of its people?

A Way of the Cross

Contrary to the growing concern on the part of many church leaders, there are vital communities of faith seeking to live out their commitments in the world. North American forms of Base Christian Communities have been gathering in urban settings in the lobbies of resident hotels, people's living rooms, and college dorms. They offer examples of ways to combine pastoral care and political involvement through a fresh appropriation of the cross. Some ethnic churches demonstrate an implicit political interpretation of the cross that can help guide pastoral theology. Through my pastoral ministry with Japanese Americans I met people who understood their experience of the internment camps during World War II as a crucifixion event. Out of this political-religious consciousness they raised up community leaders who worked for reparations, a movement that provided a form of resurrection for many who identified with Christianity. Further illustrations are found in new immigrant churches where members see their struggles in an inhospitable United States revealing the pathos of Jesus' life and death, and yet they live out vibrant expressions of faith.

Again, the African American churches that identify the struggle for racial justice with the death and resurrection of Jesus offer a powerful witness. One local example is Missionary Church of God in Christ, in Berkeley, California, where pastor Gordon Choyce gives leadership to his congregation and the surrounding community. The church is located in one of the sections of the city where homeless and jobless people come to the church doors daily. To respond to the needs that greet them every time they gather for worship, the congregation, through the guidance of Pastor Choyce, has developed a comprehensive outreach program. Together they have worked to cross denominational barriers, church and state barriers, racial barriers, and class barriers to engage in creative and effective community renewal projects. They have "taken up the cross" in order to establish affordable housing units, substance abuse programs, homeless youth programs, tutoring and job placement programs, and more. People who were "dead" are being offered new life.

Former Episcopal Bishop of New York Paul Moore writes, "One of the vocations of a Christian is to become so familiar with the patterns of God's Kingdom in Scripture and in liturgy that we can recognize it glistening in the most unlikely places and occasions in the world around us. Then, having recognized the Kingdom, we are called to join in its movement."[14] This pattern is glimpsed in the lives of vital communities of faith, such as the Missionary Church of God in Christ, who know and practice the empowering ways of the cross and resurrection and are engaged in the work of life and death, liberation and reconciliation. The work of pastoral theology involves recognizing the patterns of God's realm in scripture, in liturgy, and in communities of faith that practice faithful and joy-filled living. As we do so, we are called to join in its movement.

The church and its pastoral theologians can seek out and heal the brokenhearted burdened by historical circumstances. We can do so by providing an alternative vision of human relationships and places to practice it–if we will. By remembering the cross, with all its political and pastoral significance, we can position ourselves to witness the power of resurrection with those who are willing to face and resist the powers of death.

With Caution but Not Timidity

Some concern and much caution needs to be exercised when we approach the subject of personal and communal suffering. Above all, suffering must never be justified or trivialized by the theories through which we understand what it means to care. Dorothee Soelle is right when she says that the human goal is to "abolish circumstances under which people are forced to suffer, whether through poverty or tyranny."[15] In addition to our theories and practices, our theologies must not contribute to the perpetuation of poverty or the forces of tyranny, even indirectly.

It hardly needs to be stated that we live in a world that is torn and fragmented. Most all of us want desperately to make it different, almost at any price. But do we really stop to consider at what cost? How do we even pause to count amidst the noise and confusion that prevents us from seeing clearly? How can we find a place still enough to hear one another, let alone ourselves? The cross reaches out to hold these conflicts, distractions, and tensions. The cross causes an interruption, a jolt into silence, which can become the stillness where the unimaginable can somehow become possible again.

One of my convictions is that a theology that sees and responds to suffering in its depths offers something in itself that contributes to the alleviation of that suffering. In the beginning this could mean only a slight shift in the way someone views his or her experience. Or it might offer the courage to venture a first tentative step out of the malaise of isolation that suffering engenders.

Within the core of suffering lies the key for addressing the conditions of suffering. Again, Soelle is perceptive when she says, "Who is working

[14]As quoted by Bruce Bauer in the *New York Times Book Review*, 4 January 1998, 11.
[15]Dorothee Soelle, *Suffering* (Philadelphia: Fortress Press, 1975), 2.

on the abolition of social conditions which of necessity produce suffering? Only those who themselves are suffering"[16] Who can explain this? What motivates pain to take political form? What motivates pain to take any constructive action? This cannot be readily explained, if at all. Yet the witness is clear with profound implications for human solidarity in healing community life. The power of the wound to heal is a historical fact. This offers some new ways of understanding healing. Healing becomes understood as something other than instrumental, like an application of a scalpel to an incision or salve to a wound. It is, rather, a divine mystery, a life-giving gift, which by its very nature is organically connected with those who are suffering. It is a factor that we have less control over than we think, but more access to than we know.

While ultimately outside the rational technological boundaries of our taken-for-granted logic, healing is available through our willingness to participate in a kind of redemptive suffering that is political in nature. This way of suffering restores the faces of the vulnerable, with whom we are ultimately related, and involves us in regaining our humanity. This puts healing in the vicinity of sacrament.

However, when I say that at the heart of suffering is the source for healing, I am not suggesting what has been so often and erroneously preached, that suffering in and of itself is redemptive. On the contrary and emphatically, no! This is not the case at all. All suffering that is felt personally is influenced in some way by the ways in which we are formed socially and culturally. This historically inflicted suffering especially needs to be exposed for what it is. Critical connections need to be made between personal and internalized structures of meaning and the way we organize the way we live together. To this end, pastoral theology needs to use the tools of social and political analysis to shed new light on the conditions and contours of human pain, so that we will not reduce the suffering of people to individual problems alone. By making the connections between personal suffering and political structures central for pastoral theology, we will more fully address the needs for healing in our communities.

However, it should be noted that this view of the cross is at variance with traditional atonement theories, which have too often been interpreted in ways that can justify or glorify suffering. Particularly harmful are those associated with Abelard and Anselm, about which more will be said later. Instead of alleviating intolerable situations, these theologies have been used to augment the burden of suffering in some and encourage apathy in others. Furthermore, they have tended to take the focus off the ongoing anguish of human beings, placing it instead on the accomplishments of God through the "work of Christ." The atonement, conventionally interpreted, is not the focus here; it is, rather, how the cross interpreted politically can help

---

[16]Ibid.

illumine the historical and social factors that impact the nature of suffering and what this means for pastoral theology.

Summary

The recent reemergence of the cross, expressed in political and liberation theologies, is challenging all dominant theologies of glory in whatever form they take. Whether it is through the trust in a growing economy that weds the church to social structures that burden and strangle large portions of God's creation, or triumphant forms of ideology that justify the systems that keep oppressive social structures in place, these forms of theology must be dismantled. Theologies that elevate human will and potential to exaggerated levels must go.

The cross, interpreted politically, casts the work of pastoral theology in a different mold. It calls us not to glory, but to the harder way of naming and engaging the historical conditions in which we live, as well as our place in them. The political cross is critical to pastoral theology as it seeks to participate in the vision of a new reality marked by just communities of compassion and meaning open to the dawning realm of God. But in order to pursue this direction, it is important to look more closely at the reigning paradigm to see more clearly how it helps obscure historical suffering and the conditions that perpetuate it.

CHAPTER TWO

The Reigning Paradigm

For the wound of the daughter of my people
is my heart wounded,
I mourn, and dismay has taken hold on me.
Is there no balm in Gilead?
Is there no physician there?
Why then has the health of the daughter of my poor people
not been restored?

JEREMIAH 8:21–22 (AUTHOR'S RENDERING)

Believers of all faiths expect their religious associations to interpret suffering and provide for its relief. For Christians the church has sometimes honored this trust and responded in effective ways. At other times it has failed miserably. Too often it has been a source of suffering itself, contributing to the hardship of people by aligning with unjust societal practices and patterns of living. For example, until quite recently many churches supported laws that perpetuated racial segregation while practicing styles of worship that reenforced white elitism. Even today some communities of faith exclude underrepresented populations such as gay, lesbian, and transgendered persons, inflicting harm by showing hostility instead of hospitality to them. Still others are caught up in what might be called "practices of commerce," ways of selling faith through seductive and manipulative methods of advertising and forms of worship in order to compete for new members.

When the church uncritically reflects the wider culture's values and ways of life, it fails to offer alternative opportunities for meaningful living. It cannot even address some harmful behaviors, because it participates in them. When this is the situation, it abandons its own calling and no longer provides a sanctuary where people's lives are taken seriously. Under such circumstances life ceases to flourish, and wholeness becomes a forgotten dream.

Sometimes pastoral theologians have unquestioningly followed the lead of the church and participated in destructive practices. At other times we have appropriated cultural values from extra-ecclesial sources, particularly psychology and psychiatry, that ignore some historical and societal types of suffering. In concert with the church and through our professional associations we have limited our horizons of care and our means for addressing contemporary pastoral problems. While we address the needs of some people, the concerns of others go unmet.

Some years ago historian Sydney Ahlstrom warned that one of the many factors that helps perpetuate historical injuries is something he calls "rampant anarchic economic individualism (RAEI)."[1] This wide-ranging social orientation is supported by an exaggerated sense of individual privilege based on economic advantage. Key features include competition and a "survival of the fittest" advantage in terms of access to power and dominant forms of decision making and control. Its effect weakens our sense of community life by placing a disproportionate stress on the importance of rivalry and keeping the disparity between people in place. It helps create "corporate persons" and works to keep our cities, states, and neighborhoods in a constant state of rapid social change. This is destructive to our environment, contributing to human woe and general institutional instability and insolvency. Ahlstrom claims that RAEI along with racism are the two "root systems" that feed American social evils. Robert Bellah's widely accepted analysis of American values in *Habits of the Heart* later echoed Ahlstrom's findings, noting how our therapeutic leanings help perpetuate this individualistic ethos.[2]

A market economy based on rampant anarchic economic individualism operates to keep people unnecessarily separate and disconnected from one another. This economic orientation also keeps people in our churches, our classrooms, and our hospitals and clinics from flourishing. Furthermore, it negates some of the foundational principles that have governed pastoral theology: equality before God and unconditional regard and acceptance of all human beings. These core pastoral values cannot be cultivated apart from our economic and political relationships.

---

[1]Sydney Ahlstrom and Rodger Van Allen, *American Religious Values and the Future of America* (Philadelphia: Fortress Press, 1978), 21.

[2]Robert N. Bellah, Richard Madsen, William M. Sullivan, Ann Swidler, and Steven M. Tipton, *Habits of the Heart: Individualism and Commitment in American Life* (Berkeley and Los Angeles: University of California Press, 1985).

If our theories and practices of pastoral theology are to counter historically rooted suffering and provide a corrective to the entrenchment of RAEI and its devastating effect on people, we will need to attend to race, class, and economic factors in every aspect of our discipline. But we cannot simply add them or incorporate them into our existing theories and practices. They can not be additions. They shape who we are and inform the core of our thinking. They reveal themselves in our every pastoral action. Our alternatives will need to account for this in order to counter certain given ideas of personal identity that have helped reinforce the kind of individualism that promotes injustice. But that is not all. We need to do a harder thing. We need to examine how we have become complicit in exploiting and harming some to the promotion and advantage of others through our theories, our practices, and our professional priorities.

Pastoral theologians stand at a time in history to critically examine the practices we have fostered, to redress our own complicity in structures of injustice, and to forge new ways of attending to the needs of all people. What is at stake has fundamental implications not only for pastoral theology but also for other religious disciplines as well. While we have begun this task, we need to take stock of where we are and how we need to proceed. While recognizing the good motives that have led us this far, we need to look at how our various reform movements have failed and why.

The Lingering Psychotherapeutic View

One of our strongest challenges, I believe, is our continuing over-identification with the dominant pastoral care paradigm that emphasizes a psychotherapeutic point of view. This orientation, particularly as it is expressed through psychoanalytic schools of thought, still permeates our public and private lives to the core. It is a standpoint that has evolved out of a predominantly white, middle-class and Euro-Western ideology and reflects the cultural bias of this setting. It is a view compatible with economic individualism and is uncritical of social structures and their impact on people and their communities. It is supported by a set of myths: the myth of individual autonomy, the myth of diagnosis, the myth of insight, the myth of self-realization, the myth of science, and the myth of functionalism. These myths need to be examined and their implications exposed. They do not engage the historical and political dimensions of human suffering and therefore do not address their causes and means of relief. In fact, they help keep the societal injuries of some concealed while we address the personal needs and crises of others. All the while, the corporate well-being of us all suffers.

The Myth of Individual Autonomy

At the heart of the psychotherapeutic worldview is a strong accent on the individual person as the primary subject of inquiry and focus of interest. It is the autonomous individual who is the point of reference when looking for the causes of pain and suffering. The sources of suffering reside in the individual person and can be remedied through diagnoses and treatments to his or her mind, soul, or body. But this approach to healing is more than a program to provide clinical intervention; it also offers certain under-standings of what it means to be a human being. To be human means to be someone who is self-reliant, autonomous, independent, and free. This view, long in the making, is particularly advanced in psychoanalytic psychology, which has had a strong influence on Western thought. It still rules much of our thinking and has helped shape our many orientations to individual and family care, including pastoral care.

The myth of the autonomous individual is deeply embedded in the American psyche, fueling our national identity and powering the engines that keep our economy humming. It has generated a unique type of "American hero," perhaps best exemplified by Horatio Alger. The young Horatio came from humble origins and became a self-made man who succeeded in life against impossible odds. Through his own determination, wit, and perseverance he raised himself up "by his own boot straps" to the world of fame and victory. His life became so emblematic of what it meant to be an American that it earned the distinction the "Horatio Alger myth." There have been numerous books written about his life and scores of motivational clubs founded to promote his ideals and philosophy. Today there is even a Horatio Alger Web site on the Internet!

As the Horatio Alger myth permeates and forms our public consciousness, it provides a fitting venue for the RAEI phenomenon mentioned earlier. Alger was able to successfully compete and survive, make a name and a small fortune for himself. In subtle and not so subtle ways his rags-to-riches fable, and others like it, helps create positive biases in us toward some, and attitudes of distrust and indifference toward others. They influence whom we take seriously and those we don't pay attention to.

The ability to profit in a market economy is a sign of virtue and the measure of success. Because not everyone conforms to the Horatio Alger success story, those who do not are often seen as failures, personally and socially. They are viewed as deviant or strange. Too often they become branded as "less than" human and are alienated and rendered invisible. Or worse, they become the objects of our efforts to adjust them to what is acceptable. We ignore them, isolate them, or try to "fix" them. Through our indifference and manipulations the sorrows of people become not only intensified but also compounded.

The recent so-called religious "conversion or reparative" therapy programs aimed at preventing or "shifting" sexual preference of gay and lesbian people are examples of our culture's misguided activities. The poignant film *Ma Vie en Rose* vividly portrays the heartbreak of this mindset. The movie shows a young boy-child who loves to dress in his sister's dresses and wear his mother's makeup, and he is ridiculed and severely punished for it.

When the myth of the autonomous individual in any of its many forms provides the assumed interpretive framework for psychotherapy, therapy itself comes dangerously close to justifying and supporting rampant anarchic economic individualism as not only desirable, but normative. Some of the more positivist approaches may even promote and advance the "strive and be successful" orientation that the Horatio Alger myth idealizes. When secular therapies are drawn on uncritically to inform pastoral care, their unstated values become incorporated into our theories as well. When this happens, we unknowingly sanction contemporary expressions of harmful economic individualism. This can become particularly problematic in pastoral practices where personal growth or self-realization is our primary focus. When we confuse personal growth and self-realization and associate them with the cultural aims of economic triumph and material success, we no longer participate in their intended religious aim of wholeness. Instead, we objectify and commodify human personality and interpersonal relationships. In this way people begin to lose their "thouness," and so do we.

The Myth of Diagnosis

The myth of autonomy has also played a significant role in constructing the myth of diagnosis for identifying causes and cures of personal pathology as well as social ills. Its assumption is that if we identify and cure personal ills, then in this way we will mend society. In the diagnostic paradigm, however, the interconnection between the so-called private realm and the public world is mostly denied. When suffering is confined and defined within the private realm of the individual or family unit, an overemphasis is placed on interpersonal and intrapsychic dynamics for addressing it. When suffering results from external disasters, international conflict, community violence, and the like, we either do not address them, seeing them outside the purview of pastoral theology, or we tend to fall back on interpersonal theories of loss, grief, and conflict. These limited responses to suffering tend to make what is going on seem comprehensible and manageable. But the diagnostic approach based on the anthropology of autonomous individualism is inadequate for addressing the pervasive economic and structural malaise of our time. It is also misleading. It perpetuates a dualistic worldview in which the legacies of imposed suffering as well as their contemporary expressions are rarely recognized. Instead, people who bear the marks of injustice often become blamed for having inadequate personalities, for choosing to be victims, for having a "victim mentality." At times they are seen only as victims, incapable of altering the forces that impact their lives. In other words, in a clinical diagnostic view it is very difficult for victims to become agents capable of acting in history and critiquing their own experiences from a political-contextual point of view.

Like economic individualism, the process of diagnosing people tends to keep people unnecessarily separate from one another. The ones diagnosed are often isolated from the rest of the community. Diagnosis objectifies people by categorizing and labeling them in a way that can place them outside the boundary of what is commonly agreed on as normal by the dominants of a particular culture. In this way categories of illness, or wellness for that matter, are never culturally neutral. Many diagnoses tend to be socially stigmatizing. Moreover, those who are in positions to name, describe, and diagnose in the first place are usually the ones who have the power to determine what is normal and acceptable. Once a practice of diagnosis is established, it has the power to transform subjects into objects, making some people extremely vulnerable. Those diagnosed can easily become bearers of whatever "dis-order" or "dis-ease" the dominant members of society wish to deny. Gay and lesbian people experienced this acutely until homosexuality was removed from the seventh printing of the Diagnostic and Statistical Manual of Mental Disorders (DSM II) in 1973, and the associations still remain powerful.

Often those who are diagnosed as abnormal are viewed as "mad" or "bad." They deviate from the society's governing social values and suitable behavior. But contrary to being ill or evil, some "deviants" may be acutely in touch with reality. It is very possible that those who react strongly to insane circumstances around them are labeled crazy while those perpetuating the madness are deemed normal, perhaps even exemplary citizens. Diagnosis can be used as another way of denying historical suffering.

The Myth of Insight

A strong confidence in human insight and human freedom is foundational for the diagnostic approach to healing. Individual freedom and human insight are also indicators of liberal theology and have been positively linked with democratic culture, especially as it evolved on American soil. On this continent they have contributed to the value system informed by the American Dream, an amalgamation of the Horatio Alger myth and Manifest Destiny. Pastoral care has been extensively shaped by this modern worldview that emerged essentially from the nineteenth-century American incorporation of the earlier eighteenth-century Continental Enlightenment. A hallmark of the Enlightenment was the Kantian principle *sapera aude* ("dare to know"). This expressed the central theme of the Enlightenment thinkers: the courage to use one's own human understanding for the betterment of the world and for the alleviation of suffering. It also represented a shift in the location of authority from institution and tradition to human experience.

In the early part of the twentieth century, theologians of "crisis" (notably Karl Barth) began to challenge the liberal views concerning human freedom and insight. Reinhold Niebuhr also became suspicious of the high trust placed in human nature, and his brother H. Richard challenged the unexamined assumption that God is a supporter of human ideals and not one who stands in judgment over every finite value.[3] During the post–World War II era until the early 1970s, when the therapeutic paradigm was at its peak, even people such as Rollo May questioned the Enlightenment's assumptions of both liberal theology and pastoral care that supported freedom and insight as adequate ends for human well-being.

During the latter part of the century Lesslie Newbigin was another who continued this conversation on human wisdom and insight. While acknowledging the contributions of the Enlightenment for liberating the human spirit from many ancient fears and restraints, Newbigin also began to criticize its fundamental orientation. He claimed that the Enlightenment view of human agency rested on the "illusion of autonomy." Rather than freeing the human spirit, this illusion actually produced new forms of bondage that undermine modern men and women's confidence in the future.[4] In contrast to autonomy, Newbigin said that mutual dependence was intrinsic to true human identity. Mutuality, he believed, was the governing principle for humankind.[5] Writing in 1983, Newbigin either presaged recent trends in feminist thinking and writing or could have been influenced by this emerging theme during that time.[6]

Newbigin nuanced his understanding of mutuality by saying that in order to live interdependently in mutual relations, we need to understand the difference between bearing witness to the truth and pretending to possess the truth (insight). This means that no one group has a corner on truth. Even the meaning of mutuality will need to be constructed provisionally and tested communally. This will be hard for some, because it will involve

---

[3]E. Brooks Holifield, *A History of Pastoral Care in America: From Salvation to Self-Realization* (Nashville: Abingdon Press, 1983), 252.

[4]Lesslie Newbigin, "Can the West Be Converted?" *International Bulletin of Missionary Research* 11 (January 1987): 7.

[5]Newbigin, *The Other Side of 1984: Questions for the Churches* (Geneva: World Council of Churches, 1983), 56.

[6]Mutuality has since become a key theme for feminist and womanist theologians in recent years. Carter Heyward constructed her theology on the principle of relationship as the original reality. See *The Redemption of God: A Theology of Mutual Relations* (Washington, D.C.: University Press of America, 1982). Bonnie Miller-McLemore, Pamela Couture, and others use the metaphor "the living human web" in distinction to the more individualistic "living human document" that has been a standard of pastoral care since the early days of the clinical movement in the United States. See Rodney J. Hunter and Pamela Couture, *Pastoral Care and Social Conflict* (Nashville: Abingdon Press, 1995); Jeanie Stevenson, ed., *Through the Eyes of Women* (Philadelphia: Fortress Press, 1998). And eco-feminists and other environmental theologians emphasize the total interrelated nature of life. See Rosemary Ruether, *Gaia and God: An Eco-feminist Theology of Earth Healing* (San Francisco: Harper, 1992); Rosemary Ruether and Dieter T. Hessel, *Christianity and Ecology: Seeking the Well-being of Earth and Humans* (Cambridge, Mass.: Harvard University Center for the Study of World Religions, 2000); and Mary Elizabeth Moore, *Ministering with the Earth* (St. Louis: Chalice Press, 1998). These recent advocates for mutuality and continuity as central motifs for humane communities join with the early works of Newbigin and others in asserting relational values over detachment and separation. This is a welcome corrective that is beginning to impact pastoral theology and new visions of community.

showing those of us who are used to being in charge our propensity for devising ways to stay there. Insight becomes tamed through mutuality. "Bearing witness to the truth" suggests an unfinished and emerging understanding of which I am a part, but I am not the chief architect. Or as Newbigin expresses it, "We must understand that witness *(marturia)* means not dominance and control but suffering."[7] One does not necessarily alleviate suffering by assigning it meaning or explaining its causes. However, one can respond to suffering by bearing witness *(marturia)*. But this has not been a popular stance.

The power of insight and the promise of individual autonomy and freedom have fed North American Protestant liberal theology. And in many ways Protestant liberal theology has become coterminous with the American Dream. Unreflective of this connection, we do not as yet recognize the failure of this dream, let alone the flaws at its inception. Pastoral theology, as a child of North American Protestant liberalism, has participated in trusting insight with its pretense to possess the truth. This has been a major source of much suffering imposed by one group on another. In the form of diagnosis this has proven especially true.

The Myth of Self-Realization

The myth of the autonomous individual is maintained by a strong belief in the possibility of self-realization. As pastoral theologians uncritically adopted the psychotherapeutic understanding of life with its focus on the individual, they helped create what historian E. Brooks Holifield has called a preoccupation with the quest for self-realization.[8] Self-realization is a strong cultural force as well as religious factor in American life. It provides a certain self-determination that frees us to become creative, spontaneous, and actively engaged in the world. It is necessary for us to make commitments. But over time our emphasis on self-realization has also taken on mythic proportions that have proven to be problematic.

When self-realization becomes an end in itself, as it has over the past few decades, we minimize the impact that social structures and cultural environments have on our lives. This narrow expression of self-realization has become identified with personal growth and the enormously profitable self-help industry. But instead of producing people who are joyful and who actively participate in the world, this unreflective form of self-realization has taught people that public life is something remote and distant, a backdrop for human drama rather than the pulsing matrix out of which we grow. It promotes a false idea of public life as separate, given, and fixed and personal life as expansive, unlimited, and free.

---

[7]Newbigin, "Can the West Be Converted?" 7.

[8]Holifield, *History of Pastoral Care.* Holifield is an important source for examining the history of pastoral care in America. His critical examination of pastoral care explores how it has been influenced by various historical trends and thought patterns.

Our preoccupation with self-realization as personal growth helps maintain the strong division between the public and private spheres of human activity that we have come to experience as normal. Again, as in economic individualism, this form of separation acts as a powerful wedge to unnecessarily separate people from one another, serving to increase the suffering of those who are hurt by systems of exploitation and dehumanization. Historical injuries are seen as manifestations of personal maladjustment and individual depravation. People are condemned for having poor coping skills for addressing the very systems that starve and stifle them. In this way, self-realization has become an unfulfilled ideal for too many men and women and a growing number of children. Our prisons, psychiatric hospitals, and streets are filled with some of these people who have not been given the tools, the means, or the opportunities to live productive and meaningful lives.

When the separation of personal from public life is internalized, it feeds the destructive idea that self-realization as personal growth can be accomplished in the absence of public renewal. This is the false promise and sad betrayal by the self-help industry. In fact, this individualistic understanding of self-realization is not applicable to anyone. Pursuing it might make some of us *feel* as if we are on a path to self-improvement, but ultimately this is not the case. The question is, Can there really be such a thing as self-realization apart from public renewal? Can personal growth be furthered and identity deepened or improved at the expense of corporate well-being? I think not. What self-realization as personal growth may do, for a while, is bolster our self-image. But whether we are looking into the mirror over the bathroom sink or the mirror called life, image is a fragile imitation of who we truly are. Turn away from the reflection in the mirror and the image disappears—and if the image is all we are, we disappear too!

When religion is used to reinforce image making, it becomes a tool of the ruling classes. When pastoral theology blesses this process, it only functions, as Soelle says, "to comfort the sad, enrich personal life, and give the individual the feeling of significance."[9] Image is not the same as identity. Identity is more than image and more than personality. It includes what we long for and who we want to become, as individuals and as a people too. The fantasy of fulfillment through personal growth too often becomes confused with the popular cultural forms of "image making" as a means to self-realization. In the end, self-image does not lead to self-realization.

For many personal-growth adherents, there is no limit to our ability to change and grow and become more of whoever we choose to become. This view of personal growth sees self-realization as an extension of natural evolution, another expression of Enlightenment thinking. It is also a product of the deeply held national faith in success and progress that we have been

---

[9]Dorothee Soelle, *Choosing Life* (Philadelphia: Fortress Press), 82.

discussing. This is the Horatio Alger myth writ large and sewn deep into the fabric of the modern psyche. The nurturing of this myth can almost be understood as a kind of spirituality. However, it is a spirituality that prizes inner motivation and hard work and relies on the private and inner resources that one brings to all of life's endeavors. What tends to be reinforced in people who highly prize personal growth is a diminished ability to trust or even entertain what is external. Why should they? Self, the domestic world, and the domesticated god are all in alignment. Some talk of this arrangement as a loss of genuine transcendence.

When we are governed by the ideal of self-realization, our worlds become small, very small, as the individual self becomes large. We become our own and often sole source of knowledge. Hesitant to trust in what we do not know, we hold to what we alone can see, hear, and understand. But we lose something very important when we are not willing to trust what is outside of ourselves. We lose genuine alternatives. Even the meaning of faith becomes problematic. It is our ability to believe that there is "something more" that allows us to step outside of what is familiar into something new. Those who focus on personal growth that relies on the belief that life is self-produced and self-generated have difficulty believing that life is a gift from God to be received with gratitude.

When self-realization is disassociated from public renewal, it becomes a disposition that fosters a kind of shortsightedness that does little to encourage us to look for hope and inspiration beyond our own private worlds. This understanding of self-realization has been necessary to maintain the kind of society we have created, and it has spawned additional markets to secure its continuity. At the same time the proliferation of self-help books and quasi-spiritual remedies for healing hurting people reveals a deep hunger for meaning and the culture's readiness to look for secular and occult answers. How can pastoral theologians relate to these powerful cultural forces that have grown out of an individualistic and evolutionary orientation to life without being drawn in and seduced by them?

The Myth of Science

Personal growth, insight, and self-realization are supported by another American ideal, the optimistic belief in unlimited progress that helped motivate the nineteenth-century Industrial Revolution and continues to fuel our current advancements in information technology and "techno-capitalism." This myth of unlimited progress is manifest in our confidence in the seeming endless benefits of modern science and industry.

The scientific worldview is secular and materialistic to the core. Dismissing all transcendent aspects of reality, it attempts to reduce reality to what is observable and measurable, resulting in what the French historian Paul Hazard describes as the replacement of a society based on duties with a society based on rights.[10] This shift of our moral posture in society, accompanied by a reversal of dogma in which doubt is now the fundamental orientation to life, has helped reinforce the dichotomy between the private and public arenas as separate universes. "Beliefs" are relegated to the private sphere, whereas "doubt," expressed through systems of verification, has come to govern the public domain. An effect of this value shift is to limit one's striving for what is true, good, and ultimately real to the material world of what is observable and measurable, particularly in the realm of public life.

The scientific worldview, or scientism, pushes all transcendent interpretations of reality aside and attempts to reduce all views of reality to what can be empirically tested and described. As Edward Wimberly has pointed out, proponents of this orientation urge people to abandon their traditional beliefs and to think that their salvation rests in the liberation from their old religious ideas.[11] Although scientism has attacked the icons of faith and is being touted as a new expression of the search for the ultimate, it does not help people meet their needs for something beyond themselves. Rather, it tends to push people toward denying this need as something infantile or silly. Perhaps this is most evident in some of our clinical approaches to healing.

It is telling that today's practices of healing are not generally thought of as public practices in which all members of a society participate. And with limited exceptions, the cultivation of just and healthy social, physical, and economic environments are not considered a part of the healing arts. While there is a growing interest in the relationship between spirituality and personal healing, rituals of healing are rarely exercised in mainline churches, quasi-public places, where people come together. The further connection between spirituality, personal healing, and social well-being is only beginning to be made in the historically white churches.

Clebsch and Jaekle noted nearly a quarter of a century ago that the healing arts had been all but lost to the church.[12] However, an important recent exception needs to be recognized here. In areas of the country where the AIDS epidemic has impacted communities the hardest, such as San Francisco and New York, some churches are responding by offering healing services, public education, and advocacy within healthcare systems. Perhaps it has been the tragic outbreak of AIDS that has helped alert us once more to the connections between mind and spirit and body, and to the knowledge

---

[10]Paul Hazard, *The Philosophy of the Enlightenment,* English trans. (Princeton, N.J.: Princeton University Press, 1951).

[11]Edward P. Wimberly, *Pastoral Counseling and Spiritual Values: A Black Point of View* (Nashville: Abingdon Press, 1982), 10–11.

[12]William A. Clebsch and Charles R. Jaekle, *Pastoral Care in Historical Perspective* (Englewood Cliffs, N.J.: Prentice Hall, 1964), 29.

of our bodies as socially connected. Even so, while there are signs that a holistic consciousness is beginning to emerge in some parts of the country, we are still a long way from understanding this as normative for this society. We do not first think of people as being situated in communities, but rather as being individuals, as they are in themselves. This remains the primary focus of most people, along with the hospital, as the place where healing is effected.

The hospital remains a temple to science, where the tools of medicine are brought to the object of healing, the individual—his or her private body, his or her independent mind, and occasionally, his or her spirit. Approved, accredited, and specialized professional healers practice healing. Doctors, nurses, medical technicians, and various occupational therapists are brought together as a group of individual professionals. But they are not necessarily a "public" or a community in the sense of a people governed by a shared set of norms, visions, and values. Perhaps the hospital chaplain is added to this mix, but he or she often becomes simply another professional specialist in the hospital setting who has minimal ecclesial ties or allegiances.

Compared to the sophisticated methods of modern medicine, old religious ideas seem antiquated in the hospital setting. Next to science, faith smacks of superstition and old-fashioned folk remedies. Faith becomes shy when measured by these commonly held stereotypes. Faith becomes timid next to her more sure-minded and technically trained colleagues in the secular healing professions. Often, then, practitioners of faith begin to adopt the means and methods of their secular-scientific counterparts, in part to find an adequate language for communication, in part to secure a more legitimate role for themselves among the helping professions. However, when pastors, chaplains, and even theologians do this, they begin to sound as if they trust the same scientific values and assumptions about healing to meet the needs of people.[13]

Today, the promise of science with the technological advances it provides seems to be trusted even more and almost without question. For example, biomedical research, astrophysics, and communication engineering are gaining considerable international recognition and support. The home computer revolution only accelerates this. We point to the Search button and "click" to find medical advice or any other information, and it appears on our computer screen in an instant! The advances of science do offer a tremendous gift to people today. However, our growing acceptance of the expanding scientific world continues to push theologians to articulate a faith that is relevant, rational, and compatible with this ever-widening perspective. But will relevance and compatibility suffice?

---

[13]Fortunately, not all religious practitioners adopt these patterns, particularly as they are looked to for genuine leadership in a fast-growing and increasingly complicated health care area. But even here they will need to be careful not to succumb to reducing spiritual practices to outcome analysis: for example, "Does it work?" In other words, is the spiritual practice observable and measurable by scientific standards?

Health and wholeness involve more than science can provide. The strong identification between science and religion (or between psychology and theology) is straining thin at this turn of the century. Wimberly is perceptive when he says that people still need something to meet their needs for something beyond themselves.[14] Science alone is not sufficient for addressing and alleviating the suffering that people live with, particularly as a result of historical injuries.

Alternatives to scientific understandings of healing and disease need to be recognized in order to address the deep pain and complex nature of contemporary life. These sources must be sought outside of hospital-tested applications of physical and behavioral theory. Here, Alastair Campbell draws our attention to the additional context of love, whose ultimate aims are expressed in sacrament, prayer, and prophecy, "all of which can turn the values of humanistic love *(and science)* into only proximate goals."[15] These ecclesial-based alternates might not offer the kind of confidence that tested, proven, and legitimated medical practices offer. In fact, they introduce a certain messiness and ambiguity that removes all hope for security from the heart of our theory and practice. Instead, we are vulnerable and "at risk." But in this insecurity we may discover something else.

By turning to alternative venues, people may be offered the possibility, as Edward Wimberly says, "to recover a posture of trust in a divine whose activity is unconfinable."[16] This faith posture prompts us to examine the multiple sources of human ills and to explore fresh and imaginative responses to them. It recognizes the benefits of modern social, physical, and human sciences, but it also says something to us about the need for all children to have access to physical check-ups and immunization, as well as the need for enough food on the table for everyone to eat.

The Myth of Functionalism

Scientism has helped foster a functionalist approach to pastoral care and theology that had its beginning during the massive cultural shifts of the late nineteenth and early twentieth centuries. Urbanization, emigration, reconstruction, and the rise of modern sciences impacted the modern world in unprecedented ways and contributed to what some historians have called an "ecclesial disarray."[17] The church found itself awash in new ideas and historical tides. It was during this period that pastoral care began to incorporate various secular sources.[18] William James, Sigmund Freud, and

---

[14]Wimberly, *Pastoral Counseling,* 10–11.

[15]Alastair V. Campbell, *Professionalism and Pastoral Care* (Philadelphia: Fortress Press, 1985), 18. Italics mine.

[16]Wimberly, *Pastoral Counseling,* 10–11.

[17]Ronald E. Osborn, *Creative Disarray: Models of Ministry in a Changing America* (St. Louis: Chalice Press, 1991).

[18]Sydney Ahlstrom, *Religious History of the American People* (New Haven, Conn.: Yale University Press, 1972), 824.

others of the pragmatist school of thought figured prominently and began to have an impact on pastoral practices.

The pragmatists were most concerned with a method to settle the endless metaphysical disputes over such issues as the nature of freedom or determinism, the relationship of one to many, and so forth. They were interested in outcomes. The pragmatist asked, What practical difference does it make to answer a question one way or another? In this way beliefs were understood as practical rules for action, not as orientations for living.

James contributed to pastoral theology through his work in psychology of religion, specifically by combining the insights of biology and philosophy for moral development. Freud brought his particular interpretation of the human psyche. James asserted that habits could convert the central nervous system into an ally for human moral development, suggesting that actions formed character and were under the domain of the will.[19] Freud's discovery of the unconscious and subconscious as being instrumental for human behavior was perceived as supporting the idea that religion was a matter of attitude rather than something concerned with the revelatory nature of faith.

These theorists developed the idea that mental states were basically functional states, that is, related to external stimulation, other internal states, or the results of a person's behavior. At the same time, functionalism as an expression of pragmatism approached mental states in an empirical cause-and-effect way. It held to an extremely antimetaphysical bias. This overemphasis on physicalism left out any serious consideration of complex nonphysical input and hindered the ability to account for nonempirical phenomena. Symbolic meaning, mysticism, and other complex relationships could not be readily accounted for by pragmatic standards. As pastoral theology opened itself to these powerful cultural resources of the early twentieth century, it also inherited their basic assumptions and biases.

Developing alongside the pragmatist worldview was the gradual professionalization of the pastoral office. As mentioned earlier, this led many clergy to view what they did, and in some instances how they did it, in light of other professions such as medicine, law, and teaching. This was a natural outcome of functionalism that informed many of the professions. Over time, the norms and practices developed in nonecclesial settings have led clergy in the direction of specialization. This has helped produce entire categories of "specialized ministries" that are recognized and endorsed by various denominations. Pastoral counseling is one of these specialties that has been recognized and accredited by cognate institutions such as the Association for Clinical Pastoral Education (ACPE) and the American Association of Pastoral Counselors (AAPC), who in addition to securing

---

[19]Holifield, *History of Pastoral Care*, 187.

ecclesiastical endorsement also develop extraecclesial standards and licensing procedures for practitioners.

The drive toward specialization has influenced clergy and laity alike to view ministry as composed of different spheres of work involving different skills and talents. Pastoral care is often seen as one among many of the separate proficiencies of ministry. And the field of pastoral care itself is further conceptualized into a subset of activities commonly identified as guiding, healing, sustaining, and reconciling. This move toward categorizing and specializing has also helped create a more functional approach to ministry. Indeed, pastoral guiding, healing, and sustaining are called "functions." The skills and talents for pastoral care are intended to be pragmatic. They have an aim and are instrumental in the healing process. Without being prescriptive or coercive, they are to be useful; they serve a function.

Perhaps Seward Hiltner's interpretation of these pastoral functions, with the exception of reconciling, has influenced and captured the imaginations of pastoral theologians more than anyone else. Writing at a time when pastoral theologians were beginning to search for new ways to communicate their methods to a wider academic audience, Hiltner picked up the challenge. He was dedicated to the task of finding a method that could persuade his clinical peers as well as his academic colleagues of the effectiveness of pastoral care. And he was committed to proving that the language of psychology could also be a theological language. He was convinced that people would simply dismiss theology as something irrelevant to their thoughts and concerns if this were not the case. The relevance and compatibility of theology with psychology were of keen interest to Hiltner, as were their practical applications.

To engage his task, Hiltner drew from the process thought of Alfred North Whitehead, the correlation method and theological concepts of Paul Tillich, and the clinical posture of the one-time seminary student Carl Rogers. Rogers' emphasis on nonjudgmental acceptance and empathy became central for Hiltner during a time when pastoral theologians were eliminating anything from their theories and practices that hinted of authoritarianism. He relied on these concepts to develop his "shepherding perspective," which he introduced to pastoral theologians as the pastoral way to engage and understand people. The image of the shepherd is based on Jesus as the great shepherd whose aim is healing. It is exercised through "solicitous and tender and individualized care by the shepherd of the sheep."[20] The shepherding perspective soon became operationalized through the pastoral functions guiding, healing, and sustaining. Once established, these philosophical, theological, and clinical points of view

---

[20]Seward Hiltner, *The Christian Shepherd: Some Aspects of Pastoral Care* (New York and Nashville: Abingdon Press, 1959), 20.

became synthesized into a pivotal framework for the next generation of pastoral scholars and practitioners.

The contributions of Hiltner and others must not be dismissed, nor should their philosophical insights be lost. He and his generation addressed the genuine need to find a way to establish dialogue with other disciplines. This is still a crucial issue for pastoral theologians today, so that we do not become isolated, irrelevant, or parochial in our thinking and exercise of care. The practical aims of their functionalist approach are important, so that people who are suffering do not become objects of speculation or material for theory alone. Pastoral theology must remain close to its source and engaged in addressing the face-to-face needs of people.

Yet there remain real limits to a functional approach for pastoral theology. It is limited in long-term depth. Its preferred method of correlation often simply replaces theological meaning with psychological interpretations, which does not guarantee equivalent meaning on a nonempirical level. Symbolic orientations can easily escape functionalist descriptions. Furthermore, the functional approach has not been used to make connections between the needs of individuals and the common malaise of the larger society. It leaves the ambiguity and the uncertainties of modern life untouched, and people's longing for meaningful change continues unassuaged.

Functionalism has tended to be individually focused and one-directional in approach. As developed by Hiltner, the point of view of the shepherd perspective is that of the practitioner. No matter how nondirective the caregiver is, the shepherd perspective and the pastoral functions originate within the pastoral office or professional guild and are directed toward the client. Their creation, interpretation, and practice have not been generated from the perspective of those seeking relief from what malady is theirs. This limits the sources of knowledge we draw from for practicing our vocation and neglects the authority of those who may experience different social and historical realities from ours.

Lastly, functionalism is inadequate for the pluralistic nature and multicultural context of pastoral care. Its overappreciation of pragmatics can result in serving the dominant culture's "common sense" (or taken-for-granted-world), making it difficult to advocate for transformation within society. In this way, the pastoral functions are "dis-functional" for those suffering historical injuries. The multicontextual nature of care and theology needs to be more fully expanded and deepened to meet the demands of this time.

The Shattering of Myths in a Crumbling World

Until recently, the modern world was understood as something fore-given, and Protestant theologians were busy attempting to adapt religion to its demands. The task was to modernize the old religion and smooth down its rough edges. Few were trying to do things the other way around, critiquing society until it was better understood through the prose of the gospel and its vision of life. Perhaps they thought that by changing religion, we could change the world. It didn't work. We changed religion instead of changing the world. In the process we reduced our religious traditions, myths, and symbols and confined them to our personalities and ourselves. Perhaps we thought that by changing ourselves we could change the world. This hasn't work either. In the process we have ended up using religious concepts and images for mainly one purpose, to serve the supreme value of middle-class culture—the individual self.

Hiltner and his cohorts may be the last voices of a liberal religion, with its particular assumptions about the modern world, to guide pastoral care and theology. In their own way they were trying to salvage a world that had been unprecedentedly damaged by two world wars, the Holocaust of the Jews, and the atomic bombing of Hiroshima and Nagasaki. They witnessed the unleashing of scientific knowledge for human destruction rather than for human good and saw a terrible schism revealed in the human soul. Maybe Hiltner and the others still hoped for something different after these atrocities as they turned to a deeper focus on human nature and moved to the deeper plane of personal change. Or perhaps their move was something else, a pale reflection of giving up on God. After all, Carl Rogers was one who said, "God is dead," so why use religious vocabulary?[21]

But ultimately the world would not simply be put back together again; it had become shattered beyond repair. In the aftermath we are in a "postmodern" situation, where human knowledge is more fragmented and trust in anything such as "truth" is more provisional. Once unleashed, the knowledge of human evil and the untamable aspects of life can no longer be ignored, explained, or hidden. The question of God has become forever problematic. The world as it had been is no longer available to us, a reality we have yet to fully mourn. Previous assumptions about the care of people no longer hold when a new reality is revealed for what it is.

An unflinching belief in the promises of science left little room for the reality of human limitations and irretrievable failures. The strong accent on human knowledge and insight neglected the hard truth of human folly and life's incomprehensible tragedies. Self-realization has failed to materialize, and historical suffering is closer to us than ever. The synthesis that had been carefully knit between psychology and theology became shattered by the mid-twentieth century and is continuing to unravel at this turn of the century. And so are the myths that supported it.

---

[21]Holifield, *History of Pastoral Care*, 288.

CHAPTER
THREE

Pastoral Care at the Crossroads

A Time of Reckoning

In times of stress,
when profound structural change seems imminent,
the air fills with messages
salted on one side with a trace of panic
and sweetened on the other
with escapist unrealizable options.[1]

MORRIS MILLER

As we embark on this twenty-first century, we carry the legacy of the massive human suffering in the twentieth century. This is a time of answerability we cannot avoid. In the wake of two world wars; the unleashing of nuclear destruction on Hiroshima and Nagasaki; the Holocaust of the Jews; genocide in Vietnam; the "Killing Fields" of Cambodia; the abuse of Native Americans here and its parallel in the treatment of indigenous peoples in other parts of the world; the atrocities of ethnic cleansing in Africa and the Balkans; the ongoing threats of international terrorism and evidence of it in our own public schools;

---

[1]Morris Miller, "The Chicken-Little Syndrome and Its Implications," working paper, June 1995, page 3, as quoted in Sharon D. Welch, *Sweet Dreams in America: Making Ethics and Spirituality Work* (New York: Routledge, 1999), 133.

continuing conflict in the Middle East, Indonesia, and elsewhere; the ongoing realities of racism, sexism, and homophobia; the massive poverty and starvation throughout the world; and the ever-present ecological crisis threatening the survival of the planet, we are reminded daily of our own vulnerability. We are living during a time of reckoning. And we are coming to realize that the myths that have supported the reigning paradigm of pastoral care have failed to account for these historical realities by silencing or neutralizing its victims and individualizing hope.

By failing to adequately address expressions of historical suffering, we have also robbed ourselves of access to authentic holiness that can renew our lives and restore meaning to our days. Our theories have tended to collapse theology into psychology, creating a certain loss of depth that limits our vision. As these dimensions are cut off from our lives, we experience a tremendous sense of void. This becomes especially painful as we confront what some are calling a breakdown of symbolic meaning in our lives. This breakdown is supported in part by a therapeutic worldview that is incapable of reversing it. It helps generate the multiple losses of hope, holiness, and finally, our selves. At the same time there is an almost palpable sense of longing for something that we cannot easily name. We are facing a time of reckoning.

Days of Loss

Some perceptive voices are telling us that as a society we are losing the heart of our culture. Not only have historical atrocities disrupted our self-confidence, but as Edward Farley warns, the myths and symbols that once acted as powerful sources to bind and guide our common life are faltering under the strains of growing cultural diversity and late capitalism's market mentality.[2] This breakdown of our symbolic reality deprives people of a sense of depth in their lives and destroys our sense of connection, necessary for living in community. We are experiencing a tremendous historical transition and a loss of what once seemed stable and secure. As a result of our lack of common understanding about what this means we are being pulled in two opposing directions.

Fearing the magnitude of our loss, we begin to trivialize the symbols and traditions that we once revered. When they no longer seem useful or relevant, we become indifferent to them and discard them as antiquated relics. We adopt instead an attitude of extreme permissiveness, entertaining whatever new idea or fad captures our attention. Turning the opposite way, we raise our symbols and traditions to the level of unalterable truths. We believe that if we repeat them firmly and often and sufficiently loudly, our lives will once again become safe. We see signs of this in the resurgence of

---

[2]Edward Farley, *Deep Symbols* (Valley Forge, Pa.: Trinity Press International, 1996).

fundamentalism in our religious life. We hear it expressed in new forms of patriotism and demands for rigid law and order enforcement. And we experience it in the adamant call to return to "traditional family values."

Both our indifference to our symbols and our stubborn clinging to them point up our unsuccessful attempts to simplify the complex nature of our current circumstances. Both responses signal a loss of depth and lack of vision that lead to a kind of cynicism that becomes expressed in shallow or moralistic behavior. Neither posture provides the ground for meeting or mediating the intricacies of life. As the distance between these viewpoints increases, the tension grows. At some point the pulling apart becomes unbearable, and the center collapses. When this happens, we fall.

Our souls are housed where meaning takes shape. When we experience the loss of our deep and powerful symbols that help us know who we are and what it means to be human, we are in danger of losing our soul. This is no small thing. As our symbols fail to communicate meaning, our traditions falter; and when our traditions no longer bind our lives together, we tend to abandon them. Moreover, the loss of our symbols and traditions takes away our ability to practice rituals that invite the kind of corporate participation that renews life and bodes well for a future. What then remains? How do we counter these trends that foster estrangement from the purposes of our lives?

Whenever we disregard or idolize our traditions and symbols, we place ourselves in a precarious place of learning not to care. Learning not to care provides the seedbed for apathy. Such a basic level of mistrust and resentment in the fabric of our communal life, and the growing threat of indifference to it, acts to compound the everyday suffering of the people we meet and also our own suffering. Nicholaus Mills says that our culture is exhibiting a "triumph of meanness," and that we are a country without shared hopes and obligations.[3]

Because pastoral care has historically been concerned with the care of souls, a threat of such magnitude to the very core of human culture ought to evoke grave concern on our part today. But we are not immune to these same social trends and cultural currents, and our functionalist approach is inadequate to stem them. So how do we enter into this modern malaise without becoming caught ourselves by the vicissitudes of despair?

Despair gnaws at the human heart, defying facile answers and short-term responses to its warning. It signals to us that something deep and holy has become lost to us. Despair demands nothing less than a radical reorientation, if hope is to once again take root in the human soul.

---

[3]Nicholaus Mills, *The Triumph of Meanness: America's War Against Its Better Self* (New York: Houghton Mifflin, 1998), 8.

The Eclipse of the Holy

The breakdown of our symbols and traditions contributes to the eclipse of the holy in our lives and is reinforced by the reigning pastoral paradigm that overly accentuates the individual. In this orientation, personality and personal identity become their own ends, and, as previously noted, any genuine need for transcendence remains unmet. In the place of satisfying and meaningful expressions of faith, many people are tempted by a weak form of individual piety that, in practice, reflects the same aims of personal growth referred to in the previous chapter. This pale form of spirituality substitutes the longing for "something more" with the belief in "this is all there is," robbing people of hope and an authentic sense of the holy.

When a sense of transcendence is diminished, we no longer have holy ground on which to stand with bare feet and open hands. Instead, we are left with a barren landscape that produces cynicism on the one hand or forced optimism on the other. Cynicism and what Douglas John Hall calls "credulity" have become two functional spiritualities in twenty-first-century North America. We find these dueling belief systems at home in the culture at large and in many of our churches as well. Hall refers to them as the spiritualities of the "officially optimistic society." They displace hope for authentic depth and meaning. When they influence our theologies and practices of ministry, suffering is defused and the burdens of people become multiplied.

Both the cynic and the optimist emphasize the centrality of human wisdom and insight. The cynic does so by granting too much power to human knowledge. The cynic *expects* successful outcomes as a result of human ingenuity, and when they are not forthcoming, disappointment sets in hard and deep. When problems persist and progress stops, the world and its people are judged harshly. When human will is thwarted, the cynic sees few if any alternatives to challenging situations, no viable openings for change. The cynic sees static, hopeless situations that offer little relief to victims of suffering. For the cynic, the air we breathe becomes thin with un-dreams and dis-illusions. Holiness becomes meaningless as God becomes seen as ineffective and untrustworthy, or simply absent.

The optimist, on the other hand, sees behind every cloud a silver lining. Given a little time, things will get better. This, of course, is rarely the case. Circumstances seldom change for the good by simply waiting for them to do so, even when accompanied by positive thinking. The optimist believes in chance, benevolent fate, and the blessing of the gods. Unlike the cynic, whose high hopes become dashed when human wisdom fails, the optimist actually begins with a rather low expectation of human ability to create meaningful change. The optimist ascribes too little to human knowledge and all knowledge to an all-powerful God. All the same, whether overvalued or underestimated, the place of human wisdom figures prominently as the pivotal axis on which hope turns for both the cynic and the optimist. But the optimist negotiates with the world in ways to minimize the impact of not having his or her expectations met.

Unlike the cynic, the optimist insists on certain modes of behavior and ways of belief that are supposed to assure a certain and unfailing happiness. *Certain* is the operative term. The world is supposed to look and feel and respond in certain positive ways. For this reason, the optimist has a difficult time coping with situations that are ambiguous or contradictory to his or her perceived ordering of life. Furthermore, to maintain this "supposed order," the optimist must limit the sorts of encounters she or he has with many aspects of the world. For example, it is hard for the optimist to explain the "contrary evidence" when he or she makes the occasional wrong turn onto a street where vacant lots are littered with old couches and discarded hypodermic needles. The optimist has difficulty when someone sits next to her on the streetcar who smells bad and seems to be riding simply because he doesn't have anywhere else to go. The optimist needs to hold a tight reign on the world to make it line up with a cheerful ideal. God needs to be kept separate and apart from all opposing and harsh realities. The optimist's God "is in heaven, and all is right with the world." But this is a most difficult arrangement, if not an impossible undertaking!

Both the optimist and the cynic avoid depth. The cynic does so through an inadequate reading of life, which says that there is nothing more than what I see and experience. The optimist, on the other hand, is convinced by the equally mistaken belief that this is all there is—and it is good! Each is convinced that his or her interpretation of how the world operates, or how it should, is right. And this helps create a climate of narrow self-righteousness that works to keep their respective views intact. Both are individualistic readings of the world that deny the world and the sources of holiness available to it.

One way the cynic rejects the world is by withdrawing from its overwhelming problems to a more private and manageable environment. Caught up in what Dorothee Soelle calls "anthropological pessimism,"[4] the cynic who does not expect anything good from people turns inward to concentrate on him- or herself. Holiness might be discovered internally, in oneself, apart from the world. On the other hand, the optimist denies the world by simply avoiding its crueler aspects and only allowing certain experiences into view. The optimist believes that the environment can be successfully managed, so if the world "out there" cannot be changed, it can at least be contained. However, when something negative does break through, the optimist, along with the cynic, rationalizes, "If the world out there cannot be changed, the world close at hand can—that world being my individual self." So they both imagine. The result of these world-denying

[4]Dorothee Soelle, *Choosing Life* (Philadelphia: Fortress Press, 1981), 28.

responses is that suffering in the world remains unacknowledged and is left to fester and grow.

By accenting the wisdom and inner world of individuals, both optimism and cynicism are completely compatible with and conform to our personalized culture of self-realization. They are strong forces that feed the personal growth industry as a way to recover the holy dimensions of life.

Personal growth may seem to be the answer to a prayer for some; it sometimes substitutes for prayer for others. For those inside the dominant religious, political, and economic systems this may seem to be a workable option, but it is really a false security. Personal growth will ultimately collapse in on itself when it is disconnected from its social and relational environments. It is an inadequate spirituality that not only eclipses the possibility of authentic holiness but also obscures the suffering of people who live with the wounds from historical injuries. Personal growth avoids their suffering and therefore denies their hopes. In fact, it is precisely because individualized personal growth denies historical aspects of human suffering that it also rejects the holy, which cannot be segmented. Holiness cannot be separated from the world and all its complications. It cannot be reserved for some people but not for all. By denying the world and its historical processes, personal growth left to itself supports the status quo and helps maintain an intact and unjust social order. Holiness withers and eventually dies in such a climate, and so does hope. Hope and holiness reside together or not at all.

For those who experience an unyielding and increasingly rigid social system, personal growth is not enough. Forces that can intervene from outside the existing social order are necessary for their survival and any sense of hope for a different future. For many outside the historically dominant white middle-class society, transcendence as an expression of a true alternative to systems of injustice plays a central role in their lives. Transcendence as an intervening force for right living signifies the hope for recovering holiness and, ultimately, our selves.

The Eclipse of the Self

The concern about a diminished sense of the holy is not about the threat of secularization. Rather, it is about what happens when human life becomes isolated through self-preoccupation, allowing the dehumanizing forces that exploit and destroy to gain strength. The self, then, as well as the holy, becomes diminished rather than "realized." Through uncritical cultivation of personalistic spiritualities, the suffering of others becomes ignored and sometimes intensified. In this way inadequate spiritualities actually become self-destructive, deceptive, and harmful.

The uncritical cultivation of individualistic forms of spirituality is vulnerable to the same dangers as the cults of self-realization; they both may simply advance a quest for higher stages of consciousness or advanced forms of personal development. When spirituality is promoted to serve these ends alone, it participates in and replicates the pervasive consumer mentality that is rampant across the globe. Spirituality becomes captivated by what United Church of Christ pastor Lynice Pinchard calls the "commodity mind,"or it reflects the middle-class values that Soelle criticizes:

> Many middle-class people are seeking today for a new spirituality. They want to add something to what they already have: education and profession, upbringing and secure income, family and friends. Religious fulfillment, the meaning of life, food for the soul, consolation–all that is to be added on top of material security, as a kind of religious surplus for those who are already over privileged. They seek spiritual fulfillment of life in addition to the material blessing from above to supplement their riches.[5]

Karl Barth, in a somewhat polemical fashion, warned about the dangers inherent is some of these kinds of spiritual practices early in the twentieth century. In his commentary on Paul's letter to the Romans, he insisted on the paradoxical character of the absolute transcendence of God, which we can never reach from our side, which we can never bring down to earth by our efforts or our knowledge, which either comes to us or does not come to us independent from our efforts.[6] He is talking about grace.

The promotion of self-fulfillment through spiritual growth can become an insipid spirituality devoid of real and lasting hope. It might make some of us feel a measure of safety, because it seems to offer a way to manage our lives. But it is ultimately delusional and therefore dangerous. It cannot fulfill its promise. It will not satisfy our hunger or our longing for the lost holy in contemporary life, nor will it touch the radical suffering of some and the historical injuries of others. With its false notion of transcendence based on an overvaluation of human potential, it reinforces the twin counterfeit belief systems of cynicism and optimism mentioned above, which basically say, "Don't get involved. Mind your own business."

However, this criticism of some programs of spiritual growth is not intended to put down the renewal of religious life that is taking place in many places. We need to be encouraged by the authentic quests for the holy and alternative forms of spirituality that are being practiced not only for personal depth but also toward transforming the world. Many sincere people are retrieving older spiritual practices as well as seeking new ones in order to exercise their faithfulness and serve others.[7] They testify to the

---

[5]Dorothee Soelle, *The Window of Vulnerability: A Political Spirituality* (Minneapolis: Fortress Press, 1990), 16.

[6]Karl Barth, *The Epistle to the Romans,* trans. Edwyn C. Hoskins (London: Oxford University Press, 1968).

[7]Thank you to Joseph Driskill, professor of Protestant Spirituality at Pacific School of Religion, for his insights on these practices of faithfulness.

human need to trust. They show us that hope is not so easily destroyed. They demonstrate that even during confusing and perplexing times the propensity to trust survives in some exquisite ways in unexpected places. A faith that holds this attraction begs for expression.

In spite of these hopeful signs, we are by and large a culture that still lends itself to soft piety and formulaic responses to the complex problems we face. These attitudes lead us away from solutions altogether by allowing us to avoid ambiguous situations and turn our attention away from the historical issues that underlie suffering. They also leave little room for the doubts that surface when we face extreme forms of human suffering that defy explanations. In these ways we still banish sufferers as we try to save ourselves. To the extent we do this, we end up rejecting the holy and, ultimately, ourselves.

Spiritualities that flirt with cynicism and walk with optimism minimize and falsely explain the suffering of many people. When they are aligned with individualistic forms of spiritual growth, they also deny avenues for real healing and reconciliation. Caught in a labyrinth that leads nowhere, we lose ourselves. In order to respond, pastoral theologians will need to struggle with how we frame our relationship with the holy, how we articulate an authentic piety. This is not a new struggle, but it takes on special significance as we face these strong cultural forces and diverse spiritualities that have taken root in our contemporary landscape. We will need to pay close attention to what is happening and be careful not to join in evading suffering, lest we, too, risk closing ourselves to encounters with the holy. We do not want to hobble ourselves with an inability to express authentic faith, nor do we want to cut ourselves off from sources of healing for the wider community. As much as we talk about healing as a function, it is not. Healing ultimately springs from contact with holiness, at least this is what is confessed throughout the various faith traditions.

Days of Longing

The spirit of "official optimism" and its counterpart, cynicism, are symptomatic of the loss of our common life. The deep symbols and myths that once supported us are faltering, and the spiritualities that are trying to take their place are fragile and incomplete. These trends have been developing over time and have not gone unnoticed by pastoral theologians. Many have struggled with them and have lamented the failure of earlier pastoral reforms to address them. For example, the 1960s "reformation," which attempted to cultivate human potential and responsibility for personal *and* social renewal, ended up increasing a focus on interior life. This contributed to the inward thrust of the 1970s that resulted in the "me generation" of the 1980s. Among other factors, the New Age spiritualities of the 1990s reflected the unmet longings of these years as well as the individual approach to pastoral care that permeated them. Increasingly, pastoral theologians are coming to terms with the limitations inherent in these movements and are trying to address them.

Although the individualistic therapeutic paradigm still functions within the broad field of pastoral theology, it is being challenged and modified by an increasing number of pastoral theologians who view the person as culturally and socially formed. The psychological underpinnings that have shaped pastoral theology are being reexamined, and theology and the faith traditions are being reclaimed as central to pastoral care. While these are days of loss, they are also days of longing as pastoral theologians grapple with these issues.

The Reclaiming of Theology

The relationship between psychology and theology and how they inform pastoral care is not a new issue. David Roberts and Albert Outler debated it more than half a century ago. Roberts emphasized that psychology could be an aid to religion when he argued, "My main purpose, is to convey to someone who knows little or nothing about psychotherapy an impression of how it obtains results that in some respects parallel what religion seeks to do."[8] Roberts' position supported the idea that perhaps psychology, with its implicit "faith assumptions," was the best interpreter of the human condition.[9] Outler, on the other hand, claimed that theology should challenge and deepen psychology. In other words, theology was to be understood as the primary interpreter of life. What was at stake in these debates was the basic paradigm that would orient pastoral care and theology for the next generation. In the end, Roberts' point of view, that psychology would interpret theology, was more convincing to pastoral theologians.

Thomas Kuhn's definition of *paradigm* is helpful here. As a coherent research tradition, a particular paradigm defines the types of problems to be examined, the interpretations to be applied, the range of explanations that can be given, as well as certain assumptions about the nature of the world. For example, in the case of the scientific paradigm, the world is seen as predictable, knowable, and credible.[10] In other words, a paradigm determines how we view the world and its inhabitants. Until now, modern pastoral care and theology have relied on a therapeutic paradigm, one construed mainly from the various schools of psychology. And psychology is considered, by most, to be a scientific discipline. Pastoral care, by adopting this paradigm, has assumed this scientific worldview. The scientific worldview is based on "doubt," not the doubt that accepts and welcomes

---

[8] David E. Roberts, *Psychotherapy and a Christian View of Man* (New York: Charles Scribner's Sons, 1950), xiv.

[9] E. Brooks Holifield, *A History of Pastoral Care in America: From Salvation to Self-Realization* (Nashville: Abingdon Press, 1983), 328.

[10] Thomas S. Kuhn, *The Structure of Scientific Revolutions* (Chicago: University of Chicago Press, 1962).

the ineffable and mysterious aspects of life, but the Enlightenment view of doubt mentioned earlier, which promotes human knowledge for understanding oneself and the world around us. "Dare to know" means "doubt" what you cannot understand.

An alternative to this is a theological paradigm grounded in a faith orientation. Here, doubt is not something to be resolved but is that which confronts us and leads us in new ways of living and being. A faith paradigm offers a radically alternative standpoint and reveals our old assumptions in totally new perspectives. This implies a complete transformation of our imaginations and a shift in our political commitments. However, this theological or faith paradigm can only be practiced when there are structures and alternative systems of knowledge to support it. Outler's claim that theology, or the faith paradigm, can challenge and deepen our psychological worldview is being revisited and taken more seriously by a number of pastoral theologians at this juncture in our lives.[11]

The Society for Pastoral Theology, formed in 1985, was organized to address the need to more intentionally reclaim theology as a rightful conversation partner for pastoral care and theology. It was not formed to abandon the contributions made to the field by the psychological sciences. Within the society, too, there is a growing recognition that other social and political sciences in addition to psychology offer needed tools for analyzing and describing our social and historical contexts. This suggests a deep respect for wisdom forged through human knowledge that should not to be forsaken; rather, it is to be cultivated under the tutelage of faith. The society was formed because a growing number people within the field began to recognize that theology is needed for a depth interpretation of psychological and social scientific findings.

Yet even here, the psychotherapeutic worldview still has a powerful claim on its members. At a recent meeting, a group of seminary professors gathered to discuss some of the emerging themes in the field.[12] After examining a representative sample of syllabi for introductory courses in pastoral care and theology, one participant noted that there were very few theological texts listed as required texts on the syllabi being reviewed. As yet, theology does not seem to have emerged as a strong voice in our teaching.

Perhaps more important, the recent move to *reclaim* theology belies the deeper and potentially more serious problem that has plagued the field of pastoral care for some time. If something has to be reclaimed, it has not been there. This acknowledges that something other than theology–for

---

[11]One among many is Don Browning, particularly his *Religious Thought and the Modern Psychologies: A Critical Conversation in the Theology of Culture* (Philadelphia: Fortress Press, 1987).

[12]Before its annual meeting in 1999, a group of pastoral theologians met in Denver, Colorado, to look at how the introductory courses in pastoral care and theology were being designed and taught in various seminaries across the country.

example, psychology–has primarily informed our theory and practices. This raises critical questions about what our aims are and how we go about achieving them. If something other than a faith perspective informs our starting place, it makes sense that there will be a loss of depth, theological meaning, and sense of the holy.

In order to engage pastoral care from a theological perspective–in other words, to interpret our lives through a theological paradigm–we still need to rediscover what George Lindbeck calls our "grammar" of faith. This is not just a matter of learning the words that others have said or producing a scheme of how these words fit together in some coherent manner. Or as mentioned earlier, it is not about correlation, even a critical correlation between theology and psychology or any of the other social sciences. It means discovering in this postmodern, and what some call post-Christian time, that absurd posture of trust in something more than human wisdom, yet revealed, in part, through human understanding.

The confidence of faith is always absurd, because everything in our experience tries to convince us to place our trust somewhere else. To risk this kind of trust means we do so through our longings–and sometimes our tears. All our discussions about how to relate theology and psychology, or any other academic discipline for that matter, really belie our deep hunger to touch and be touched by what lies deeper than any synthesis and beyond any correlation. Our search for foundations, adequate methods, and whatever we point to that can stand as core literature in our field is really an overture to something that is more than all of these together. It is a search for that something, or someone, who might breathe life into our feeble gestures, hope into tired limbs, and healing into our fractured bodies and communities. This search for our rightful beginning place has something to do with discovering our authentic piety. This is a confessional posture that involves cultivating a theological paradigm to guide our work.

The Reclaiming of Tradition

Theology cannot be done in a vacuum. It involves being in conversation with the traditions of our faith as well as contemporary life experiences. If the loss of traditions and the breakdown of our symbolic life are threatening our well-being, this task becomes monumental. Recognition of this state of affairs has prompted some pastoral theologians to seek out the classical traditions of pastoral care in order to recover them for contemporary use.

Thomas C. Oden's *Care of Souls in the Classic Tradition* is one example of this search for an authentic foundation to meet the longings of people today.[13] However, his approach has not paid careful enough attention to the differences between the historical period being retrieved, its worldviews

---

[13]Thomas C. Oden, *Care of Souls in the Classic Tradition*, Theology and Pastoral Care (Philadelphia: Fortress Press, 1984).

and assumptions, and our contemporary context to which it is being applied. Too often the past has been arbitrarily chosen and not "critically retrieved" as a resource for current pastoral practices. We cannot simply appropriate traditions or knowledge from one context and transfer them to another without examining their inherited worldviews and cultural biases. We cannot treat pastoral insights or spiritual wisdom of one era as if they were timeless truths for all situations. They are not. New times require fresh perspectives. As a corrective to this limitation, some pastoral theologians are beginning to examine the emerging literature on postmodernism and the implications of deconstruction for pastoral care and theology.

Claiming Postmodern Insights

The impact of the pluralistic nature of our world today, as much as any other factor, helps leverage the need for critically examining the dominating forces of an individualistic, evolutionary pastoral paradigm. At a preconference gathering before the 1999 Annual Meeting of the Society for Pastoral Theology in Denver, Colorado, the impact of postmodernism on the field of pastoral care and theology was the main topic for discussion. Participants began to find the deconstruction of modernism through the tools of literary and textual criticism of given theories a helpful and necessary way to engage the multidimensional world in which we live. They also found them helpful for critiquing the tyranny of essentialist theories embedded in pastoral care.[14]

However, it is helpful to recognize that postmodernism is a philosophical expression for the theological breakdown of our symbolic life, as noted by Ed Farley. Deconstruction is a method to examine this particular phenomenon, not an answer to it. It is important to distinguish between the two. Without making this distinction, deconstruction as a method becomes confused with a particular philosophical orientation. Deconstruction then becomes seen as an end in itself and not as a tool for providing an opening for something new. When this conflation happens, deconstruction takes on an unintended role and begins to create its own form of rigidity for approaching texts. In this fashion it can become cynical and nihilistic.

Postmodern thinking is very "here and now" centered, very time-limited, specific, local, and oral. It does not locate authority in the past (traditions) and does not place an emphasis on the future (vision). In fact, the deconstruction of modernism can be engaged in a way that only acts. Without a past or traditions, such actions risk becoming rootless and perhaps meaningless. Without a future, hope is dimmed, and the climate ripens for the spirituality of cynicism mentioned earlier.

Furthermore, as pastoral theologians we need to be mindful that the secular postmodernist's "faith in the particular" might represent a historical

---

[14] As a participant of this conversation, I appreciated the lively discussion and the valuable insights that were shared.

culmination of the humanistic movement in philosophical terms: faith in "human knowledge in particular." It is not a method that counters faith in the autonomous individual. It does not alter some of the basic assumptions of the Horatio Alger myth. By uncritically adopting the methods of deconstruction that presuppose this philosophical bias, we could find ourselves advancing the psychotherapeutic paradigm rather than radically altering it. We could, then, even find ourselves supporting the destructive rampant economic individualism mentioned earlier, rather than challenging it.

As we entertain postmodern critiques and methods developed in other disciplines, we need to ask the hard question, Are we still feeling the need to prove that pastoral theology is a legitimate academic field? If this is a concern, we need to carefully discern when and how we adopt procedures and methods developed in cognate branches of learning. We need to ask when and how they further the aims of pastoral care and theology and when they serve primarily to bolster the field within the academy. The danger is that if language and logic and second-level analysis become too reified and disengaged from the concerns of our shared community life, we will again eclipse the real suffering of people.

The insights of postmodernism and the methods of deconstruction are valuable and necessary, but they need to be appropriated carefully. While they can help us describe and analyze the fragmented, pluralistic, and fluid nature of our modern world, a faith perspective is still needed for a depth reading of it. Theological sources that can address the ambiguous, uncertain, and provisional understandings of life circumstances need to be cultivated more than ever before for our current situations of loss, dislocation, and identity confusion.

Engaging the Politics of Identity

In our cultural morass there is a growing loss of identity amidst a politics of identity. This will be a key challenge for pastoral care and pastoral theology as identity becomes an ever more critical issue for all people in the twenty-first century. No one group of people will represent a normative majority. We will need to come to terms with this reality and the fact that our identities involve more than our individual selves. This new self-understanding will require forging fresh forms of self-realization within our changing cultural context. It will involve recapturing what it means to be a citizen and imagining creative ways to live this out. Membership in the new world will become an even more important concern for pastoral theologians as we traverse the terrain between public and private domains. We will need to attend to new ways of approaching what Steven Carter terms "civility," that social and political way of living together in which we are willing to make many "sacrifices for others" as a "signal of respect," even love, for one another as full equals before God.[15]

---

[15]Stephen L. Carter, *Civility: Manners, Morals, and the Etiquette of Democracy* (New York: Basic Books, 1998), 12.

Pastoral Care at the Crossroads

Our cultural context is more than a postmodern dilemma. It is more than the breakdown of superpowers where there is no clear enemy. Amidst a multiplicity of realities, there are persistent injustices that continue to plague us. Historical injuries are acerbated by what we might call the "moving target of responsibility," where blame or cause resists our every attempt to rest accountability. Pastoral theology is caught in these crosscurrents.

Pastoral care is practiced under the shadow of a failed American Dream. We thought we could build a society that succeeds where others have not, but in fact the dream has failed many of its citizens. The "Life, liberty and the pursuit of happiness" dream of our founders has become a nightmare for a growing number of people. The belief in the ability to prosper through hard work, and a trust in something vaguely defined as "progress" is experienced as pain for a large number of people who work and still do not prosper. In truth, and in practice, progress means profit. And profit is the bottom line.

By substituting profit for people and success for symbols, late capitalism has been able to subvert our very desires and dreams. Instead of deep satisfying relationships with neighbors and friends, our environment, and our God, market success has become our aim and reason for being. Economic growth confined to private and individual initiative is our highest national good. Where religion blesses this process, Soelle says, "it only functions in order to comfort the sad, enrich personal life, and give the individual the feeling of significance."[16]

Pastoral theology has, perhaps unknowingly, been powerfully supportive rather than critical of these processes. In the United States pastoral theology has been strongly identified with and influenced by Protestantism as it developed on North American soil. As Ernst Troeltsch demonstrated in his *Protestantism and Progress,* Protestantism became closely allied with capitalism.[17] It is perhaps unavoidable that pastoral theology as a product of North American Protestantism shares at least some aspects of this relationship with capitalism and, by implication, its tendency to objectify people. Where this is the case, our response to our current impasse cannot simply be reform or the recovery of practices of care that have been lost. Pastoral theology cannot "restore" what it has not established—a true and just alternative.

We need to recover an alternative ecclesial lens and reconceive pastoral practices that can engage people of faith in the complexities of modern life at this beginning of the twenty-first century. We need to recover collective

---

[16]Soelle, *Choosing Life,* 82.
[17]Ernst Troeltsch, *Protestantism and Progress: The Significance of Protestantism for the Rise of the Modern World* (Philadelphia: Fortress Press, 1986).

practices that foster self-realization within the renewal of religious life. While we need to do this in dialogue with secular insights and knowledge, we need to do it without becoming uncritically attached to them. Unless we do so, we are in danger of offering too little too late to those who suffer historical injuries.

Hints and Glimpses of Something New

At the beginning of the twenty-first century, something new is breaking into the world of pastoral theology that holds the promise of meeting some of the challenges of our time. Although not fully developed, the contours of an emerging paradigm suggest that pastoral theologians are starting to recognize how the rights of the individual are often tied to public privilege. The autonomous individual as the centerpiece of our theory and practice is beginning to be joined by a growing awareness of his or her social context. This means that a fresh notion of "peoplehood," not just the individual, may become the reference point for pastoral care and theology in the future.

Underrepresented communities in the U.S. have been instrumental in forging this new awareness and are becoming more vocal in their challenges to the norms of pastoral theology that promote individualistic and private views of care. Feminist voices have led the way by articulating a relational meaning of identity, as shown by the growing body of literature in the field, such as *Through the Eyes of Women; Women in Travail and Transition;* and *Feminist and Womanist Pastoral Theology,* to name a few. As mentioned earlier, the works by Archie Smith, Jr., *Relational Self* and his more recent *Navigating the Deep River,* and Larry Graham's *Care of Persons, Care of Worlds* draw from narrative, systems theory, and interdisciplinary methods for addressing people within their social and cultural contexts. Edward Wimberly writes out of an African American faith tradition and speaks forcefully about the rich pastoral resources and the theological contributions of the black church, pointing out the communal nature of pastoral care and theology. Larry Graham and Joretta Marshall are now writing pastoral theology that addresses the needs of gay and lesbian communities.[18]

---

[18]Jeanne Stevenson-Moessner, ed., *Through the Eyes of Women: Insights for Pastoral Care* (Minneapolis: Fortress Press, 1996); Stevenson-Moessner and Maxine Glaz, eds., *Women in Travail and Transition: A New Pastoral Care* (Minneapolis: Fortress Press, 1991); Bonnie J. Miller-McLemore and Brita L. Gill-Austern, eds., *Feminist and Womanist Pastoral Theology* (Nashville: Abingdon Press, 1999); Archie Smith, Jr., *The Relational Self: Ethics and Therapy from a Black Church Perspective* (Nashville: Abingdon Press, 1982); Smith, *Navigating the Deep River: Spirituality in African American Families* (Cleveland: United Church Press, 1997); Larry Kent Graham, *Care of Persons, Care of Worlds: A Psychosystems Approach to Pastoral Care and Counseling* (Nashville: Abingdon Press, 1992); Edward P. Wimberly, *Relational Refugees: Alienation and Reincorporation in African American Churches and Communities* (Nashville: Abingdon Press, 2000); Graham, *Discovering Images of God: Narratives of Care among Lesbians and Gays* (Louisville: Westminster John Knox Press, 1997); and Joretta L. Marshall, *Counseling Lesbian Partners* (Louisville: Westminster John Knox Press, 1997).

The emerging pastoral paradigm is beginning to recognize the complex interplay between people and their social and cultural environments, their institutions, and their systems of government. Pastoral theology cannot be separated from this historical context. Pastoral theology, too, is socially constructed. Furthermore, this means that the findings of pastoral theology have political implications. This makes pastoral theology a political theology.

As people and their communities become primary sources of theological knowledge and the focus of pastoral inquiry, human suffering resulting from oppression and injustice will challenge our conventional ways of conceiving theory and practice. As this happens, liberation, both in personal and political terms, will become the test of our pastoral methods and theories. Personal healing will be related to communal well-being. Although it is difficult to imagine the needed new social order that will allow all people to flourish, it is clear that a functional approach to theory and practice will not suffice.

We clearly need to move away from pastoral functions that maintain old ways of living and engage in less familiar but freeing practices that allow for something new to come into being. We will need to practice what we cannot predict until the outline of a new vision begins to form, a vision where dominant voices might not be the chief architects. This says something about living and working in faith, resisting taken-for-granted insights, and reclaiming an authentic piety that walks the way of unknowing. The way of unknowing points to a faith orientation that acknowledges the limits of human understanding.

Toward an Alternative Approach to Pastoral Theology

If we are experiencing an "eclipse of the holy," where do we turn? What faith posture can we assume? It needs to be something other than a doctrinal position or a fixed set of beliefs that serve to guide our actions. Perhaps we need first to recognize that faith is not something certain, or else it wouldn't be faith; it would be called something else. Faith invites us to encounter what we do not know. It leads us through hints and guesses into unexpected places. Such "trusting insecurity" is a posture of radical faith we tend not to practice when we feel materially comfortable and socially secure. But it is precisely this radical faith that risks everything, even academic credibility, for the sake of something genuinely new. We need to recover this posture of faith, along with a renewed sense of future. We need to cultivate a corporate ability to imagine and dream once more.

We need a faith posture that assumes life in its totality, with no strict dichotomy between our private and public realms or barrier between who we are as believers and who we are as citizens. We need a faith that is as concerned with economics and the social order as it is with prayer and sacraments. In other words, we need a faith stance that does not separate the pastoral from the prophetic. Only then will we recover the holy in our midst and a deeper appreciation of ourselves. A pastoral theology that can guide an alternative approach to pastoral care requires this faith point of view.

A political interpretation of the cross offers an alternative lens for pastoral theology today. The cross recognizes and respects the limitations of life, not just progress. The cross acknowledges suffering and untold tragedy. Yet it puts a question mark next to anything that seems to suggest complete understanding or a "last word" approach to life. A political theology of the cross offers a place to stand when we cannot see the new vision that is forming. It means we believe that there is something more even when we don't fully know what it is. The cross simply calls us to take a stand, to break with neutrality and passivity and account for whose side we are on. In this way Paul's injunction "to take up your cross" is a call to join the struggle for justice. Or as Soelle says, "Put yourself on the side of the damned of this world."[19]

Douglas John Hall has called the theology of the cross the "thin tradition" that has always been present in some form throughout the history of Christianity. It has functioned to critique reigning ideologies and the church's tendency toward abuse. He is not talking about times when the church has distorted the meaning of the cross and used it to subdue dissent or impose imperialistic aims. Instead, a theology of the cross as the "thin tradition" offers an interpretive framework for entering into historical ambiguities in order to engage people who are suffering. The "thin tradition" is a political interpretation of the cross. Soelle rightly agrees, "The cross is the place where Christians stand when they begin to become aware of the civilization of injustice, and of estrangement as sin."[20]

We are living in perilous times and fragile settings, waiting for a new heaven and earth. We are longing for a new home and an answer to the eucharistic prayer where "We pray for a vision of the day when sharing by all will mean scarcity for none." A political interpretation of the cross offers this hope and a way to enter it. The cross offers a way for pastoral theology to recover the holy and find new practices of care that help us live into our counterstory.

---

[19]Soelle, *Choosing Life*, 53.
[20]Ibid., 47.

CHAPTER
FOUR

"In a Dark Time the Eye Begins to See"[1]

Interpretations of the Theology of the Cross, Part One

*The theology of the cross can never be a brilliant
statement about the brokenness of life; it has
to be a broken statement about life's brokenness,
because it participates in what it seeks to describe.*[2]

DOUGLAS JOHN HALL

In an out-of-the-way nightclub, an eighty-year-old African American woman sings about a life of poverty and sorrow and survival. When she finishes her set, she says, "I don't want to sing the blues, but I got to." And she adds, "I know this isn't a church, but thank the Lord." She sings from the depths of her soul, and her listeners recognize that she is saying

---

[1]Theodore Roethke, "In a Dark Time," *The Collected Poems of Theodore Roethke* (Garden City, N.Y.: Anchor Press/Doubleday, 1975), 231.
[2]Douglas John Hall, *Lighten Our Darkness: Toward an Indigenous Theology of the Cross* (Philadelphia: Westminster Press, 1976), 117.

something very true about struggle and hope and, ultimately, self-determination.[3]

Contemporary feminist folk singer Holly Near says that she gave up singing the blues written for women. She said it wasn't because she couldn't sing the music, but that she found it hard to get behind words that say things like "Beat me, kick me, I'll go anywhere you want me to and won't mind."[4] So instead of singing songs that reinforce pain, she writes her own version of the blues, singing that she won't live in pain anymore. Her listeners hear something strong about resistance, defiance, and hope for a life freed from abuse and unnecessary sorrow.

Both these artists sing about their experiences of suffering and uninvited pain. They tell the truth about their lives, refusing to remain silent about something that is unhealthy for them and others. Through their music they resist what is unjust and harmful. A political interpretation of the cross can do no less. It must begin with truth telling, and "truth hearing," and end by resisting the unjustly imposed suffering that is so prevalent in our world. In other words, a political reading of the cross cannot simply be a statement of belief that can be taught to someone so they can consider its relative merit. It begins with a different and rather messy approach to theology, one that first takes seriously those who are saying something about the incredible hardships they live with.

Robert McAfee Brown challenges all North American theologians who are overly confident of their positions when he quotes one of Elie Wiesel's characters: "When a Jew says he is suffering, one must believe him, and when he is afraid, one must assume his fear is justified. In neither case does one have the right to doubt his word. Even if one cannot help him, one must at least believe him."[5] Brown says that this honest recognition of the reality of suffering of another, in this instance a Jewish person, provides the starting point for theology. Suffering means, "When we hear the cry, 'I'm hurting,' we must take it seriously." This is messy. This holds the very real possibility of calling into question everything we might think we already know, because this tilts the location of authority away from us toward those whose understanding is formed under different circumstances.

When Brown talks about believing someone who is hurting, he means taking them so seriously that we are even willing to be judged by their

---

[3]James H. Cone, *The Spirituals and the Blues: An Interpretation* (Maryknoll, N.Y.,: Orbis Books, 1991). Cone talks about how black music creates a new political and theological consciousness that is liberating and counter to the racist laws of white society, pp. 5–7.

[4]Holly Near, "Get Off Me Baby" (lyrics by Holly Near; music by Holly Near and Jeffrey Langley, 1973) on *A Live Album* (Ukiah, Calif.: Redwood Records, 1974).

[5]Robert McAfee Brown, "Liberation Theology: Paralyzing Threat or Creative Challenge?" in *Mission Trends No. 4: Liberation Theologies,* ed. Gerald H. Anderson and Thomas F. Stransky, C.S.P. (New York: Paulist Press; Grand Rapids: Eerdmans, 1979), 214.

experience. We may in fact discover that we have been a party to the very conditions that contributed to their suffering in the first place–and that is a painful revelation. Some feminist theologians know this difficult lesson well, as we have had to face how our own methods and styles of doing scholarship have not only excluded the voices and wisdom of women of color but have added to their hardships.

The song of an old African American blues singer commands the same starting place as the Jew who says he is suffering. So does the protest voice of a feminist songwriter. We must believe them. They not only sing their own songs, they invite us to hear the voices lying hidden in the stones that cry out. These voices, and those of others who experience pain but only know how to sigh, demand to be heard. They insist on relief from their suffering. Any pastoral theology that attempts to understand and address their circumstances will need to take their suffering most seriously by being willing to participate in their struggles for relief. By doing so, it will participate in reviving hope for all people, because in the end we are inescapably related to one another. And if it is true that we are experiencing an eclipse of sacred depth, only as we move together will we be open to receiving the holy again in our time. A political interpretation of the cross offers a faith posture that can help lead pastoral theology in this restorative direction. But first it is important to say what this orientation of the cross is not. Although not completely separate from them, it does not represent a continuation of the traditional atonement theories of the cross.

Traditional Interpretations of the Cross

As stated in the first chapter, any interpretation of the theology of the cross must be approached with caution. The cross is a stumbling block. It is a central symbol of the Christian faith, for many a symbol of hope and salvation. And it is itself a symbol of violence and humiliation, a symbol of failure from the perspective of its use in Roman executions. It is a mean and grotesque symbol that cannot be "prettied" or denied. It is a symbol that some wish could be discarded and that others simply ignore.

The cross has been used as a symbol of imperialism (during the crusades), and it has been used to keep subjugated people "in their place," assigned to them by the dominants of the culture. Women have been especially vulnerable to this oppressive interpretation of the cross when we have been led to believe that it is virtuous to "bear your cross" in the form of enduring abuse from our husbands or other significant, and sometimes not-so-significant, people in our lives. We have been told to "bear your cross" under intolerable and unfair working conditions. It is to this theme of oppression that the folk singer objects when she declines to sing the "traditional" blues written for women. This oppressive interpretation of the cross is a distortion and a violation of human trust and dignity. It is not a life-giving theology of the cross; it is a travesty of the cross that privatizes suffering and participates in its continuation. A political interpretation of the cross that pays particular attention to both historically imposed and unjust experiences of suffering is needed to address this distortion.

There are two interpretations of the cross from the Middle Ages that have dominated Western Christianity and have helped perpetuate the "un-freedom" of those already suffering unbearable burdens. One is the satisfaction theory of atonement associated with Anselm's substitutionary redemption, and the other is Abelard's moral influence theory, based on sacrificial love. These two strands from Christian tradition reflect the doctrines of atonement most frequently referenced by Protestants as well as Catholics. These motifs reflect an emphasis on the transcendent reality of faith as manifested and embodied in a special institution, the church. They assume a special and sacred society that interprets the nature of its life through these doctrines.

The doctrines of atonement assume a certain relationship between God and the world and human beings from a hierarchical worldview. They do not foster mutual relations among people, between people and God, or within any of the whole, animated realm of God. Such an arrangement inhibits people from advocating on their own behalf and resisting conditions that are harmful. To paraphrase Martin Luther, the doctrines of atonement create the dilemma: How do those of us who are the subject of imposed suffering ever possess a righteousness that would enable us to stand in God's presence? A political interpretation of the theology of the cross turns this question around. It says that it is precisely those who are the subject of suffering who are able to stand in God's presence. Because the starting place of the cross engages this question, suffering critiques all theologies of atonement that have been used to further pain and injustice.[6] An interpretation of the theology of the cross that Douglas Hall calls the "thin tradition" is an alternative to the traditional theologies of the cross and has political implications.[7]

A "Thin Tradition" of the Cross

Douglas Hall calls the theology of the cross the "thin tradition" because it has never been a dominant theological theme throughout the history of

---

[6]John Macquarrie, *Jesus Christ in Modern Thought* (London: SCM; Philadelphia: Trinity Press International, 1990), 400–403. Macquarrie also questions the validity of atonement theories that presuppose ideas of God that are questionable from a Christian point of view. He means "theologies which represent God as angry and offended, or as a punishing God intent on exacting the penalty for sin." He notes particularly the theologies of Anselm and Calvin that present "satisfaction" and vicarious suffering theologies of atonement.

[7]Hall, *Lighten Our Darkness*, 113–15. Hall used the term *thin tradition* to talk about the cross of Christ. He sees this as a way of proclaiming the possibility of hope without shutting out the data of despair.

the church.[8] But neither has it been completely absent. The "thin tradition" seems to surface during times of strife and social unrest. It often provides a way to describe these periods. But it also serves to challenge any prevailing interpretations of them that distort or minimize their impact on people. It emerges when the vision of a sustainable world becomes blurred for people who have lost access to the holy and hope for a different future. In the midst of disastrous circumstances it has functioned as solace to suffering people and a critique of oppressive ideologies. The theology of the cross as the "thin tradition" seeks to take the human situation in history seriously, and by so doing it offers the promise of life.

The political cross stands as a corrective and a companion throughout the history of the church and calls for the church and its theology to be the embodiment of the gospel of liberation. As such, it not only reflects the reality of imposed suffering in our midst, it refracts the assumed and "false" world that relentlessly perpetuates it. The language of the cross does not simply repeat, it opens and changes present experience from the perspective of the history of oppression. It truly calls for a new day. As Dorothee Soelle says, "The call to take up the cross is the call to join the struggle. Take sides, break with your neutrality, put yourself on the side of the damned of this world."[9] In this way, a political interpretation of the cross challenges the church and pastoral theology to become more faithful to this gospel reading, especially in the midst of strong cultural forces that tempt us to remain contented with the way things are and complacent about radical change.

The "Thin Tradition" in History

"When a man, no matter who, is tortured and put to death in as cruel a manner as by crucifixion, it must lead to a crisis of human civilization."[10] With these words Hans-Ruedi Weber approaches the cross, its tradition, and interpretation. These words say that even the suffering of one human being must be taken absolutely seriously, not only because that one human being is ultimately important but also because the suffering of one has far-reaching implications for all. It calls into question who we are fundamentally and who we can trust when the suffering of another comes by our own human hands. When the forces of evil combine to eclipse the noonday sun, everything is called into question. Herein lies the real "scandal of particularity," the place where faith, from the point of view of this particularity, begins. Here, too, resides the political significance of the cross. This earliest example of the cross is intimately tied to the suffering and

---

[8]Ibid.

[9]Dorothee Soelle, *Choosing Life* (Philadelphia: Fortress Press, 1981), 53.

[10]Hans-Ruedi Weber, *The Cross: Tradition and Interpretation,* trans. Elke Jessett (Grand Rapids: Eerdmans, 1975), 1.

hope of people and represents the origin of the "thin tradition" of the cross in history.

The "thin tradition" of the cross has always been a minority voice within Christianity. It originated in crisis and has resurfaced at times when people are facing extreme cruelty, tyranny, and domination. The "thin tradition" reappears when people experience an "eclipse of the holy" and the loss of hope. It emerges again when people are confused about who they are and where they belong. It is a tradition that has been called on to renew hope, recover the holy, and provide more authentic ways for us to know who we are. These themes–the recovery of depths and the renewal of hope–have always been associated with the renewal of corporate life, through naming evil and working to restore right living. These are themes of the "thin tradition" that can be called on today to interpret the cross politically for pastoral theology. But first, this particular orientation to the cross needs to be understood historically.

Crucifixion and the Early Church

Whatever else Christian tradition and its interpretations have taught about the crucifixion of Jesus, there is general agreement that the event actually occurred. It is commonly understood that Jesus and his companions lived during a time of religious and political unrest. Violent rebellions and their even more violent repressions marked the comings and goings of their everyday life together. Although in tension with Jewish authorities at the time, Jesus was not crucified by the Jews. The crucifixion was not a Jewish punishment; in fact, Jews abhorred this form of capital punishment, preferring instead death by stoning.[11] The crucifixion was a political event in which temple and palace joined together to accuse Jesus of being an anti-Roman activist in order to reject him and his message. Jesus was crucified under Pontius Pilate, an official of the Roman government. The citizens of Rome, in all their diversity, gathered in attendance to watch the proceedings.

To understand the meaning of this event today, it is important to remember that those who witnessed the crucifixion directly and those who heard about it later understood what was taking place within the Hellenistic world. The Hebraic world of communal living was being torn asunder by the cultural upheavals of assimilation taking place in the region. There was considerable resistance to the emerging Greco-Roman metropolis, with its shifting values and cultural exchange. A whole way of life was under siege as disruptive forces were at work causing widespread fear and alienation among the people. Loss of familiar ways increased their sense of loneliness and threatened to overwhelm them as they tried to make new adjustments.

---

[11]Ibid., 8–9.

While the corporate nature of community life was under attack and new forms were emerging, our current understanding of the human being as autonomous cannot be attributed to this time and place. The cross did not come from a context where people primarily thought in private or personal terms. The cross was an instrument designed for torture in a world of strong, conflicting, cultural forces, where shifting anthropologies were shaping the life of the early followers of Jesus.

It is also important to remember that as the early church tried to understand its own experience and the significance of Jesus' passion, there was no uniform interpretation of Jesus' death.[12] This is still the case. The early witnesses and believers drew from the existing Hebrew Scriptures along with pre- and extra-canonical writings to find images and language to convey their experiences with meaning and force. As they did so, they began to use some of what they found in novel ways to interpret their own particular situation. Again, we still do this today when we preach, teach, and offer pastoral guidance.

Yet, when any tradition is brought forward and adopted for new settings, it brings with it the various meanings that had previously shaped it. Even when certain of these meanings are not featured, they remain dormant within the language and symbols of the tradition and thus remain a part of the ethos of a community through its myths and rituals. In this sense, tradition is less about the recording of historical facts and concepts and more about a living and changing mythos: the collection of stories and legends, ideas and beliefs that inform a people about who they are and what their lives mean. What is part of the fabric of a community's myth, although hidden in the background, always has the potential of coming to the foreground, depending on the circumstances. This way of appropriating tradition was at work in the life of the early church as it sought to express the meaning of Jesus. Even the earliest accounts of the death of Jesus stem from the memory of him as interpreted through scripture, tradition, and other available sources.[13]

New Testament scholars assume that the gospel writers and Paul had access to various common resources.[14] Among the sources that they used to interpret the meaning of Jesus were the lament/praise Psalms, the third

---

[12]Ibid., 52–53.

[13]See John R. Donahue, S.J., "Introduction: From Passion Traditions to Passion Narrative," in *The Passion in Mark: Studies on Mark 14–16*, ed. Werner H. Kelber (Philadelphia: Fortress Press, 1976), 8–16. He also quotes Raymond Brown, *The Gospel According to John*, Anchor Bible 29A (Garden City, N.Y.: Doubleday, 1970), 787–89: "Critical scholars of diverse tendencies (Bultmann, Jeremias, and Taylor, to name a few) agree that the Marcan Passion Narrative is a composite and one of Mark's chief sources was an earlier consecutive account of the passion," 8ff.

[14]Weber, *The Cross*, 31. Key texts included the Hebrew Old Testament, some intertestamental books of wisdom, apocalyptic texts, and precanonical material.

Servant Song of Isaiah (Isa. 50), and the fourth Servant Song of Isaiah (Isa. 53) as well as precanonical accounts of Jesus' life and death. Through the lens of these writings some New Testament scholars contend that the early church saw Jesus as the Suffering Righteous One, or the Suffering Servant prefigured in the scriptures they knew.[15] Herman Waetjen identifies this theme as an essential one, especially for understanding what was going on when the Twelve gathered to share the passover meal with Jesus. Through this reading of Jesus as the Suffering Righteous One, they understood him to be transforming the passover meal into a meal of the new exodus. Waetjen notes that when Jesus declared that one of the Twelve would betray him, he was quoting from Psalm 41:9, the same verse quoted by the Qumran Teacher of Righteousness in 4QH 5:22–24. Here, the righteous individual suffers injustice even at the hands of his friends.[16] Through this understanding of Jesus as teacher of righteousness, they identified him with the Suffering Servant, or Suffering Righteous One, and understood their meal with him as the new exodus.

These scriptural and extrascriptural sources functioned to inform the lives of the believers in significant ways, providing them with interpretations of Jesus that genuinely spoke to them. Some sources were offered as eyewitness accounts of Jesus' life and crucifixion, while others functioned within the worship life of the people as liturgical acts recalling the events (anamnesis).[17] Still others served as prophetic and apocalyptic understandings of the crucifixion, suggested by the image of darkness from the sixth until the ninth hour when it finally ended (Mk. 15:25–34). This apocalyptic understanding was a bold interpretation of Jesus' death that suggested that this seemingly insignificant event would have vast and ongoing importance.

Early Interpretation of the Suffering of Jesus

Significantly absent from these sources is the soteriological rendering of Jesus' death, "He died for our sins." Any transactional or Adoptionist

---

[15]Marinus de Jonge, *Christology in Context: The Earliest Christian Response to Jesus* (Philadelphia: Westminster Press, 1988), 176–79. Here, de Jonge refers to the influence of the Third Servant Song as influencing Mark 10:34; 14:65; 15:19. Drawing from the Wisdom of Solomon 2:12–20 and 5:1–7, he also positions Mark's use of "son of God" within the conception of God's vindication of the righteous man found in the book of Wisdom. De Jonge also discusses the cry "My God, my God, why hast thou forsaken me?" in light of the tradition of the Suffering Servant and suggests that even before Mark's rendering of Jesus' passion this tradition of the suffering righteous was influential in interpreting events in Jesus' life leading to the cross (177).

[16]Herman C. Waetjen, *A Reordering of Power: A Socio-Political Reading of Mark's Gospel* (Minneapolis: Fortress Press, 1989), 208.

[17]Weber, *The Cross,* 48. The eyewitness account of Simon of Cyrene testifies to the historical fact of the crucifixion without giving it any specific theological meaning. But Weber suggests that even the memory of this event and the fact that it was not repressed indicates its theological significance for the early church.

meaning is not attributed to his death and is not a part of these traditions. Nor do these sources suggest a kind of salvation that is esoterically exclusive, limited to a restricted number of individual people. Furthermore, there was no conception of a Messiah who would suffer for the sake of others in a substitutionary way. In fact, the oldest interpretations available did not carry any soteriological meaning in the strictest sense.[18]

Herman Waetjen looks at the suffering of Jesus in a different way. In light of the Righteous One of the Song of Isaiah mentioned earlier, he suggests that Jesus appropriated for himself the role of sacrificial victim. But he makes the point that this identification is only to be understood within his teachings on equality and justice within authentic community: "Jesus' sacrifice is not simply a substitutionary martyrdom which results in God being moved to spare the guilty. The offering of his life or self (psyche) is an eschatological ransom which delivers the creation from its bondage to sin and death by reconstituting the relationship between God and human beings."[19]

A similar observation is made by Marinus de Jong. He points out that 4 Macabees helps us understand how the early followers of Jesus interpreted the events of his death and resurrection. In 6:27–28 and 7:9, 37 the martyr who sacrifices for the sake of God's ordinances is the obedient servant who can bring about a turn in the fate of the people who have fallen away from righteousness.[20] The ethical conduct of the community is implied in these interpretations of Jesus' life and death, not the immortality of an individual soul. People were challenged to counter superficial signs of wealth and prestige that work to deny life and destroy human bonds. Instead, they were offered a way toward true transvaluation of values, where the first become last and the great become servants of all. This is the standard ethical requirement of the realm of God, and even when history defies it, history is forced periodically to turn over its own values and validate it.[21]

The later atonement theories do not abandon these strands of tradition. They show a remarkable variety of interpretations reflecting the historical periods and circumstances in which they evolved. For example, not every theology of atonement carried the notion of vicarious redemption (Anselm). And vicarious redemption was not always a form of sacrificial love (Abelard) as it was developed in the Middle Ages and assumed by many practicing Christians today. Today, Asian theologian C. S. Song discusses an alternative

---

[18]Ibid., 40, 50, 55. Also, de Jong, 181. Here, he discusses the role of the early martyrs who died for God's laws, thus bringing about a turn in the fate of the people. This is an understanding of martyrdom that can be seen as sacrifice for the sake of justice, not as substitution for the perpetrators of injustice. It is a tragic rendering of a martyrdom, not an explanation for the satisfaction of wrongs that have been done.

[19]Waetjen, *Reordering of Power*, 178.

[20]de Jong, *Christology in Context*, 181.

[21]Reinhold Niebuhr, *Beyond Tragedy: Essays on the Christian Interpretation of History* (New York: Charles Scribner's Sons, 1937), 200.

understanding of the atonement from the perspective of the crucified God. He writes that the endless suffering in the world cannot be understood in light of Christ's vicarious suffering. Rather than a God who vicariously suffers and dies *for* the world, God suffers and dies *with* the world. For Song, vicariousness is replaced by identification.[22] In this way he is in accord with Waetjen's understanding of Jesus' assuming of the role of the Suffering Servant of Isaiah 53 as he identifies with his fellow human beings.[23] He is also close to the understanding of Christ that Dorothee Soelle talks about in *Christ the Representative.* Here, she clearly opposes the atonement theories that, as she sees it, lead to Christian apathy or justification of suffering. For Soelle, Christ in no way takes our place, but he does represent us.[24] In a similar vein, Song agrees with the idea that suffering cannot be justified by our theological arguments. He adds that when God is not seen as an explanation of human suffering but understood as one who identifies with human suffering, we are enabled to face ultimate situations of life with equanimity.[25]

Over time, three traditions of the cross gradually evolved: Jesus' death as the Suffering Righteous One, Jesus' death as judgment and a turning point in history, and the tradition of "He died for us." These traditions have not grown into distinct and separate beliefs; instead, they interweave and inform one another. Little debate has ensued over whether or not Jesus was a good and righteous individual. Few would argue that his life and death have not had an incredible impact on the course of human history. But how people have understood "He died for us" has been a major point of contention across worshiping communities as believers try to live their lives faithful to the gospel.

The "He died for us" tradition contains the Greek preposition *hyper,* which can be translated as "for us" or "for our sins." But *hyper* can also be translated as "in favor of," "instead of," "in view of," and "for." Clearly, all of these meanings can be applied to "He died for us." But the meaning "instead of," in the sense of "as proxy," does not have to be the only one focused on. In fact, Weber insists that the phrase "instead of" in the sense of "as proxy" misses its original intent. He suggests that *hyper* can best be translated as "for the redemption/eradication of sins."[26]

When "for the redemption/eradication of sins" is kept in relationship to "in view of," this statement is well within the understanding of ethical judgment on the community. Jesus did die "instead of" someone else, but not as a proxy. He died instead of Barabbas, Mary, Pilate, the Roman

---

[22]Choan-Seng Song, *Third-Eye Theology* (Maryknoll, N.Y.: Orbis Books, 1979), 165–66.

[23]Waetjen, *Reordering of Power*, 235.

[24]Dorothee Soelle, *Christ the Representative: An Essay in Theology after the "Death of God"* (London: S.C.M. Press, 1967).

[25]Song, *Third-Eye Theology,* 165–66.

[26]Weber, *The Cross,* 61.

soldiers, and many others. This still implies that "He died because of our sins." Jesus died because of our unwillingness or inability to save him, join him, see him, free him, and follow him. At that point, Jesus was without friends. And so was God.

But Jesus' death instead of another's death is not simply the death of an innocent victim rather than a guilty one. No, again this would be an individualistic understanding of the dynamics between the person and the community inappropriate for Jesus' day. It also leaves the meaning of the crucifixion at a level where the death of Jesus could be interpreted only as the death of an innocent victim.[27] It is doubtful that the death of one faultless, injured party would warrant much attention, let alone hold our interest over time. Nor would such a death necessarily become attached to the image of Messiah, let alone a Messiah who endured suffering.

As stated previously, the earliest sources for interpreting the crucifixion drew from themes that emphasized the prophetic and apocalyptic dimensions of Jesus' death. There was no conception of a Messiah who would suffer for the sake of others within any of these earliest sources drawn from to interpret Jesus' death. There were no indications in these particular sources that the death of an innocent victim had or has any redemptive value whatsoever. Such an interpretation would have been a deviation from the understanding of Jesus as the righteous one of God.[28] Jesus was not understood as a naive, harmless, or foolishly trustful person. On the contrary, he was an active and bold visionary. He offended people, including those in official positions of authority. He made outrageous claims! He could be known as the Suffering Righteous One because he acted without evil intent to serve the cause of justice through the power of love. This means that redemption does not lie in the fact of Jesus' death. Redemption says something about how Jesus lived and why he died as well as something about the life of the community in which he lived and worked and found his meaning. In other words, redemption is no *fait accompli* on Jesus' death; it has something to do with the possibility of new life for the community, for its survival, preservation, and well-being.

Jesus lived doing the risky business of incarnating love and doing justice. That makes his life a sign and his death a challenge toward the "eradication

---

[27]Rudolf Bultmann, "Paul's Demythologizing" in *The Writings of St. Paul,* ed. Wayne A. Meeks (New York: W. W. Norton, 1972), 418–19. Here, Bultmann discusses the significance of the cross as judgment of the world and deliverance of humanity: "So far as this is so, Christ is crucified 'for us', not in the sense of any theory of sacrifice or satisfaction." He goes on to say that this event of the cross not only has past historical validity but contemporary historical significance in that it challenges those who hear it. In this way the cross and the resurrection represent an inseparable unity.

[28]Macquarrie, *Jesus Christ in Modern Thought.* In talking about the interpretation of Christ's suffering in 1 Peter, Macquarrie makes it clear that there is nothing desirable or praiseworthy in suffering as such. "There is not masochistic glorification of suffering for its own sake," 137.

of sins," injustice, and lovelessness in the world.[29] In this sense, the cross shows that both judgment and redemption are linked together through the possibility of seeing reality for what it is and naming it. They are also linked to the knowledge that the same reality that causes hardship and suffering can be changed. The cross represents a devastating social and political event; as such it ushers a terrible holiness into the world. But strangely it brings hope in its wake. However, this means that the crucifixion, as well as any rendering of the resurrection, says something about the life and meaning of a community in order for hope to become real in history. This can be seen in the struggles of the early followers of Jesus after his death.

The Cross in Mark's Gospel

Of the early writers, the author of Mark and Paul are regarded as interpreters of the cross in the way being discussed. Of the four gospel accounts, Mark is generally acknowledged to be the oldest, thus placing it closer in time to the events it narrates. The author of Mark drew from the Psalms of lament 22, 38, and 69 and the Fourth Servant Song of Isaiah as well as precanonical passion accounts and other collections of traditions about Jesus to interpret him as the Suffering Righteous One alluded to in scripture.[30] It is not surprising that because the author of Mark devotes the greater portion of his gospel to the passion of Jesus, it has been understood by many to be an extended passion story. In fact, some contend that the crucifixion is key to comprehending Mark's entire message.[31]

The author of Mark was writing at a time when the early church was anticipating the imminent return to Earth of Jesus as Son of the Human Being. Many of the early followers were experiencing persecutions because of their faith and were in desperate need of encouragement. This may offer some insight into the observation that of the four gospel accounts, the prophetic-apocalyptic readings of Jesus' death are fully included in this account and not in the others.

Mark's gospel draws suffering clearly into the center of its narrative. This is no accident. Nor is it simply an arbitrary starting place. The Jewish-Christian author of Mark was most likely writing his work after the

---

[29]Edward Schillebeeckx, *Jesus: An Experiment in Christology* (New York: Seabury Press, Crossroad Books, 1979), 310. Here Schillebeeckx concurs "that Jesus felt his death to be (in some way or other) part and parcel of the salvation-offered-by-God, as a historical consequence of his caring and loving service of and solidarity with people."

[30]Weber, *The Cross,* 99.

[31]There are exceptions to this reading of Mark. For instance, Mary Ann Tolbert's literary-critical study of the gospel of Mark focuses on the Parable of the Sower: "Jesus, the Sower of the Word." She finds this parable key to illuminating the work of Mark. However, different methods yield different insights that can enrich and deepen the multiple meanings of a text. See *Sowing the Gospel: Mark's World in Literary-Historical Perspective* (Minneapolis: Fortress Press, 1989).

destruction of the Jerusalem temple (A.D. 70). The forty years between Jesus' death and the gospel of Mark were the years of the greatest violence and bloodshed in Israel's history, culminating in the Roman victory over the Jewish nation. Not only did the author of Mark probably bear witness to the crucifixion of Jesus, he also lived through the downfall of his country. During Mark's lifetime, Israel ceased to exist as a political nation until the establishment of the state of Israel in 1948.[32] It is against this painful backdrop that the author of Mark develops his story about the cruel death of the man from Galilee. And it is the author of Mark who designates this same message, "The beginning of the *Gospel* of Jesus Christ, the Son of God" (Mk. 1:1, author's translation). If this is good news, what is bad news! Immediately following this introduction, the gospel of "good news" begins with a call to repentance, a challenge to turn completely around and see what is real and to act responsibly. Ironically, the gospel is filled with example after example of the failure of Jesus' followers to meet this challenge. Mark offers a particular political interpretation of the cross that describes as well as challenges the life and times of these early followers of Jesus.

Four metaphors in Mark reveal the shape of the political interpretation of the cross: (1) "The Suffering Righteous One" is the Messiah who endures suffering, proselytizes, and ushers in a new era of justice and compassion; (2) the "realm of God" is the new era that will counter the expectations of the religious and political authorities; (3) "the way" is the way of Jesus' life that the disciples are invited to follow and participate in; and (4) "Galilee" is that particular place where Jesus' ministry began and where the disciples are told they can meet him again. The cross of Mark is local, particular, participatory, orally communicated, and active.

Mark's Suffering Righteous One

The author of Mark may have been addressing the messianic prophets who were feeding off the war years with an ideology that negated the idea of a suffering Christ. His concern may have been to reveal these messengers as false prophets who attached themselves to a messiah who is beyond historical contingency. In an age of such harsh tribulation in which the author of Mark lived, the message of a Messiah protected from the anguish of the people could not have ushered in the realm of God; it would only have served to deepen the pain of the followers. Then as today, to say that there is peace when there is no peace is false hope. The author of Mark is clear that his project about distinguishing false hope, built on illusion and lies, from a new hope for a future is grounded in facing reality and addressing it.

The charge of blasphemy for which Jesus was crucified was a result of his identifying with the people and thus incarnating a suffering Messiah. Mark shows Jesus' life as revealing a vulnerable God who enters into history

---

[32]Werner H. Kelber, *Mark's Story of Jesus* (Philadelphia: Fortress Press, 1979), 13.

and bears the cost of loving fully and acting justly. This is not a glorification of suffering or a lifting up of suffering as a virtue in and of itself. No one, not even the Messiah, is asked to suffer simply for the sake of suffering. Jesus' example was contrary to this mistaken idea. His suffering meant something different. He did not give up the way of justice even when injustice was done to him. He lived the power of love and justice by not succumbing to injustice in order to break the cycle of violence perpetuated by an "eye for an eye" way of life. Furthermore, he claimed this possibility for others as well. Jesus claimed the vulnerability of a human being whose power lay in the truth of right relationships, a truth that contradicted the dominant view of the Messiah as a triumphant Lord coming in power and might. The charge of blasphemy was in reality an attempt to silence this truth.

The author of Mark offers a Messiah who is the Suffering Righteous One that understands and accepts human vulnerability. He integrates the realities of suffering and death in his narrative, believing this is central for a peaceful coexistence that can yield compassion and justice.[33] By facing the reality of death, one can choose to live in a way that recognizes that life is precious. The gospel of Mark places the emphasis on the reality of historical suffering and death, not the dream of power and success.

The Suffering Righteous One is a metaphor that can be retrieved for pastoral theology today. It offers an alternative to the shepherd model that has dominated pastoral care for a long time. This does not mean that the shepherd image is no longer helpful; rather, the Suffering Righteous One can offer new perspectives with different implications. This will be explored in more detail in chapter 9 as a way to help ground pastoral theology more fully in its prophetic tradition.

The Realm of God

The Messiah who suffers does so as the one who "bears witness" *(marturia)* to the creation of the realm of God. This bearing witness is not passive by any means. It is involved and intentional; it acts out the way life ought to and can be lived. Mark illustrates the contours of this realm through examples of inclusiveness: Jesus' feeding of the multitude, his traveling across the lake beyond any single town to the Gentiles, his abandoning rituals and taboos that kept some people as outsiders, his responding to the Syrophoenician woman's request to heal her daughter. This latter is especially significant because healing in Mark is a sign of restoring justice, recognizing differences, and including outsiders.

The expected realm of God of the religious authorities included an image of a ritual of enthronement sealed by the anointing of the new Messiah King. In Mark, Jesus enacts an alternative ritual, signified by the "irregular anointing" by the woman at Bethany. The realm of God that Jesus initiates

---

[33]Ibid., 52.

is contrary to a majestic kingdom ruled by a high priest. Instead of this royal scene, his was to be a table fellowship, inclusive of those who were usually excluded or kept to the margins—women, lepers, tax collectors. But inclusivity is painful; in a pluralistic world such as we have today it becomes even more excruciating. It is hard to accept differences, especially when they challenge our own views and ways of doing things. The realm of God in Mark demonstrates that accepting this pain of inclusion means bearing witness to a different form of power—relational power. C. S. Song recognizes this when he, too, interprets the rending of the curtain of the Temple as a sign of inclusiveness that is central to the dawning reign of God:

> The ruptured curtain made an end to a God wrapped in a cloak of mystery ensconced in the darkness of the Holy Place, and inaccessible to children, women, peasants, workers, prostitutes, and pagans. It abolished the barriers that had for so long separated the God of Israel from the God of the nations. The death of Jesus, which tore open the curtain of the Temple, could now be linked to the despair and hope, suffering and joy, death and life, of the millions and millions of persons who pass through the world from the beginning to the end of time. The ruptured veil is the symbol of hope for those who have had to wait patiently and desperately in the outer court for such a long time for God's saving words for them.[34]

The pain of inclusion breaks through old ways of dividing and excluding people and holds open the promise of living together into the new realm of God. This promise, born of the pain of inclusion, can also help lead pastoral theology as it opens up to new voices, theories, and contexts.

The Way

Mark's emphasis on "the way" of Jesus underscores for the followers of Jesus that to walk "the way," like him, means to incarnate love and justice in the world. In Mark the disciples are being prepared to carry on "the way" in Jesus' absence. This is also the message to the gospel reader today. What Mark does not say is that Christian life is in the *glory* of the risen Lord. For Mark this is an illusion and the source of the disciples' misunderstanding. Instead, the emphasis is on Christian living, which means to follow Jesus on "the way." This means relinquishing any notion of entitlement or privilege, any attitude that suggests one is free to cultivate his or her own comfort and contentment at another's expense.

One meaning of the cry from the cross is that it is a final relinquishment of any notion of entitlement.[35] The cry from the cross critiques any attitude

---

[34]Choan-Seng Song, *The Compassionate God* (Maryknoll, N.Y.: Orbis Books, 1982), 95.
[35]John Blackwell, *The Passion as Story: The Plot of Mark* (Philadelphia: Fortress Press, 1986), 75.

that quests after power or proofs of superiority by displays of force. The cry from the cross critiques the kind of attitude that prompts the powerful to say, "God is on our side." It forsakes any form of extrahuman intervention. At the sound of this cry, the absence of superhuman power to intervene and rescue demands a response from human beings. God works in history, or as Soelle says, quoting Latin American liberation theologian Juan Segundo, "God is a Society."[36] The message of the passion in Mark is that through our imaginative participation in the passion story, our behavior will be oriented toward "the way" of easing and transforming the human condition through just actions and by loving fiercely and tenderly. For pastoral theology to imaginatively participate in the passion story, it, too, will need to orient itself toward just actions and risky love.

Galilee

The gospel of Mark ends with Mary Magdalene, Mary the mother of James, and Salome visiting the tomb where Jesus had been buried after the crucifixion. When they arrive, they find the tomb empty except for a man who is standing there waiting for them. He knows they are looking for Jesus, and he tells them that Jesus is not there. He tells them to go and tell the disciples that Jesus has gone on to Galilee and that they will see him there. But the women say nothing to anyone, for they are afraid.

Now Galilee is not a center of power. It is not the hub of religious and civil activity; it is simply a place where people live and struggle to survive. In Mark it is the place where the way of love and justice begins to be practiced. And it is to Galilee that resurrection points. Yet if we go to Galilee, we are inevitably led by "the way" to Jerusalem, the place where corrupt power is confronted. The gospel ends in ambiguity, with *ephobounto gar,* "for they were afraid."[37] We are not told if they went to Galilee or if Galilee still awaits their arrival. There is no offer of certainty that the disciples ever got the message even after the crucifixion. But we are told that the answer lies in Galilee–the possibility for resurrection, the reincarnation of "the way" of love and justice. The one thing we do know is that the way to Galilee is a corporate pilgrimage. It involves the disciples, in the plural.

Where is "Galilee" for pastoral theologians today? This is an important question. As we try to answer it, we will find ourselves going more and more to places outside the halls of power, away from the places of security, leaving the familiar haunts that have affirmed who we were in the past.

---

[36]Dorothee Soelle, *Choosing Life* (Philadelphia: Fortress Press), 90. Here, Soelle quotes Juan Luis Segundo, S.J., *Our Idea of God* (Maryknoll, N.Y.: Orbis Books, 1974) in order to talk about resurrection as God's love forming society in history.

[37]Norman Perrin, *The Resurrection According to Matthew, Mark, and Luke* (Philadelphia: Fortress Press, 1977).

Mark's "Night Vision"

The passion story in Mark is paradigmatic; it discloses truth. It exposes an act of violence accompanied by a new shade of night coming into the world. This scene depicts the truth that violence, the fruit of injustice, perverts the sacred order of all life. The night eclipses the noontime sun, symbolizing the overturning of the whole order of life. When all is destroyed in such a way, all is open for question. In this case the cross does not reveal heavenly splendor but the human violation of love and justice.[38] On the cross, historically imposed suffering exposes the structures of violence, the inhumane way people treat one another. This message is solace to victims in that at least their suffering is recognized. It is real and not just something left hidden and denied. It is also an indictment of perpetrators who may not even recognize their complicity with evil.

Mark is a story about unnecessary suffering that demands an answer. But there is no unambiguous resolution, only a clear depiction of the human condition and the possibility of some kind of action in response. Because the individual and the community were understood as an organic entity in Mark's time, and because Mark boldly wrote from the perspective of "cosmic judgment and historical turning point,"[39] the crucifixion in Mark can be understood as an all-inclusive and comprehensive event. By implication, the possibility of resurrection, then, depends on an equally broad understanding and corporate response.

The resurrection is about the courage to vindicate suffering, the willingness to see the truth and walk the way of love and justice. Jesus does not respond to violence with violence but with truth. He does not fight on the level of his adversaries, nor does he flee. His is not simply a passive reply, but a truthful and courageous response. In Mark the cross signifies the challenge to perceive and understand the human condition as it is and to do something about it. Mark reminds us that wherever temple and palace, church and empire, church and society are joined, "Jesus" is put on trial.

Paul's Theology of the Cross

What Mark portrays in story, Paul presents in theory. Whereas the author of Mark narrates the passion story, Paul can be understood as the first to articulate a theology of the cross. Paul uses the theology of the cross as *criterion* in his letters to the Corinthians and as *justification* when he addresses the Galatians.[40]

Cross as Criterion

In Corinth, the Christians were being influenced by those who linked Jesus with the Wisdom figure of the Hebrew Scriptures and intertestament

---

[38]Blackwell, *Passion as Story,* 53.
[39]Weber, *The Cross,* 106.
[40]Ibid., 65, 80.

writings, interpreting Jesus as the risen Lord in a way that promoted an attitude of superiority. Christians were exhibiting behavior in which they exalted themselves above their neighbors. They had left the cross behind in their self-satisfaction. They had little interest in Jesus the human being and his way of the cross. Theirs was a one-sided faith based on a tradition in which only the risen Lord mattered (1 Cor. 15:3–5).[41] Paul sarcastically writes of their spiritual enthusiasm: "Already you have all you want! Already you have become rich! Quite apart from us you have become kings!" (1 Cor. 4:8).

When the gospel became distorted and misunderstood in Corinth, Paul could no longer proclaim the creedal formula of 1 Corinthians 15:3–5. In his opening address to the Corinthians Paul leaves out the "for us" and simply proclaims that Christ has died. Period.[42] There is no allusion to Christ's resurrection. To believe the word of the cross alone means salvation. The Corinthians are told to learn to judge themselves, their brothers and sisters, their age, and the world around them through the cross.[43] Here, Paul's understanding of the cross as a stumbling block can be understood as "the cross becomes the crisis of the world." It becomes a criterion to describe and judge the world. This is a confessional theology that becomes important for later developments.

Cross as Justification

Paul shifts his emphasis when he addresses the Christians in Galatia. The Galatians were deserting the gospel because of their misunderstanding of Christian freedom. They were in a crisis over how to remain faithful after baptism when the second coming had not yet arrived. How could they continue to live without transgressing God? There were those who objected to the teachings of Paul's gospel of freedom and looked for other answers. Paul's theology of the cross challenged the Galatians' human striving through justification by law. Paul insisted that the law lives by observing faith. Unlike the emphasis in Corinthians, Paul's message of the cross to the Galatians did not focus on their transgressions. Instead, he sought to instill in them a sense of confidence that the Spirit was leading them. Justification came through faith. This, too, became a consistent theme in the development of Christianity.

Time and again, the cross has been that persistent symbol that has drawn people back to what is central and true in the Christian faith. Like Paul, the Reformer Martin Luther retrieved the "word of the cross" as

---

[41]"For I handed on to you as of first importance what I also in turn had received: that Christ died for our sins in accordance with the scriptures, and that he was buried, and that he was raised on the third day in accordance with the scriptures, and that he appeared to Cephas, then to the twelve." This creedal formula is considered to be one of the earliest articles of faith.

[42]1 Cor. 1–4, in 1:18–25 and 2:2.

[43]Weber, *The Cross*, 76.

central for the particular times in which he lived. For him justification by faith came as a new revelation during a time when genuine holiness was at risk in the hands of corrupt religious leaders and hope for meaningful ways of living was being diminished for believers.

Martin Luther's Theology of the Cross

Justification through faith surfaced again in a new and powerful way during the Protestant Reformation. The imagination of Martin Luther in particular was sparked by this tenet of faith, and it became a foundation for his theology of the cross. In fact, Luther coined the phrase *theologia crucis,* and it is his name that is most closely associated with "theology of the cross."

The era in which Luther lived was marked by the upheavals in Europe that began in the latter part of the Middle Ages. From the last third of the thirteenth century until after 1450, most of Europe was suffering from severe economic depression.[44] One of the major causes of the economic depression was an ecological crisis. The land used for farming had been overused and exploited without being replenished. There was not enough productive farmland to support the needs of the people. In addition to this, war, violence, disease, and social and political upheaval contributed to the malaise and pervasive unhappiness of this time. Perhaps the most graphic example of suffering during these later Middle Ages was the bubonic plague, which erupted in 1348 and destroyed nearly one third of the European population.[45] Although the disease had its greatest impact some one hundred and fifty years before Luther's time, there were still outbreaks of the epidemic until the seventeenth century.

It is not surprising that the disruptive events of these years had people thinking that perhaps it was the end of the world. While this proved not to be the case, it did help generate the disintegration of the medieval thought world. The comprehensive worldview of medieval Catholicism began to crumble, as its worn-out practices no longer addressed the changing world around it.[46] As people began to look for a new way of understanding human life and motives, a shift gradually began to occur in the minds of the believers toward a more inward religion. They began to seek refuge through personal communication with the holy as they longed for a more intense religious experience of God.

This move toward a more personal religion was in accord with the emerging concept of humanism that was taking root in Europe. It was

---

[44]Norman F. Cantor, *Medieval History: The Life and Death of a Civilization* (New York: Macmillan, 1963), 577.

[45]Lewis W. Spitz, *The Renaissance and Reformation Movements: Volume 1, The Renaissance* (St. Louis: Concordia Publishing House, 1971), 12.

[46]Cantor, *Medieval History,* 578.

believed that this new assessment of the power of human intelligence could help restore order to a devastated continent. While this movement asserted human freedom against sacerdotal power, it also helped foster a kind of religious individualism that fed into the triumph of the nation-states.[47] There was a new notion of *polis* developing that depended less on religious sources and more on secular principles for governing relations among individuals and communities.[48] The old religious framework of meaning for holding the social fabric together was beginning to crumble. This does not mean that religious influence was absent from public life, but it was beginning to have a less encompassing role in the governing of people's lives.

This was the broad historical backdrop of Luther's writing. Unlike the author of Mark, who tells the story of the passion as the cosmic challenge of the gospel for all, unlike Paul whose insistence on a theology of the cross was to challenge those who attacked the church, Luther's *theologia crucis* was an attack from within the church. He was not crying out against immorality or economic exploitation, he was protesting against the abuses of medieval Catholicism. His was mainly a doctrinal quarrel, a religious conflict.[49] But that was not all: Luther's burning question was, How could guilt-ridden humans ever possess a righteousness that would enable them to stand in God's presence?[50]

Luther's struggle was to reconcile a wrathful God and the human need for salvation. For him the ways of the medieval church were of no help and only drove him deeper into despair. At the same time, his answer would not come by way of self-help. It would not come through his own remedies or through the church's sacraments, especially the sacrament of penance. And for Luther, reconciliation would not come through the way of the mystic who yields him- or herself to God, because yielding still suggested an element of human effort and verged on speculation. For these reasons, the mystic's approach especially was not open to Luther.[51]

Using the language and images of faith from a different anthropology and a different theology than that of the early church, Luther came to an understanding of the cross in keeping with the traditions of Mark and Paul. The righteous God of Luther is consistent with the crucified righteous One of the earlier evangelists. Luther's understanding of divine forgiveness can be seen in light of this tradition of the righteous One, which demonstrates that incarnated love need not be compromised by the forces of evil, even

---

[47]Ibid., 588.

[48]Stephen Toulmin, *Cosmopolis: The Hidden Agenda of Modernity* (Chicago: University of Chicago Press, 1990), 97.

[49]Roland H. Bainton, *The Reformation of the Sixteenth Century* (Boston: Beacon Press, 1952), 24.

[50]Roland H. Bainton, *Here I Stand: A Life of Martin Luther* (New York and Nashville: Abingdon Press, 1950), 32.

[51]Bainton, *The Reformation*, 32.

at the point of risking life itself. For Luther, as for Mark and Paul, there is no "reason" that love should prevail. It is a miracle, if you will, when it does. Like that of Mark, Luther's theology allows for ambiguity. Hope after the crucifixion is a matter of faith, not certainty. In fact, Luther's conception of the resurrection is framed within the *theologia crucis* and can only be understood from this point of view. That is, Luther avoids speaking about the resurrection in a way that implies that the human condition of forsakenness into which Jesus as the "Christ entered unreservedly, has been surpassed."[52] Instead, forgiveness and forsakenness come together through divine human solidarity in the face of suffering. In other words, only by recognizing and addressing human suffering can the holy that becomes eclipsed over and over again in human history be retrieved.

In 1518 Luther gave his Disputation of the Augustinian Order at Heidelberg. It was in this document that *theologia crucis* and *theologia gloriae* were first used to distinguish two opposing ways of regarding faith. The theology of glory was Luther's maxim for what he was protesting against in search of a true theology. It refers to the attempt of human beings to know directly and unequivocally the power and glory of God. For Luther, such direct knowledge identifies faith with reason and reason's supposed way to salvation. A theology of power and glory falsely elevates human wisdom and confuses faith and works:

> Just as the theology of glory prefers works to sufferings, glory to the cross, power to weakness, wisdom to foolishness, so philosophy would rather investigate the essence and actions of the creatures than listen to their groanings and expectations.[53]

Through his condemnation of *theologia gloriae* in all its forms, Luther denounced the whole scheme of medieval Scholasticism and the triumphalism of papal Christendom. Over against a *theologia gloriae,* Luther proclaimed the *theologia crucis.* Theses 19 and 20 reflect this development in Luther's theology:

> 19. The one who beholds what is invisible of God, through the perception of what is made, is not rightly called a theologian.
> 20. But rather the one who perceives what is visible of God, God's "backside," by beholding the sufferings and the cross.[54]

---

[52]Hall, 122.

[53]Quoted from Luther's works in Walther von Loewenich, *Luther's Theology of the Cross* (Minneapolis: Augsburg, 1976), 69.

[54]John Dillenberger, ed., *Martin Luther: Selections from His Writings* (New York: Anchor Books, 1961), 502.

For Luther, the cross is not simply one aspect of theology, it is the center that provides the perspective for all theological statements. "For Luther the cross is not only the subject of theology; it is the distinctive mark of all theology."[55] The main features of Luther's *theologia crucis* can be summarized as follows:[56]

The theologia crucis *is a theology of revelation.*

This is Luther's position in direct opposition to Scholasticism. Luther was not interested in speculations about the attributes of God aside from living acts. "At the cross every fictitious conception of God is destroyed."[57] Here, Luther's emphasis on revelation takes history seriously.

The theologia crucis *is an indirect revelation.*

In Thesis 20 Luther alludes to Exodus 33:23, where Moses does not directly view the face of God. This emphasizes Luther's opposition to the primacy of reason, which looks to find God manifested in power and glory, whether in nature, including human nature, or in history. Instead, Luther has a concept of the "hidden God"–God hidden in unexpected places. These "hidden and unexpected places" include one's neighbor in Luther's theological understanding. "Indirectness" includes "my neighbor" as an unexpected place to meet God. Through my neighbor, or by way of my neighbor, God is revealed to me. Luther even claims, "My neighbor is Christ to me."

For Luther, then, human relationships are crucial for God's revelation. This means that we are never to approach our neighbor as someone to possess or control. Control and ownership are incompatible with neighbor, and with God. This way of indirectness by which we meet God through relationship with our neighbor depends on mutual respect. From the perspective of the cross, this mutuality stems from the recognition that we all suffer and we all die. Only at this place of humankind's most profound vulnerability is salvation possible.

The revelation of the theologia crucis *is recognized in the sufferings and the cross of Christ, not in works.*

Here, works refers to both God's created works of the natural order and creations of the human mind. Luther is rejecting both the moralist and the rationalist who expect to find God through reasoning alone. He rejects approaches that reflect on moral nature in general and forget the particular, specific, and concrete experiences of human beings. And in contrast to the

---

[55]von Loewenich, 17.
[56]Alister E. McGrath, *Luther's Theology of the Cross* (Oxford: Blackwell, 1985), 150–51.
[57]von Loewenich, 69.

prevailing natural theology of his day, he denies the ability to discern God's purposes through contemplating the pattern of the created order.[58]

The knowledge of God who is hidden in this revelation is a matter of faith.

In order to understand Luther's experience of a hidden God, it is important to remember that Luther was wrestling with his inability to experience mercy in the face of a wrathful God. He struggled personally and painfully for his faith. After a particularly intense period he wrote,

> For more than a week I was close to the gates of death and hell. I trembled in all my members. Christ was wholly lost. I was shaken by desperation and blasphemy of God.[59]

It was only after trying to confront his despair head on, and to no avail, that he discovered his "indirect" approach, which finally gave him some relief. He writes of it this way,

> To give up the argument is of itself an act of faith…an expression of confidence in the restorative power of God, who operates in the subconscious while man occupies himself with extraneous things.[60]

When Luther's understanding began to shift after these events in his life, his theology of the cross made him able to speak of his total faith experience of finding "hidden" in this fearful God a merciful God. His omnipotent and omniscient God "hid" a merciful and vulnerable God who entered history and actively participated in human suffering to alleviate it. Luther knew this firsthand. His theological confessions reflect his struggle between faith and experience. For Luther, experience can only stand in contradiction to faith. By 1525, as a result of his own theological journey Luther was forced to concede that God might not have spoken the final word in Christ.[61]

For Luther, true faith is the opposite of the kind of exultant confidence found in a theology of glory. For Luther, what is most vital is most hidden. But "hidden" doesn't mean absolutely eclipsed; it means that what we see through the eyes of faith is what is most true and just and loving. And we know this indirectly only by hints and glimpses. But this also means that a true faith involves temptation, because it never overcomes doubt. *Theologia crucis* can stand in the shadow of doubt within the gates of temptation as it

---

[58]Because Luther did not articulate an ethic of the cross, this aspect has led to some confusion in understanding the implications of his theology of the cross for social ethics.

[59]Quoted in Bainton, *Here I Stand,* 361.

[60]Ibid., 364.

[61]McGarth, 172.

searches for what is most important in suffering and negation. Although not called so by Luther, such a theology is political, for it is capable of illuminating the historical realities involved with suffering and doubt.

God is particularly known through suffering.

Luther stresses faith and doubt to counter the "works and reason" emphasis of the theology of glory. A theology of works opposes even the thought of suffering, and for Luther, the one who looks only to the mountains and skies does not search out those in pain. But to know God in suffering is not to advocate passive suffering or to glorify suffering in any way. To do so would simply be a more damaging form of the theology of glory. The point Luther is making is that those places in human life and history where suffering is experienced have deep significance for knowing God and discovering the holy. To affirm that we know God in suffering means that God is active in the suffering of the world. God chooses to be where suffering is. God seeks to relieve suffering not necessarily through a direct and triumphant overcoming of suffering, but through the hidden transformation of suffering that can sometimes come as a surprise. Again, though it is not Luther's aim, this has political implications.

While Luther's theological breakthrough opened many possibilities, his *theologia crucis* has limitations. For example, he never developed an ethic of the cross. His exegesis of the Magnificat linked his concern for justice with *theologia crucis,* but he never pursued this.

> For if he is not wise but poor in spirit, my kindness is with him, if he is not mighty but brought low, my justice is by his side to save him...at that very point of suffering.[62]

His exclusive focus on doctrine prevented him from developing the social and political implications of this thought. As a result, *theologia crucis* fed a form of resignation to the ills of society during his lifetime and helped reinforce a kind of quietism and inward thinking among religious seekers. A particularly tragic case in point is that his theological insights were never translated to adequately address the oppression of German peasants of the sixteenth century. Although one can point to nondoctrinal reasons for this, such as the particular relation of the church to the state and the revolutionary uprising of the left wing of the Reformation, the implications of his theology were not carried into the political realm. African American theologian James Cone notes that while Luther spoke out against the princes for their role in the Peasant's Revolt, he strongly denounced the peasants for their breach

---

[62]Jaroslav Pelikan, ed., *Luther's Works* (St. Louis: Concordia Publishing House, 1956), 21:332.

of law and order. Speaking from a black church perspective, Cone says that Luther's condemnation of the Peasant Revolt sounds very much like white churchmen's condemnation of ghetto rebellions.[63]

What was markedly new in Luther's reform was that instead of the hierarchical church as the incarnation of Christ, the power and the authority of the Bible began to inform the understanding of divine incarnation through an inward experience of faith. Through this, emphasis began to be placed on the emotional life of the individual in a new way. A greater importance was being placed on the role of unearned grace, the duty of love and patience, and the significance of suffering.[64] In these ways the cross points to the relationship between holiness and suffering. It shows a way to recover the lost depths and personal orientation. At the same time, however, when a theology of the cross is not interpreted socially or politically, it can promote private individualism and other-worldly piety, something Luther never intended. When this happens, the cross as the power for transformation in the world is trivialized and becomes replaced by an elevated and floating cross, an object of sentimentality. Although this danger and distortion of the cross is not inherent to the theology of the cross itself, precautions need to be taken if a political interpretation of the cross is to be explored for pastoral theology today.

Toward the Political Cross

The earliest recorded reflections on the cross in the New Testament were made during an era of crisis when people were experiencing confusion about their future and where the holy was located. The gospel of Mark and the early writing of Paul in particular addressed discouraged and dispirited communities who questioned the role of discipleship under adverse conditions. Personal torment and historical crisis attended Luther's thinking as he questioned whether or not discipleship was possible at all. Again, adversity prompted a renewed interest in the cross in the twentieth century. The first serious studies of Luther's theology of the cross for contemporary Christians began after World War I, when people tried to come to terms with the massive suffering experienced around the globe. They continued

---

[63]James H. Cone, *Liberation: A Black Theology of Liberation* (Philadelphia and New York: J. B. Lippincott, 1970), 72.

[64]See H. Richard Niebuhr, *Social Sources of Denominationalism* (New York: Holt and Company, 1929), 34. In this classic work, Niebuhr discusses the problems associated with emphasizing the spiritual realm by the church. The spiritual realm of influence by the church tended to ignore the real economic and political sufferings on the part of the peasants of Luther's day. The "priesthood of all believers" did not deliver them from the political and economic inequalities they were facing. In fact, the peasants were encouraged to submit to and to obey their oppressors in the spirit of Christian self-sacrificing meekness.

with renewed interest and intensity after World War II, as people failed to make sense of the enormity of human evil unleashed during this time.[65]

Douglas John Hall and Dorothee Soelle are two contemporary theologians who were deeply impacted by this time in history and the ensuing events during the last half of the twentieth century. Both of them have been strongly influenced by Luther's *theologia crucis* and have drawn from his insights to develop a political interpretation of the cross to address the situations facing people today. Both Hall and Soelle recognize an increasing loss of hope in many places in the world as a result of this world-changing time. They address what they believe to be some of the causes of this loss, particularly in North American and European settings. Both agree that all theologies of glory, especially certain forms of unsubstantiated optimism, are misplaced and are actually detrimental for recovering authentic holiness in our lives. It is to their development of *theologia crucis* in political form that we now turn in order to instruct a pastoral theology that takes historical suffering seriously.

---

[65]Jürgen Moltmann, *The Crucified God* (New York: Harper and Row, 1974); Kazoh Kitaori, *The Theology of the Pain of God* (Richmond, Va.: John Knox Press, 1965); Kosuke Koyama, *Mount Fuji and Mount Sinai: A Pilgrimage in Theology* (London: SCM Press, 1984). These are a few works that address the theme of the theology of the cross since WW II.

CHAPTER
FIVE

The "Thin Tradition" of the Cross for Contemporary Settings

Interpretations of the Theology of the Cross, Part Two

The cross of Jesus is for us not an empty symbol but a point of entry into the pain of the world.[1]

DOUGLAS JOHN HALL

To embrace the cross today means to grow into resistance. And the cross will turn green and blossom.[2]

DOROTHEE SOELLE

The sheer magnitude and massiveness of human suffering that reached new proportions during the mid-twentieth century exceeds all normal categories of reason and has called into question many of our philosophical traditions and theological orientations. Since the deployment of nuclear

---

[1]Douglas John Hall, *Confessing the Faith: Christian Theology in a North American Context* (Minneapolis: Fortress Press, 1996), 133.
[2]Dorothee Soelle, *Theology for Skeptics: Reflections on God* (Minneapolis: Fortress Press, 1995), 104.

89

weapons, we have known that is possible for humans to annihilate life on this planet as we know it. Through the design and construction of Nazi death camps more than six million Jews were killed, exposing the evil that humans are capable of perpetrating against one another, both through willed implementation and by compliant nonresistance. We have passed through a time that has changed our world and us in an irreversible manner. In order not to feel impotent in the wake of such an overwhelming revelation of human bankruptcy, some have tried to fool themselves into believing that such events are inevitable, that the repercussions are grossly exaggerated, or that the events did not happen at all![3] Without language or thought categories to describe, let alone explain, the shattering of human comprehension, others are left with the horror of silence. Douglas John Hall and Dorothee Soelle are two contemporary theologians who speak to all feeble attempts at denial and also to the impossibility of ascribing meaning to these atrocities. They introduce a theological interpretation of the cross, to address the rupture of contemporary human consciousness and the shattering of divine-human community. This "thin tradition" of the cross speaks to the loss of hope precisely when people are experiencing an "eclipse of the holy."

Douglas John Hall articulates a contextual interpretation of Luther's theology of the cross for North America in the wake of twentieth-century atrocities.[4] His question is posed within what he calls our contemporary "malaise that has been a long time in the making."[5] He deals with whether or not there will even be a future in which to exercise discipleship. Dorothee Soelle speaks from a European perspective as well as from her experience of living in the United States and Latin America. Both theologians address the eclipse of the holy, the loss of hope, and the possible recovery of self through a renewed discipleship founded on the way of the cross. Both continue an interpretation of the cross that recognizes holiness as being intimately related to suffering and its relief. Each has a certain urgency. Their treatments of the cross have political implications that can help inform pastoral theology today.

Douglas John Hall

Douglas John Hall constructs a theology of the cross within the "thin tradition" for the North American context. As he does so, he draws on Reinhold Niebuhr's critical assessment of theology during the early 1950s.

---

[3]Elie Wiesel, *A Jew Today,* trans. Marion Wiesel (New York: Random House, 1978), 52–53. Here, Wiesel discusses Sorbonne professor Robert Faurisson, who claimed that no Jew was ever burned anywhere, and that Anne Frank's *Diary of a Young Girl* was a forgery.

[4]Douglas John Hall, *Lighten Our Darkness: Toward an Indigenous Theology of the Cross* (Philadelphia: Westminster Press, 1976), 15.

[5]Douglas John Hall, *Thinking the Faith: Christian Thought in North American Context* (Minneapolis: Augsburg Fortress, 1989), 35.

Niebuhr insisted that Christians should never regard the tribulations of a civilization with detachment. Nor are Christians permitted to identify the meaning of life with the preservation of their own particular culture. On the contrary, the obligation of the Christian is to fashion a shared life along the order of the realm of God. Religious loyalty to an eternal meaning and destiny should not deter Christians from this concrete aim, their "historical obligation."[6]

Hall identifies an angst that lies not far below the surface of contemporary life when he asks, Is what one hopes for really possible? This existential question is a version of Luther's doctrinal question, How can guilt-ridden humans ever possess a righteousness that would enable them to stand in God's presence? Hall's heightened contextual consciousness makes his basic question more than a rhetorical probe into our complicated social dilemma. Hall sees people trying to answer this question about whether or not hope is possible today in various ways, many of which seem to reveal either naive optimism, cynicism, or nihilism. His theological motivation is to find an alternative response to these futile options. Drawing from Luther, he proposes the cross, stumbling block that it is, as the only source of authentic hope today.

Hall poses his question about the possibility of hope within the North American context, where he notes an absence of real hope in what he calls the "officially optimistic society."[7] The "official optimism" of North America tries to maintain an illusion of hope by convincing its people to trust in progress, have confidence in different expressions of what he calls "mastery," and have faith in various symbols of success such as personal and material prosperity. As discussed earlier, these foundational building blocks of our national identity are crumbling as the myths that support them dissolve. In other words, "official optimism" tries to shore up what is failing, and by doing so it becomes a defensive maneuver and a symptom of our extensive denial. Instead of hope, then, our "official optimism" feeds its opposite—despair—because it conceals the truth. The result is that North Americans who have learned to expect a certain level of abundance in both material and personal matters are experiencing these expectations no longer being met—and they are afraid.

Hall is saying that North Americans are experiencing a conflict between their expectations and the reality of their experiences and do not know how to deal with it. He points out that, in an attempt to deny this conflict, we have almost completely expunged the word *can't* from our vocabulary, and we go so far as to scorn those who point out the limits of human power.[8]

---

[6]Reinhold Niebuhr, *The Nature and Destiny of Man,* vol. 2 (New York: Charles Scribner's Sons, 1953), 307f.

[7]Hall, *Confessing the Faith,* 463.

[8]Hall, *Lighten Our Darkness,* 39. During my early experience in clinical training, we were told that anytime someone used the word *can't,* we could suggest that they change it to *won't.*

In fact, candidates for political office who do not reinforce an expansive vision for the future of our national life cannot expect to win elections.[9] He locates the loss of real hope in this discrepancy between the expectations that many North Americans have learned and digested almost without question and the experiences we actually live with. Furthermore, this loss of hope becomes exacerbated when we have no consensual framework of meaning (myths and symbols) within which to address our dilemma. When this is the case, our loss of hope goes unnamed.

Usually what we expect and take for granted doesn't shift until we become challenged. Our worldview doesn't change until it begins to fail. And the symbols and metaphors we use to order our lives follow a similar pattern. They fall out of use when they no longer capture the spirit of our lives and times. This was the situation of early Christianity; it happened again in the Middle Ages; and this is true for today as well. It has also been during these critical turning points in history, when people feel they have reached a profound limit and are searching for a way to express it, that the theology of the cross has emerged time and again.

It is also a common experience that when a framework of meaning begins to crumble, whether it is that of an individual, a community, or a whole country, those going through it often believe they are living during "end times." The end of the world feels close at hand, even if it is only "the end of the world as we know it." Hall identifies this outlook as having a strong hold in North America today, although it is not named as such. It plays a part in the loss of our deep symbols discussed earlier. Yet even when it is not recognized and named, it creates an insidious dis-ease, low grade malcontent, and a festering apprehension that breeds distrust in everything and everyone. Official optimism tries to mask these misgivings. But pervasive and unacknowledged suffering (because that is what this is) does not go unexpressed; it finds alternative expressions and creates other "names," powerful ones and destructive ones such as "Auschwitz," "Hiroshima," "Vietnam," "Birmingham Jail," "Bosnia," "Northern Ireland," "Matthew Shepherd," "Columbine High School," and "Dioxin."[10] These names point to terrible atrocities. But they are also names for our self-deception and our own self-destruction, even if we call them something else.

The officially optimistic society dares not call reality by its true name. Yet Hall says that this is exactly what we need to learn to do. We North

---

[9]Hall, *Confessing the Faith,* 463.

[10]Elie Wiesel captures this when he writes: "Our generation…is the generation of Auschwitz, or of Hiroshima, tomorrow's Hiroshima. The future frightens us, the past fills us with shame: and these two feelings, like those two events, are closely linked, like cause to effect. It is Auschwitz that will produce Hiroshima, and if the human race should perish by the nuclear bomb, this will be the punishment for Auschwitz, where, in the ashes, the hope of man was extinguished." Elie Wiesel, *Legends of Our Time* (New York: Holt, Rinehart and Winston, 1968), 180.

Americans need to learn to recognize the bankruptcy of our corporate value system and the harm it has caused others as well as ourselves. However, self-awareness of our failure will not suffice. Insight on this level will not be enough to address the experience of conflict and pain that is inevitable when we do realize our loss. Nor will exposure to the pain that our system inflicts on people guarantee any kind of transformation in our beliefs and lifestyles. It hasn't in the past. Quite the opposite, denial in the form of apathy, numbness, or madness has often resulted, and there is no reason to believe this will not continue into the future.

Madness, or mental illness in its many guises, is far-reaching in our culture. Some critics of traditional mental health positions even suggest that societal ills actually determine far higher incidents of mental illness for all classes than we are willing to concede. Perhaps people guilty of road rage or air travel rage, or those who create computer viruses give evidence of this. Mental illness in all its forms can be seen as an extreme expression of the absence of hope. If this is our situation, Hall asserts that authentic hope is never possible through denial but only through an exposure to reality that can lead to transformation and new possibilities. "Authentic hope comes into view only in the midst of apparent hopelessness and probably over against what announces itself as hope in a given society."[11]

Hope emerges when there is a sober recognition of the reality that needs to be healed, not denied. Hall predicts that North Americans will, of necessity, come to a conscious recognition about this need for healing in our national life. But this process will not be automatic. It will involve our becoming critically self-aware, which will be painful, producing acute discomfort and suffering.[12] Hall's vision for what is needed in North America is consistent with the insights of Walter Brueggemann. Brueggemann also recognizes the need for North Americans to come to terms with the contradictions in their domestic life and their place in the world. He points out that our honest assessment and awareness of this will involve pain. But he is also clear that the biblical record demonstrates that the way to new life often involves grief. It is the task of the prophet to help the community to grieve, he says, that something new might be born in their midst.[13]

Hall rightly observes that the dominant forms of Christianity in North America have been incapable of providing resources or environments that deal with limits, failure, and suffering, particularly the suffering caused by historical injuries. Many mainline, predominantly white Christian groups have so exclusively identified with the expectations of modernity, which place confidence in expansive progress and human wisdom, that they have

---

[11]Hall, *Lighten Our Darkness,* 114.
[12]Hall, *Thinking the Faith,* 19.
[13]Walter Brueggemann, *The Prophetic Imagination* (Philadelphia: Fortress Press, 1978).

become paralyzed when these no longer address the new problems they face.[14]

This is not to say there is an absence of social concern in American Christianity. Many of our liberal denominations are committed to social justice ministries and are making important contributions. While this is true, others are limping, not having cultivated comprehensive enough theological warrants to garner local support to sustain their programs. Without an alternative faith posture with clear theological grounding, pastoral interventions risk becoming vacuous activities lacking in moral vision. When this happens self-righteousness becomes a real threat to what is really a deeper longing that has yet to discover its moorings.[15]

In contrast to our prevailing stalemated ethos of despair, Hall suggests an alternative, the perspective of the cross. The cross provides an orientation that affirms the possibility of hope without shutting its eyes to the data of despair. The cross can generate a theology of hope because its point of departure is precisely the limits of human accomplishments, the brokenness of human spirits, and the fracture of human community. "It [the cross] places its hope in God's transformative solidarity with fallen creation, with the world in its brokenness."[16] Or as James Cone puts it, "Jesus' cross is God's solidarity with the poor, experiencing their pain and suffering."[17] These observations mean that any understanding of hope cannot be expressed without a deep and critical reflection on the history and culture of the victims of oppression and our part in its creation.

The black church community, Asian American communities of faith, and other racial ethnic communities as well as some of the emerging new forms of church–such as the Metropolitan Community Church, Women-Church, and North American experiments in Base Christian Communities–give expression to this kind of hope that looks long and hard at all of life. The theology of the cross is not an answer, and it is not a doctrine; it is a faith posture and a way of seeing that gives political expression to *fides quaerens intellectum* in communities of faith seeking to make a difference for themselves and the world in which they live. It challenges any one-sided emphasis of the modern world that identifies faith with a "seeing is believing" perspective and leaves things the way things are. From the perspective of the cross, the aim of religion in all its expressions is not to overcome the persistent conflict between expectation and experience, as though we can

---

[14]Hall, *Lighten Our Darkness*, 35.

[15]John Thomas of the United Church of Christ expressed just such misgivings during a panel discussion at the January 2001 Earl Lectures, Pastoral Conference in Berkeley, California, sponsored by Pacific School of Religion.

[16]Hall, *Thinking the Faith*, 28.

[17]James Cone, "An African-American Perspective on the Cross and Suffering" in *The Scandal of a Crucified World: Perspectives on the Cross and Suffering*, ed. Yacob Tesfai (Maryknoll, N.Y.: Orbis Books, 1994), 58–59.

simply "get over it." It is not even to overcome suffering by covering it up with something else that momentarily eases someone's pain. That is merely a digressive tactic to deflect our attention somewhere else. According to Hall the hope of "overcoming" is an illusion that ends up domesticating hope by echoing the dominant culture's accent on optimism with its denial of reality. The cross points to the different reality, which says we are not healed lightly.

Hall's constructive theology of the cross for the North American context challenges any prevailing notion of progress with its attending image of mastery. He calls for a new image of the human being that moves away from the figure who stands "higher" than others and becomes more and more in charge of his or her own destiny at the expense of others and nature. In fact, the cross means to tell the truth that this image of the human being as powerful and controlling has failed! When Hall first introduced this idea nearly twenty-five years ago, he suggested that there were deep impulses awakening within the human soul intimating that this false image must be cast off. And indeed there are many who have nurtured this impulse to maturity, particularly by rediscovering and pointing out the value of our bodily nature and the close connection between our well-being and that of the earth and biosphere.

Hall gave words to a growing awareness that is being expressed in contemporary feminist and womanist literature, as well as by a growing number of historians and theologians who have a renewed interest in the physical body. It is becoming widely recognized that we have made a false dichotomy between mind and body, and this bifurcation has governed Western anthropology for too many years. This dualistic way of thinking helped create the unhealthy image of mastery in the first place and continues to perpetuate its destructive power in our fragile human and natural ecologies today. Mind over body, the rational over the emotional, the abstract above the material, humans before nature–these are but a few of the ways this image is expressed.

Hall talks about the new identity that is emerging as including a fresh discovery of human "animality." This awareness of our animal nature is not found through cults of the body, but through nurturing a genuine appreciation of the beauty and grace of the human body as one animal among the species.[18] This means learning to accept completely the extra-rational and bodily creatureliness of being human. It also means searching for a new and different relationship between humankind and nature. Perhaps the failure of our image of "humans as masters" is most evident as we come to know just how much we have despoiled nature. As we learn to respect our bodily nature Hall believes we can learn regard for nature and treat our natural world not as something to overcome, as though it were inferior

---

[18]Hall, *Lighten Our Darkness,* 176.

or evil, but as something to treasure as holy and part of ourselves. As the environmentalists remind us, when we harm nature, we destroy ourselves. When we recognize our animality and accept our creatureliness we learn to live with limits and not expect undue privilege in any realm of life.

A new image of what it means to be human involves searching for an alternative rationality to the one given to us by the Enlightenment. Hall asks, What does it mean to think?[19] He rejects purely rationalistic and calculating modes of thought, suggesting instead that a new way of thinking involves the whole person in the thinking process–body, mind, and soul. This is not an invitation to abandon clarity and focus in human reflective activity; rather, it is an attempt to free rationality from narrow experimental knowledge and forms of logic that overly rely on linear argument based on principles of noncontradiction. A new way of thinking will pull the mind back into the body. This more unitary way of knowing will be a more involved process where the thinking person becomes closely related to what she or he is thinking about. Drawing on the Italian Marxist philosopher Antonio Gramsci, Cornel West has referred to someone who thinks in this manner as the organic intellectual. An organic intellectual is an engaged activist.[20] This way of knowing is far more relational, and also more risky, because it involves thinkers in a process in which they take part, but not one they necessarily originate. The holistic way of thinking of the organic intellectual is more than a rational process, but not separate from it. Clear analytical thinking is crucial and corporal. Through a commitment to action, the new thinking human being–the organic intellectual–bears witness in thought, word, and deed. One embodies what one sees and knows.

The new form of thinking, at least in the way Hall is imagining and knows, cannot be conceived as an individualistic exercise. That is, the image of what it means to be a person will not be found in isolated settings, but will become known in community. A theology of the cross that critiques notions of mastery will search for a "community of knowers," where its members turn from mastery to cooperation, from grasping to receiving, from independence to interdependence. Unless we all move in this direction, we simply will not last very long on the face of the Earth.

The lingering ethos of mastery still governs much of our lives, so the contrasting terms are often unfamiliar and jarring to our everyday ears. One alternative is to speak of the "power of the weak." This antiquated yet fresh proclamation challenges the whole language system of triumphalism. In a religious sense triumphalism, however it appears, feeds off an implicit theology of glory. This is certainly the theological underpinning of mastery that generates an inner sense of privilege and entitlement and finds its outward expression in destructive forms of imperialism. Mastery is thinly

---

[19]Hall, *Thinking the Faith*, 14.
[20]*Christianity and Crisis* (March 19, 1984).

disguised in various economic programs of globalization that elevate the lives of some and further impoverish the lives of others. But to speak of the power of the weak is to counter these forces. It reintroduces the concept of *skandalon* as a way to profoundly question the degenerative projects that inform our society. This is the scandal the cross points to today. The point where the bankruptcy of human projects of greed and arrogance becomes known is the cross of Jesus that defines God's alternate way of being as wholly inglorious.[21]

The cross critiques values that promote selfish interests that harm others. Whether it is in the realm of material avarice, social relations, or other ways we organize our lives, "whoever wants to be first must be last of all and servant of all" (Mk. 9:35). Although this quote from scripture has been misused to create social classes to serve while others benefit, this is not what it means. The servant in this illustration counters all notions of elitism and mastery that we have been talking about. Instead, it speaks of being a servant of faith, not glory. Instead of military victory, it assumes the triumph of faith as the way of Jesus. The triumph of faith, not triumphalism, must always remain willing to be "broken."

The triumph of faith intimates the realm of God brought forth through justice with an ethic of love. This is the cross lifted up by those working for justice, not the floating cross that never touches the ground or the lives of suffering people. As an object of this faith, which is always willing to become broken for the sake of something else, it can never support projects of nationalism or any other kind of *ism*. The triumphalism of culture is an ideology that makes an object out of every aspect of creation. Theology of the cross opposes this objectification and instead talks about the journey of God to the periphery—to the place of the skull on the outskirts of Jerusalem; to the cracks in our communities where our torn safety nets no longer protect; to the margins of society where people still wait to be seen, heard, fed, and honored. This point of departure for theology of the cross is solidarity with those who suffer. This is the heart of a political interpretation of the theology of the cross.

Douglas Hall's rediscovery of the theology of the cross offers a faith paradigm that can address the crisis of modernity experienced in North America's officially optimistic society. Basically, it is a critique of ideology. In this way he retrieves the tradition of Paul, who uses the cross as a criterion to judge the behavior of the Christians in Corinth who were exalting themselves above their neighbors. He is also in line with Luther, who judged the Medieval church's excesses by the criterion of *theologia crucis*.

One limitation of Hall's analysis is that he often addresses the North American context as though it were a homogeneous whole. Not every North

---

[21]Douglas John Hall, *Professing the Faith: Christian Theology in a North American Context* (Minneapolis: Fortress Press, 1993), 286–87.

American experiences the same conflict between expectancy and experience, because not everyone has the same expectation of the American Dream in the first place. When Hall talks about the outcome of the "cross-consciousness" for communities of faith as a heightened vigilance for oppression and injustice, he is really speaking to the crises of the dominant culture. His strong belief is that the situation of people who are oppressed will not be changed until the crisis of the majority has been confronted.[22] Although his position has merit and considerable following, others are less convinced that members of the dominant culture will change their views or behavior by becoming more aware of their role in perpetuating systems of injustice. In fact, as Katie Cannon observes, relying on Euro-American analytical concepts as a point of departure is to ensure there will be a distortion of what is being analyzed.[23] Audre Lorde makes us particularly aware of this with her well-known saying: "The master's tools will never dismantle the Master's house."[24] Sources of change and new life most likely will originate outside the dominant household in very unexpected ways and places. The question is, Will we be willing to receive them?

At the same time, Hall's theology of the cross can contribute to pastoral theology by offering a criterion to judge any implicit values that promote harmful ideologies in our theories and practices. His interpretation can also alert us to the possibility of excesses or distortions that may be hidden in the way pastoral theology is evolving. He reminds us that everything we think and do ultimately has consequences beyond our own private lives and communities, and therefore has political implications.

But the political realities of difference—whether based on ideology, race, gender, class, or sexual identification and orientation—must be more fully acknowledged when talking about the North American context. Suffering takes place during a particular time in a particular place under concrete historical circumstances. For this reason we can never preach the cross divorced from history or in general terms. The cross must be preached differently in different contexts, always representing a challenge or criterion for a definite situation. The different experiences created by class, race, gender, or sexual orientation will need to be more clearly in the foreground of any theology of the cross for North American pastoral theology. These factors play prominently in how people experience the loss of hope and the creation of new meaning.

---

[22]Hall, *Thinking the Faith,* 157.

[23]Katie Cannon, *Katie's Canon: Womanism and the Soul of the Black Community* (New York: Continuum, 1995), 106. While Cannon is drawing on James Cone's concern that the academic tools of white theologians are inadequate for studying black religion, her observation holds true for the limitations of Hall, who relies on these same tools to provide an adequate means for addressing the ills of society.

[24]Audre Lorde, *Sister Outsider: Essays and Speeches by Audre Lorde* (New York: Crossing Press, 1985), 110.

Dorothee Soelle

For the early Christian communities, the cross became paradigmatic for believers who were trying to locate the holy as they were undergoing trials and tribulations. Luther's theology of the cross challenged the speculative and aggrandizing theologies of the church of the late Middle Ages, especially its doctrine of God that convinced many believers that they were unworthy of salvation. Hall draws on the theology of the cross for understanding the disillusionment he sees people experiencing across North America. For him, the cross has social implications for addressing the nature of hope, its loss, and its recovery. Dorothee Soelle makes use of these same themes as she turns to the cross to address issues of unnecessary and historically imposed suffering.

Soelle's theology of the cross unites personal and political affliction. In her understanding, holiness can only be recognized within this union, and hope can only be realized by responding to the situations in which they occur. For her, suffering is always related to a particular time and place; it is historical. For this reason it can not be generalized, because it always has a human face. In her theology, the cross brings together mysticism and political awareness in a way that offers people a way to interpret their experiences and speak about them.

Soelle's thinking has been formed within her community of faith. She comes from the Lutheran tradition, but she is by no means a middle-of-the-road Lutheran. To say she is "left of center" is to miss her radical orientation by a significant number of degrees. She is a member of a small worship community, *Politisches Nachtgebet,* a political evening prayer group that meets in Cologne, West Germany. It is a group that seeks to bring faith, social analysis, and political action together.[25]

Dorothee Soelle was born in Germany in 1929, and she grew up in the midst of World War II. She identifies herself through the reality of Auschwitz. She began her address to the Sixth Plenary Assembly of the World Council of Churches in Vancouver, B.C., by saying, "I speak to you as a woman who comes from one of the richest countries of the earth, a land with a bloody history, stinking of gas which some of us Germans still cannot forget." By claiming this historical identity, she confesses her own participation in the horrific suffering her country inflicted on innocent people, even though she, personally, was too young at the time to have even known what was going on.[26]

---

[25]Dorothee Soelle, *Political Theology,* trans. with an introduction by John Shelley (Philadelphia: Fortress Press, 1974), vii, viii. In these meetings the focus is on a problem of immediate political or social interest. Through analysis of the problem, scripture, reflection, and prayer, the community decides what can be done, what immediate action can be taken.

[26]Ibid., 92. Here, Soelle notes that it is not enough to criticize social problems–for example, property rights; we "powerless" (meaning irresponsible) individuals must be able to clarify how we are entangled in the general structures.

Soelle is quick to say that she is insulted, humiliated, and disgusted by the evil her country brought forth in the pursuit of a "master race." Anyone who would minimize these past atrocities or anything that could lead to future brutalities appalls her. She is extremely critical of the accumulation of power and the worship of power in any form.[27] She rejects the theology of "almighty God" (*theologia gloriae* in Luther's terms), because it represents a theology that legitimates the very conditions she abhors and works to eliminate. Instead, she looks for a different basis of power in Jesus, who died on the cross. On the cross Jesus had no one who could rescue or free him. He was absolutely powerless. But for Soelle, this powerlessness is not hopelessness. Instead, it is the source of his counter-being, his inner authority. The power that Jesus shows is the "power of the weak," the power of love, a weaponless power that is stronger than death.[28] Along with Douglas Hall, she rejects any imperialistic anthropology and all ethics of mastery. War and its aftermath are all too real for her.

War, the suffering of war, and the conditions that lead to armed conflict are constant themes in Soelle's writings. At one point she says, "Once I understood Auschwitz, I joined the peace movement." She wrote her classic work *Suffering* toward the close of the Vietnam war.[29] In this work she writes of her anger and bitterness against the American bombings and mass murder of people in Southeast Asia. Along with Elie Wiesel, Robert Lifton, and others, she makes a connection between Vietnam and Hitler's Germany. She writes, "Vietnam carries on the story of Auschwitz. For here, as there, people saw, but did not see, heard, but did not hear."[30] The threads that unite these acts of violence are human apathy and its companion, willed ignorance.

Similar to Hall, Soelle is concerned about the future of the world. Like Hall, she is concerned with large issues such as population explosion, unemployment, nuclear war, and more. But unlike Hall, she does not understand these in ideological terms or as primarily resulting from conflicting values. Where Hall talks about the illusion that arises for people when they face a discrepancy between expectation and experience, Soelle talks about finite beings with infinite demands.[31] Although these may sound similar, Soelle makes her point in a radically different manner. Instead of starting with large concepts and their conflicting ends, she begins with the specific lives of people.

I read recently about a woman who works at a machine in a factory. Her foreman has the habit of coming up on her from behind, and

---

[27]Dorothee Soelle, *The Strength of the Weak: Toward a Christian Feminist Identity* (Philadelphia: Westminster Press, 1984), 97, 101.

[28]Ibid., 98.

[29]Dorothee Soelle, *Suffering,* trans. Everett R. Kalin (Philadelphia: Fortress Press, 1975).

[30]Ibid., 47.

[31]Ibid., 147.

whenever he does this, her whole body shrinks in startled reaction. This has happened six or seven times a day, however many times the foreman has come by, for thirty years. The woman has developed a tic from this, and now others see her simply as "someone with a tic."[32]

For Soelle, the suffering of one human face is linked to the large issues that beset our world. The woman in her example suffers from being subjected to the ongoing harassment by a man who has power over her movements, while she works at a job that does not inspire her, in a society that does not value and respect her. Soelle is concerned about suffering, which has social and political causes that invade the lives of individuals. It is from this perspective that she asks, Where is the crucifixion happening today?[33]

Soelle's orientation is consistent with that of Robert McAffee Brown. Along with Brown, Soelle insists that we must take suffering seriously, and when we do we must respond. But what is an appropriate response? Soelle is clear that by no account can suffering be justified. She is emphatic when she says, "From a Christian point of view, suffering does not exist in order to break our pride, demonstrate our impotence, or take advantage of our dependency."[34] Furthermore, the purpose of suffering is not to direct us to a God who achieves greatness by reducing us to insignificance.[35] This would make God the great cosmic sadist! The sadistic god stands above history and behind all forms of apathy and cynicism. This is a god that not only gives support to all forms of mastery and control, it also cultivates climates of isolation. Suffering cannot call on this god who increases rather than alleviates our pain.

Soelle does not focus on the theodicy question, How can an all-powerful, all-loving, all-wise God permit suffering, especially suffering of the innocent? She argues that this preoccupation with the motives of God is unanswerable and diverts our attention and energy away from people who are suffering. She accepts that suffering is a part of the world as we know it and asks what it means, where and how we can eliminate its causes, and how it makes us more human.[36] She makes a distinction between suffering we can and cannot end. Those for whom suffering cannot be alleviated must not be abandoned. However, historical injuries and other forms of imposed suffering are preventable. They are not to be tolerated or sanctioned by any measure. Indeed, they need to be addressed and eliminated. The human goal, according to Soelle, is to abolish circumstances under which people are forced to suffer, whether through poverty or tyranny.[37] This was the

---

[32]Ibid.
[33]Ibid., 2.
[34]Soelle, *Strength of the Weak,* 29.
[35]Ibid.
[36]Soelle, *Suffering,* 5.
[37]Ibid., 2.

point of Jesus' life and ministry. In Jesus we know a different God, one who does not stand above history but participates in human struggle. "Jesus is the indwelling presence of God in the world."[38] Jesus reveals God who is an oppressed victim, a "human being of sorrow," in solidarity with the weak. It is through discipleship with this one who was tortured to death that we learn to understand our own lives.[39]

Soelle moves away from Jesus as understood through substitutionary atonement theology by introducing the language of representation. Representation does not substitute one person for another. Through representation we do not lose ourselves in someone else. We do not forsake our ability to respond to others and their situations. Instead, Jesus as the human being of sorrow is Christ the representative, who re-presents human identity. Christ reminds us what it means to be an authentic human being. We know who we are by recognizing who this Jesus is who does not impose himself on us. Instead, Christ restores our identity by showing us who we really are and who we are capable of becoming. We know Christ the representative who does not replace us but who identifies with us in our struggle for fullness of life. In discipleship to this Jesus we, too, can represent what it means to be human without needing to replace anyone else and his or her strivings for authentic life. In this way, representation is an aspect of what Soelle calls "solidarity with the strength of the weak," which takes its cue from mystical love learned through the political cross.[40] Unity and solidarity are central to representation, which means human identity is honored and not exploited or destroyed in any way.[41] This is the basis for a solidarity that can empower and not inhibit or try to conform people to our way of thinking and acting.[42]

Like Luther, Soelle objects to speculative theology. There is "no such thing as a truth that can be acquired in detached, contemplative observation...[truth is] only [discovered] in practical relation."[43] Similar to Luther's *theologia crucis,* Soelle's truth of the cross discloses reality. But unlike Luther, she interprets the cross in a way that points to the truth about the political context of suffering. She asks, "What are the social and political causes of suffering and how can these conditions be eliminated?"[44] Herein

---

[38]Ibid., 145.

[39]Soelle, *Choosing Life* (Philadelphia: Fortress Press, 1981), 47.

[40]Soelle, *Strength of the Weak,* 98–103.

[41]Soelle begins to develop this theme in her early work *Christ the Representative* (Philadelphia: Fortress Press, 1967).

[42]John Macquarrie, *Jesus Christ in Modern Thought* (London: SCM; Philadelphia: Trinity Press International, 1990), 401–2. Macquarrie agrees with this interpretation and sites Soelle, who makes the distinction between Christ's representative role and substitution. He goes on to say that the representative nature of Christ's activity means that "we can think of him as repenting for the whole race as their representative, and as one who in true solidarity with the race knew something of the alienation that sin has brought about."

[43]Soelle, *Political Theology,* 73.

[44]Soelle, *Suffering,* 3.

lies the source of hope. Hope for the future is rooted in the current realities of today, in naming them and doing something about them instead of perpetuating them. In this way the gospel is not about pinning our hopes on otherworldly landscapes; it is something that heightens our consciousness about our present historical setting. It means holiness has this-worldly contours; hope is historical; and our very identities are tied to this. This gospel message counters all illusions that tempt people to become content and satisfied and may not be a soothing message at all. A political interpretation of the cross affirms that the truth about reality is open to the future precisely because it prods people to combat their apathy. In so doing it creates new anguish while inspiring new projects of intervention that seek the transformation of historical suffering.[45]

A life free of suffering is a myth. Using Hall's language of expectation and experience, the lived discrepancy between these creates a loss of hope for people that stems from a belief that life can be free from suffering. This loss of hope, then, not only denies suffering but also rejects the idea that there can be any value in suffering at all. Such a view necessarily ends in indifference and cynicism. Apathy is the result of the inability to recognize, let alone feel, suffering. The denial and repression of our own suffering and indifference to the suffering of others feeds systems of domination and oppression, which determines that "Someone" *must* bear suffering. And that "Someone" *must* be someone else! This is a misappropriation of the so-called "divine must" of the cross in the human guise of apathy and greed.

Soelle asks, Who is it that conceives of Christian life as life without suffering? She places her judgment on certain liberal theologies (which she calls Bourgeois) that overlook judgment and reduce the aim of Christian life to a private affair. From this perspective freedom from suffering means freedom from pain, which in fact means freedom from commitment to other people and causes not directly related to oneself. It means getting through life easily and well…and untouched.[46]

Next, she asks, Who is working to abolish the social conditions, which of necessity produce suffering? It is not those who are free from suffering, those who are incapable of suffering, or those who are unwilling to see the pain of others. Nor is it those who have been destroyed by misfortune. It is only those who are experiencing suffering themselves, who do not deny, soften, explain, or divert their attention, who are working to eliminate conditions that produce suffering.[47] But how does this occur? Soelle asks two questions: How do we move from mere passive endurance of suffering to productive suffering? and, Under what conditions can suffering make us more human?[48]

---

[45]Soelle, *Political Theology,* 69.
[46]Soelle, *Strength of the Weak,* 27–28.
[47]Soelle, *Suffering,* 2.
[48]Ibid., 3.

Where Hall argues that the word *can't* should *not* be eliminated from our language, Soelle takes a different position. She observes that those who are working to eliminate suffering do, in fact, seek to eliminate certain kinds of limitations on people. When "I can't" becomes the internalized "you can't" of the dominants, it needs to be eliminated. The "you can't"– as in, "You can't have access to decision-making processes, have your experiences validated, have a decent salary for the work you do, get married like heterosexual couples," and so forth–must go. When looked at from the perspective of those who are told in words, actions, and policies that they do not count, "I can't" does indeed need to be expunged from our vocabulary. In other words, this internalized *no* feeds a sense of helplessness in people who then become willing to endure hardship at any cost, because they *learn* to believe that there is no alternative. This is an enforced ideology of helplessness applied to some and not to others. It is a mockery of the authentic human limitation and vulnerability that is a part of everyone. In the end, it enforces false limitations and extra vulnerability on some while protecting the privilege of others.

An internalized no only produces cynicism and despair. A political interpretation of the cross counters this internalized no by providing a more radical no that teaches a revolutionary yes. It is a yes that says no to discrimination and injustice and is motivated by love and righteousness. Soelle sees this revolutionary yes in Paul's letter to the Romans (Rom. 6:12–14; 4:10). Here, Paul says that in Christ we are capable of righteousness; we can put our capabilities, our potentialities, our vital energies at life's disposal. "We can make ourselves weapons of righteousness, the instruments of peace whom God uses."[49] In other words, no one is strictly at the mercy of circumstance; we are created to live in resistance to what can potentially destroy us.

Hall's inquiry into the nature of contemporary hopelessness begins with his view on the conflict inherent between expectation and experience. He begins by looking at what is involved in people's expectations in North America. He rightly shows that there is something basically wrong with the social and philosophical underpinnings of our national vision. But in a certain sense he begins with speculation about the reason for hopelessness– the givenness of expectation and the discrepancy that one experiences in life in relationship to this. Hall assumes the nature of this expectation. In other words, he speculates that there is a certain expectation that is true for all North Americans. Historically, such an approach has not alleviated hopelessness or helped instill a new sense of purposeful living. Even "understanding" has not been a strong motivation for changing the conditions that adversely affect communities.

---

[49]Soelle, *Choosing Life,* 28.

Soelle, on the other hand, struggles with the phenomenon of the finite being with infinite yearnings. While this is still a philosophical question, she begins with lived experience. Here is where she locates the motivation to transform the conditions of historical suffering in the world. Her premise is that people struggle with the experience of being determined biologically, culturally, and socially, and at the same time, the experience of being an "I" in relationship to a "Thou." Being an "I" to another is to know freedom, to experience a taste of eternity, to have one's yearning for transcendence affirmed. Therefore, the "I" must first of all be seen and heard. The way out of powerlessness begins initially with the experience of "I" making a difference to another. This experience of making a difference to another is a political statement. It has particular implications for those who have been silenced and made invisible. The recognizing of the "I-ness" of people starts the political process of bringing into view and bringing into speech the faces and voices of those who suffer. This begins a practice of transforming suffering that is endured into "active suffering." This is the link between the personal and the political.

This first movement out of powerlessness begins with what Soelle calls the first phase of suffering, suffering that is mute. At first, the recognition of pain can be too deep for words. The first experience of an "I" making a difference to another evokes the abyss of isolation that has been all too familiar. Perhaps the only sound of this early recognition is moaning or wailing. The plea is to be seen, to be heard, and to be believed. At this time, "respect for those who suffer *in extremis* imposes silence."[50] This is a silence called for on the part of the one who is in the presence of suffering. It is not the muteness of the sufferer. It is a silence necessary on the part of those who are used to talking and who take it for granted.

The silence evoked by respect recognizes the presence of holiness that precedes all words; the "I" in search of a "Thou." Respect invites the presence of holiness and is not possible apart from it. It honors the "I" of someone, which is necessary before he or she can learn to articulate his or her own needs and desires. Or as Soelle says, "If people cannot speak about their affliction they will be destroyed by it, or swallowed up by apathy."[51] Only through respectful silence on the part of those willing to hear are the silences of the mute ones broken and speech made possible once more. Speech in its many forms begins to dispel muteness and leads to the second phase of suffering, which Soelle calls lament. The chaos and isolation of muteness begins to find form through lament.

When people are in severe depths, they often see themselves as being abandoned by everyone. Soelle reminds us that all extreme suffering takes us even further and evokes the experience of being forsaken by God. Lament

---

[50]Soelle, *Suffering*, 69.
[51]Ibid., 76.

offers a form for naming these expressions of alienation and then offers a way to retrieve and honor one's stillborn yearnings by analyzing, accepting, and therefore transcending the situations and structures that banished that person in the first place. Lament seeks to reestablish communication and communal connections, and it leans toward change. Learning to lament allows suffering to find expression. As words come, acceptance and analysis of the situations that cause suffering begins. Accepting what really exists is what "accepting suffering" means. But instead of promoting helplessness and feelings of powerlessness, this kind of acceptance does the opposite. It engenders courage in the face of adversity, hope for something different, and actions for positive change. Herein lies the transforming power of suffering.

The movement from muteness and isolation into lamenting and communication is a political movement that leads to the possibility of actions for change in existing personal and social structures. Through communal awareness and solidarity, actions are organized to transform the conditions that cause and perpetuate suffering. The pressure of suffering turned inward, which is what helps produce muteness in the first place, is transformed into the pressure of suffering turned outward for change. This is active suffering that bears witness to what life is like for people and to the possibility for a different, more hospitable world. This is a suffering that is no longer mute; instead, it has become vocal and powerful through being expressed and shared. Shared suffering produces a strong corporate witness capable of wielding the political pressure necessary to abolish the conditions that create unjust suffering. This communal response is an expression of the transformation of powerlessness into active witness. And the transformation of powerlessness into active suffering is the power of love. Love is people accepting reality and transforming it.[52]

The work of love is dangerous work. The transformation of historical injuries helps make for what Johannes Metz calls a "dangerous memory," one capable of releasing the silence-breaking cry that invokes a political consciousness. Once awaked, there arises within the political consciousness of suffering people the memory of humankind's passion history. This is not just a memory that reflects the past; it is a memory that refracts our present experience from the perspective of the crucified of history and their uprisings. This powerful memory opens and changes our perspectives on suffering and offers strength and courage to respond. Instead of cowardice and apathy, it teaches us to become ready to act for change; that is, to carry out the act of suffering through our willingness to bear witness *(marturia)* and not withdraw.

There is no choice between suffering or not suffering. The question is not, Why do we suffer? It is, For whose sake do we suffer? Accepting

---

[52]Ibid., 92.

suffering places the accent on the greater cause of eliminating unnecessary misery, on discovering the ways that suffering makes us more human. The meaning of suffering becomes known through just and loving deeds and actions. This is where personal suffering becomes integrated with a larger vision, where the personal becomes political. It is when people see this union in the death and resurrection of Jesus that the cross both strengthens and consoles.

But what about situations in which nothing can be done, where the destruction of life and hope has taken a toll far beyond our human ability to endure and survive? Even when people suffer senselessly and are destroyed, their suffering must be addressed. Although their experiences should never be trivialized through explanations that seek to answer what cannot be told, they must be granted our full attention. Where nothing can be done, Soelle says, a different kind of compassion is called for, a radical sort of solidarity—a compassion that joins with the suffering.[53] Where nothing can be done, at least one can bear witness in this way. We must stay and not turn away. We must not turn our eyes or our hearts away from harsh reality, for by doing so, we betray the sufferer and ultimately ourselves. When we can indeed do nothing to change the circumstances of suffering, bearing witness means that the marks of that suffering will sear our own souls. We become changed.

The cross means breaking the long chain of silences. Jesus' cry from the cross, "My God, my God, why have you forsaken me?" (Mk. 15:34) is the cry that breaks the conspiracy of any attempt to civilize injustice that renders its victims invisible. In keeping with a political interpretation of the cross, the most accurate Easter vision is one of Jesus stumbling from the tomb, limping toward the resurrection on broken feet, wounded in the struggle for justice and love but not defeated. This is a vision in which wounds of suffering are not healed lightly, and resurrection still awaits it full expression.

Dorothee Soelle has brought a needed correction to the understanding of the theology of the cross for today. By emphasizing the political nature of suffering, she has moved the theology of the cross away from personalistic and passive interpretations. Focusing on specific experiences, she avoids generalizing or abstracting human misery. She treats particular historical settings in which suffering occurs. She reveals the human face of suffering, and by so doing challenges any temptation to justify passive and apathetic responses to their situations.

Others have joined in this emerging political orientation to suffering, particularly voices from various underrepresented communities. Katie Cannon, mentioned earlier, examines Zora Neal Hurston's sermon "The wounds of Jesus" to demonstrate how the goodness of God brings a

---

[53]Ibid., 7.

liberating redeemer whose potency eases the burden of black people's affliction. In this work, Calvary is given an ethical interpretation consistent with the political theology of the cross that we have been discussing. Calvary reveals the nature of evil that humans commit against one another as a "flagrant opposition to Divine Goodness."[54]

Cheryl Kirk-Duggan also interprets suffering through an ethical analysis that challenges all theories that fail to account for hope for all who endure conditions of misery and affliction. She suggests that we need to form coalitions of trust that never forget "the reality of the most heinous suffering and our part in the malevolent affair."[55]

M. Shawn Copeland insists that any theology of suffering from a womanist perspective involves resistance. "With motherwit, courage, sometimes their fists, and most often sass, Black women resisted the degradation of chattel slavery...with sass, Black women turned back the shame that others tried to put on them."[56] And African theologian Mercy Amba Oduyoye also talks about resistance as a critical means for addressing suffering. She goes so far as to say that women in Africa know that they will need to be ready to risk even death in order to resist death. She points to Esther as the prototype of the strong woman who practices active resistance (Esth. 4:16). She also speaks of other women who simply "refuse" to comply with dehumanizing factors. Their resistance takes a different form: "They face the cross in the hope that the humanity of women will rise from the silence and peace of the graveyard."[57] Korean theologian Chung Hyun Kyung carries this theme of resistance to Korea, where she tells of the tremendous courage of a Korean comfort woman who lived through unimaginable hardships and survived. In her old age the woman learned to forgive all her tormenters. How could she do this? Chung Hyun Kyung only says that "she cut the vicious cycle of violence and revenge with her power, which I cannot easily name."[58] She goes on to say that it was this Buddhist woman who brought her lotus flower to bloom out of her suffering. She was not a Christian, but one could still say that the lotus flower was a sign of holiness that emerged not as an explanation, but as a blessing and hope for her renewed life.

---

[54]Cannon, *Katie's Canon*, 106–8.

[55]Cheryl A. Kirk-Duggan, *Exorcizing Evil: A Womanist Perspective on the Spirituals* (Maryknoll, N.Y.: Orbis Books, 1997), 46.

[56]M. Shawn Copeland, "Wading through Many Sorrows" in *A Troubling in My Soul: Womanist Perspectives on Evil and Suffering*, ed. Emilie M. Townes (Maryknoll, N.Y.: Orbis, 1993), 124.

[57]Mercy Amba Oduyoye, "Spirituality of Resistance and Reconstruction" in *Women Resisting Violence: Spirituality for Life*, ed. Mary John Mananzan, Mercy Amba Oduyoye, Elsa Tamez, J. Shannon Clarkson, Mary C. Grey, Letty M. Russell (Maryknoll, N.Y.: Orbis Books, 1996), 167–78.

[58]Chung Hyun Kyung, "Your Comfort Vs. My Death" in *Women Resisting Violence*, 137.

Summary

If the cross stands as a paradigmatic event that can illumine the depth and contours of human suffering, it must be interpreted historically in all its particular manifestations. Crucifixion, and the promise of resurrection, takes specific forms for different contexts, always interrogating the unique circumstances in which they occur. But because of this demand for specificity, a political rendering of the cross that provides a depth reading of a particular event can also speak to other people and other situations over time. Deep speaks to deep. The depth of particularity reveals the possibility of our communion. In this way accessing the particular can open a way for people to come together in solidarity. The crucifixion of Jesus provides this depth reading and hope for solidarity and has held political significance for Christians living in extreme circumstances all over the world.

Because the cross is historical and political, the truth it reveals is contingent and provisional. It exposes the relational and contextual demands of meaning, identity, and hope. Because meaning is always grounded in history and experience, it is here that holiness is revealed, not through other speculative worlds. This is to say that the cross offers a radical assessment of human existence and relationships. This fundamental orientation is the only way that a theology of the cross can be reclaimed today. Otherwise, it will become simply another ideological system of propositional truths that no longer relates to the questions and conditions people face.

A political interpretation of the cross that takes historical injuries and imposed suffering seriously focuses on the intersection between social structures and human experience. It calls reality by its name and dares to say what it sees. The cross critiques all systems and symbols that prevent this seeing. Yet such a theology knows that to really see means to suffer. But suffering alone is not sufficient. Seeing and critically analyzing are not enough. Naming and suffering are not redemptive on their own terms. A political reading of the cross means suffering has an aim and the cross represents a strategy, or as the author of Mark talked about in his early gospel, it offers a "way." The disciples of Jesus in every time and place are invited to follow the way of love and justice in the world.

Theology of the cross is fundamentally a confessional theology. It views the cross as central for understanding who we are and what life is about as Christians. As a posture of faith, it seeks out analogies in Jewish and Christian history and tradition to illumine present experiences, not to explain or justify existing social orders. In this way theology of the cross is not a cause-and-effect theology or a question-and-answer theology. Nor does it seek to correlate ancient truths and metaphors with contemporary worldviews. Instead, while drawing on the resources of faith, it critiques the tradition itself as well as modern life. The truth of historically imposed suffering means that a theology of the cross will be driven by the quest for justice to question every norm, convention, principle, and institution in our society. In doing so, it even questions our assumptions about history itself and any method that claims certainty—even its own. As such, the cross participates in projects of deconstruction and liberation that can inform pastoral theology.

A political theology of the cross means that the relationship between social ethics and pastoral theology needs to be explored for a broader understanding of healing. This will mean seeing personal suffering as indeed historically imposed and linked to social issues. This orientation will involve pastoral theology in recovering a notion of discipleship as the way for engaging other voices within the public forum. This means that pastoral theology will find its identity in a woman who is beaten, in a teenager who is caught up in drugs, in a Vietnam veteran without a home, in the blues and protest songs of contemporary singers. Here is where we will find our identities and learn to understand our own lives.

The cross provides pastoral theology a way to deal with the reality of failure. The way of the cross recognizes the impossibility of *securitas*. Instead, the paradox of the cross offers a way to explore the deeper meaning of hope. Most critically, this will help us examine in what ways the theories and practices of modern pastoral care and theology have tended to identify with and preserve dominant American—and by implication, Western—culture. The cross provides an alternative way.

Fundamentally, a political reading of the cross for pastoral theology will also require a political interpretation of pastoral theology. This will involve reexamining the meanings of some of the traditional images and metaphors for pastoral care. The metaphor of the Shepherd, particularly the treatment given by Seward Hiltner and his followers, needs to be reexamined through the lens of Mark's suffering righteous one in order to honor the pastoral requirement of justice for those who experience historical injuries.

The four pastoral functions of healing, guiding, sustaining, and reconciling need to be reevaluated, taking into account the challenges and promises of the political cross. In order to do this, it will be valuable to see how sustaining and guiding have been practiced in communities of faith, particularly during times of unrest. It will be important to ask what has been the role of reconciliation, which until recently has been ignored by many pastoral theologians. Through a new approach to these functions, they may be better understood as practices of communities of faith over time rather than as actions of a particular caregiver. In fact, healing may not really be a function at all, or even a practice. Rather, healing is a gift, received as a kind of vindication of suffering. It is a foretaste of the realm of God and therefore tied to worship and the fruits of reconciliation when understood within an ethic of justice grounded in love.

CHAPTER
SIX

A Critical Point Directed at a Suffering World

A Political Cross Informs Pastoral Theology

Justice without mercy is tyranny.
Mercy without justice is weakness.
Justice without love is pure socialism.
And love without justice is baloney.[1]

CARDINAL JAIME SIN

Alastair Campbell says, "Pastoral care is, in essence, surprisingly simple. It has one fundamental aim: to help people know love, both as something to be received and as something to give."[2] Love is the word we speak when we are called out of our mundane routine into something new and wonderful. When we experience this, life becomes amazing and holy. Love is also a word we say when the ordinary all of a sudden takes on fresh and unexpected meaning. We call this holy too. Carter Heyward points out

---

[1]Cardinal Jaime Sin. Quoted in the *Seattle Times*, 9 May 1987.
[2]Alastair V. Campbell, *Professionalism and Pastoral Care* (Philadelphia: Fortress Press, 1985), 11.

that the root of all forms of love is relationship.[3] Love is the sacred movement that takes place between and among people in mutual relationships. Pastoral theologians honor this word and its aim when we develop theories that promote practices that support mutual relationships. But mutual relationships require a climate in which love is more than a feeling or something we merely "fall into."

Mutual relationships are established when the claims of justice are put into practice. Otherwise, love is nothing but "fancy," a passing whim; or in the words of the introductory quote, "Love without justice is baloney." The vision of just and compassionate environments in which mutual relationships are possible inspires the kind of pastoral practices that help people know *just love.* A political interpretation of the cross informs pastoral theology so people can learn and know *just love* as something to be received and as something to give.

Love, as that holy movement between and among us, is not something we have or possess. Rather, it possesses us, motivating us to make commitments and become involved with others. Love pulls us out and moves us beyond where we have been until we find ourselves somewhere we have never been before. That is why love and transcendence are often associated with each other. In this way, love is not something hypothetical or abstract; it involves connection, giving and receiving, becoming trustworthy and open to being changed. One only knows love by becoming vulnerable within time and through particular relationships. This means that love is tied to history with all its contingencies, making the struggle to know love, particularly *just love,* complicated. This means that transcendence is definitely not neutral, nor is it a *tabula rasa* on which we merely project our own wishes and points of view.

Too often the unjust forces within history diminish human life and purpose and distort love, making it appear as something it is not. There are social and political contexts that inhibit and even stop the sacred movement between and among us. This is tragic and sometimes evil. Yet almost miraculously at times, within these restrictions the movement of love continues to seek expression, sometimes through struggle and protest, and other times through sheer tenacity. These expressions of love are about justice. They challenge any interpretation that would allow love to lapse into sentimentality or mere speculation, which in the end is the same thing. They show that love and justice cannot be separated and still be meaningful.

A political interpretation of the theology of the cross is about the inseparability of love and justice. Dorothee Soelle draws this point out when she talks about the relationship between mystical love and political involvement. In this relationship, the mystical power of love embodies the

---

[3]Carter Heyward, *Touching Our Strength: The Erotic as Power and the Love of God* (San Francisco: Harper and Row, 1989), 99.

New Testament concept of *agape* as political solidarity.[4] An orientation to pastoral care with love as its aim does the same thing when it links compassion for the suffering people to injustices in the world that harm them. It recognizes that the suffering of individuals is related to the political realities that impinge on their lives. Pastoral care with this in mind requires a theology that illumines the requirements of love within the conditions of justice for love to flourish. This very demand of love involves us in working with people to transform their suffering so they can know love as something to be received and as something to give—and so can we. Such an aim is risky. It requires time, energy, participation, and vulnerability to establish settings in which mutual relations can be fostered. And this may indeed require a kind of compassion that is more physical than the emotion of empathy; one that bears suffering—physical, social, and spiritual—on behalf of and with the people we learn to call "friends." A political interpretation of the cross is about this risky form of love that addresses the historical injuries inflicted on individuals and communities through working to transform their experiences and ours.

Liberalism and the Limits of Love

The cry of suffering people is a challenge and a point of departure for pastoral care and theology. The reality of this cry and the aim of pastoral care "to know love" stand in a stark and shocking relationship to each other. The gulf between the magnitude of historical suffering of people and their yearning for wholeness has not been eliminated. As mentioned earlier, for those of us who are Protestant, part of our inability to bridge this gap may reflect our strong reliance on certain existentialist strands of liberal theology.

Liberal theology in the United States has been criticized for accommodating itself to modernity. It has also been, out of necessity, a strong proponent of the separation of church and state. However, while protecting the freedom of religious expression, this boundary has also reinforced the wedge between economics and politics and the private lives of people. The state addresses politics, the church individual souls. This has not only helped diminish the church's prophetic voice in society, it has also helped strengthen the idea that the individual person is private and free, capable of finding relief from all forms of suffering through personal religion. These private notions of salvation have eclipsed the corporate nature of liberation associated with the in-breaking realm of God.

By adopting the liberal religious paradigm, particularly as it has functioned on American soil, pastoral theologians have largely ignored the collective nature of sin and its interpretation as injustice. Sin as injustice

---

[4]Dorothee Soelle, *The Window of Vulnerability: A Political Spirituality* (Minneapolis: Fortress Press, 1990), 107.

has not been seen as a primary cause of suffering. Instead, individual guilt has. Until recently, this has generally been accepted without question, even when the causes of suffering have not been attributed to the one experiencing it.[5] Either you personally do something wrong and you suffer because you are guilty, or somebody does something wrong to you and you become injured as a result. Someone else may be the guilty person who is the perpetrator, but nevertheless, from this position it is individuals who cause suffering either to themselves or someone else. It is individuals who are guilty and need to be held morally accountable. This view has a long history and has been emphasized to the neglect of our growing awareness that structures of society also cause collective as well as individual harm to people and communities. It was this approach to sin connected to individual guilt that led Seward Hiltner to eliminate the pastoral function of reconciliation from his understanding of the shepherding perspective.

Historically, reconciliation has been an area of pastoral care that recognizes a believer's erring ways and the need to make amends. But when Hiltner was writing, there was a strong movement to abandon any kind of authoritarian approach to people, including the assigning of blame. He particularly found that ascribing guilt to people in need was contradictory to a pastoral attitude of unconditional love and acceptance. In addition for Hiltner, the shepherd, by definition, deals with individuals. Where external forces of injustice are at work that require making judgments, they are seen as problems of society to be dealt with elsewhere, not within the shepherding perspective.

When Hiltner abandoned judgment in practice and eliminated reconciliation from the shepherding perspective, he basically withdrew pastoral care from public life and cut off its prophetic roots. Hiltner identified strongly with liberal theology to ground his position and support this orientation. While the recent trends in pastoral theology mentioned earlier are seeking to rectify this loss of the prophetic tradition, the omission of reconciliation from pastoral theology for a significant length of time has created a vacuum that is difficult to overcome. In addition, our continued indebtedness to the liberal paradigm, until very recently, has also contributed to our not paying attention to sin, especially sin manifested as injustice. In the meantime, the deep cries of the wounded in our midst have remained largely unheard. As Soelle notes, "This liberal myth never really functioned for the oppressed."[6]

---

[5]This position led Seward Hiltner to eliminate the historical pastoral care function of reconciliation from the shepherding perspective of pastoral care and theology. For a complete discussion of the different perspectives he identifies as appropriate for pastoral theology, see his *Preface to Pastoral Theology* (Nashville: Abingdon Press, 1958).

[6]Soelle, *Window of Vulnerability,* 112.

Love Becomes Politically Active

A political interpretation of the cross provides a corrective to the liberal paradigm and an alternative lens for addressing the deeper layers of the wounds in our communities. From the perspective of the cross, the painful relationship between the reality of suffering people and the yearning "to know love" is informed by a vision of where these meet—a just and compassionate society. Here is where Douglas John Hall's understanding of the discrepancy between expectation and experience becomes politically active. The pain that people feel at the disjunction between their experiences and their vision becomes a motivating force to transform their suffering by working to create an environment that supports mutual and just relationships.[7]

The cross stands as a powerful symbol of the suffering of people and of their yearning to know love. Through Jesus on the cross, the yearning to know love painfully embraces the suffering of broken community. The cross profoundly demonstrates the fundamental meaning of human and divine suffering. In Jesus' experience of death on the cross, the significant issues of public and private life come together. Economics, politics, religion, dreams and the demise of dreams, the meaning of sickness and health, who is on the inside and who is on the margins, the meaning of dominating power and an alternative expression of vulnerable power—all of these and more come together at the foot of the cross. The cross is a political symbol of reality in all its starkness and ambiguity. It represents inflicted death by criminal actions and the tenacious power of life under such extremes. The conditions of contemporary life in which people are pushed to their limits find points of contact with this setting in scripture. The cross becomes paradigmatic for our own time.

In an unjust world, love cannot avoid suffering. Love cannot escape suffering if it seeks the liberation of people. In our world it is not love that causes, seeks, or produces suffering. Instead, it is the unjust circumstances that produce suffering. Dorothee Soelle states it this way:

> Love does not require the cross, but *de facto* it ends up on the cross. *De facto* Jesus of Nazareth was crucified. The cross is no theological invention but the world's answer, given a thousand times over, to attempts at liberation. Only for that reason are we able to recognize ourselves in Jesus' dying on the cross.[8]

Jesus' suffering on the cross invites us to view suffering not as private pain alone, but as part of the historical and communal fabric within which

---

[7]Soelle, *Suffering*, trans. Everett R. Kalin (Philadelphia: Fortress Press, 1975), 101. Here, Soelle draws from the mystical expression of the cross, in which God is always experienced as with the sufferer. This destroys ideologies of punishment and an overemphasis on guilt. This interpretation offers strength and consolation and an ultimate ground for solidarity.

[8]Ibid., 163–64.

our lives are formed. The ongoing question is, How does a political interpretation of the cross help us to do this? How is this orientation helpful to pastoral theology?

The cross stands with us and, at the same time, over and against us. It confronts us with the question, Who is on the cross, and why is he or she there? This is the first question before all other questions, and it is the one that involves us in the task of self-criticism. Within the field of pastoral care and theology, this means that we must engage in a self-critical assessment about the values and assumptions we profess explicitly and implicitly through the theories and practices we use. As a discipline we must ask, Who has a complaint against us? With this question we raise the issue of who is cared for and who is not. Who is served? Who is included within the framework of our descriptions, analyses, and practices, and who is excluded? Who finds a voice? Who remains silent? Or worse yet, who is silenced? And most importantly, whose burden is multiplied by the way we go about our business? It is not enough to criticize social structures unless we are able to clarify how we are entangled in them. Furthermore, it is not enough simply to name our relationship to social structures unless we are willing to acknowledge how we profit from conforming to the norms that keep those structures in place. Only by listening to those who have a quarrel with us and by engaging in such self-critical activity can pastoral care and theology address the historical and contemporary practices that continue to wound and divide people. If we listen to those who have a complaint against us, our theories and practices will be transformed more fully into the knowledge of liberating love. From this posture, pastoral theology begins with confessing its collusion in harm and its inability to "save itself" as it seeks to participate in a tradition of *fides quaerens intellectum,* perhaps better understood for today as *pain seeing understanding.*

To view suffering as part of the social and communal fabric of our lives means that we must learn to accept and understand ourselves within our increasingly diverse and pluralistic context. This means that in some circumstances the cross will stand against us, contradicting all we thought was certain. In other situations the cross will confirm and comfort, giving definition and direction to those who struggle. Historical suffering means different things to different people, while at the same time it shows that no one person's suffering is unrelated to another person's pain. As a consequence, this "stumbling block" aspect of the cross guides pastoral theology in a somewhat paradoxical manner.

A theology of the cross speaks a different word to those who create and perpetuate unjust structures and practice oppression than it does for those who suffer the direct consequences of them. For those who hold power over others in a particular society, the political cross speaks the word of judgment and demands change, usually in some form of relinquishment of power and control, followed by acts of reparation for past wrongs. In this case the cross is prescriptive. It pronounces judgment in the hope for *metanoia* on the part of the abusers. Judgment speaks the word that only God is God, and no one else is God. Any system that perpetuates human dominance, in whatever form, is false. Tyranny gives a distorted reading of life and must be changed. For those who dominate others, a political interpretation of theology of the cross prescribes limiting those powers and the people who wield them. Such a prescriptive interpretation of the cross is necessary, so that the causes of suffering can be prevented from being projected onto and into the victims or the excluded and executed ones of our society.

Projection can be a powerful way of describing someone else in light of our own unacknowledged wounds, prejudices, and disillusionments. Through projection, others become distorted images of us. Historical and cultural projections are particularly harmful in this regard. They become extremely potent when they are allowed to remain nameless within the private sphere, where they often become diagnosed as paranoia, inferiority complexes, or grandiosity. It is the carriers of our historical and cultural projections who finally become the scapegoats and victims of injustice.

Unfortunately, when projection fosters this falsely privatized and compartmentalized way of living, people in positions of power learn *not* to feel their brokenness. We do not feel the need to grieve what we do not even know we have lost. We forget how to mourn, and by doing so remain numb to the pain that is in us and in others around us. A political theology of the cross breaks this cycle. It provides a way to name what is being projected and urges it toward public expression. The eyes of this faith begin to see the deep, broad, and intricate system of power that serves the few who hold the reigns and drive the caravan. We also begin to recognize our own culpability. The prescriptive aspect of the theology of the cross creates a painful awakening, but it is always toward the restoration of right relationships.

For those who are oppressed or marginalized in any way within a particular culture, a political theology of the cross is not prescriptive in the same way it is for the dominants. For those who suffer historical injuries, it is first of all descriptive. The political cross illumines the societal contours of suffering. It reveals the political, ideological, and economic factors that impact people adversely. By identifying the social and cultural aspects of personal pain, the cross moves those who are suffering away from the internalized descriptions and social positions that have been given to them by others. The political cross helps people name reality that originates outside of them.

Seeing the relationship between one's own suffering and the social conditions that create and perpetuate it can help people find new descriptions and alternative meanings for themselves. This leads to a different prescriptive nature of the cross for people who are experiencing injustice. By naming the sources of their affliction, the political cross prescribes mobilizing the power of suffering to tear down and eliminate the oppressive structures that have been internalized. The aim is to fully *objectify* structures of oppression, externalize them where they belong, in order to begin to dismantle the oppressive structures in society that mitigate against all people and God.

This externalizing of internalized suffering makes what can be called the "order of suffering" painfully visible. It places those who suffer clearly before those who prefer not to see them. But to see, to really see, is to be moved! This is what it means to bear witness. This is what it means to awaken the heart of compassion.[9] To be moved is to see the structure of the cross in the political order of suffering today.

Yet the cross that calls for the dismantling of unjust social structures is more than a subjective process of being moved. At the same time, it is clearly not just an objective process. It moves beyond a subject-object understanding of relationships. It is found in between subject and subject in the *yearning* for right relationships. Such yearning reflects the desire, the *passion,* for mutuality. It invokes the theological imagination that involves us in the dismantling process in order to reconstruct reality from a new point of vision. However, this dismantling process is always a biased and a committed process, because the starting place is the cry of suffering that breaks open our false notions of objectivity. Dismantling, then, is not only the process of deconstructing theories that support unjust views of human interaction; it begins with the humane task of removing people from the cross, or as Choan-Seng Song says,

> The Mission of the Christian church is to work toward eradication of the cross and the disappearance of it within the church itself, in the society in which it is located, and in the world in which people of different nations strive for justice, peace and freedom.[10]

Love Becomes Biased

The implications of this faith posture for pastoral care and theology means making a "preferential option" in practice and theory for whoever is suffering, particularly those who bear the pain of oppression, exclusion,

---

[9]Brita Gill-Austern uses this phrase "awaken the heart of compassion" to talk about the aims of spiritual direction. Conversations during the fall, 2000, Andover Newton Theological School.

[10]Choan-Seng Song, "Christian Mission Toward Abolition of the Cross" in *The Scandal of a Crucified World: Perspectives on the Cross and Suffering,* ed. Yacob Tesfai (Maryknoll, N.Y.: Orbis Books, 1994), 147.

poverty, and collective harm in any form.[11] The cries of these people provide the warrants for starting with a political interpretation of the cross. This perspective does not allow for a "neutral" stance, but requires a conscious bias and commitment on the part of those who would join in movements to transform human pain. It involves risk, because it means being involved in the very lives of those who suffer, even those who may point an accusing finger at us. This is a relational orientation that requires a confessional posture of faith.

The bias and commitment toward those who suffer not only renders caregivers vulnerable, it also contributes to an alternative understanding of our vocations. Someone who is biased and committed works in solidarity with those who suffer, in private consultation and public policy and direct social action. This involves a conscious religious decision. This biased interest contradicts somewhat the value of disinterest found in much of the pastoral literature, which says that a certain disinterest is necessary in order to relate to someone in need. An example of this is found again in the writings of Seward Hiltner. He alludes to the problem of disinterest when he warns against the temptations of empathy:

> It is human for us to place ourselves empathetically in the position of the sufferer…Human as it is, [this] reflects more of our own empathic suffering than the sustaining of the sufferer…This is human, but at this time it is mistaken.[12]

Echoes of this concern can still be detected in the discussions amongst pastoral theologians around issues of transference and counter-transference between a caregiver and the person seeking counsel, overidentification with a client or parishioner, and certain boundary issues. While these concerns are valid and necessary for an appropriate empathy that does not

---

[11]"Preferential option" is a phrase used by liberation theologians when they argue that through Hebrew and Christian scriptures it can be shown that God has demonstrated a "preferential option for the poor" in the history. Latin American theologians Leonardo Boff, Jon Sobrino, and Gustavo Gutierrez and North American theologian Robert McAfee Brown are a few who began using this perspective for theology. I am using this phrase in a more inclusive sense. While still recognizing the warrants for an option for the poor in history, I also include in this phrase other people who are harmed by marginalization and subject to oppression from various sources, not limited to poverty. For example, middle-class people who have suffered harm because of environmental hazards; women from all classes and racial/ethnic backgrounds who have been beaten and raped because of male violence; and all forms of racism, militarism, nationalism, ageism, and heterosexism, as these contribute to the suffering of people living in the twentieth century.

[12]Hiltner, *Preface to Pastoral Theology,* 122. Here can be seen the strong influence of Carl Rogers on Hiltner's thought. Rogers, in discussing the necessary attitudes of the counselor, maintains that empathic responses on the part of the counselor indicate that the counselor is perceiving the hates and hopes and fears of the client through a process without the counselor's experiencing those hates and hopes and fears. See Carl Rogers, *Client Centered Therapy* (Boston: Houghton Mifflin, 1951), 29.

violate pastoral relationships, they can also be misleading. They can allow us to interpret these therapeutic dynamics in ways that are self-serving. Instead of protecting the vulnerable, disinterest can become a luxury of the one in a position of offering care or an excuse not to get involved. In these instances, distance erroneously protects the caregiver from those who are suffering. In truth, it more accurately serves to maintain the position of the caregiver who, in practice, is opposed to full mutuality. In other words, disinterest can serve the interests of the privileged. The problems that attend empathy are really also about issues that tend to keep suffering personal, in the individual, private, and therefore hidden.

Disinterest, as we are talking about it, is really a product of Enlightenment thinking that values rationalism and supposed scientific objectivity. While a pastoral care and theology that relies on disinterest is supposed to be unbiased, neutral, and fair, it can lead instead to an ethic and practice of adjustment between people and society. Influenced by a liberalism that tries to play the *mediator* between church and society, religion and culture, an ethic of adjustment often ends up serving a kind of harmony between church and state, the individual and society, the privileged and the impoverished. In this way, those who cannot or will not adjust, those who "don't fit," become excluded at the expense of the whole. But when even one person is diminished, we all are impoverished.

A political interpretation of the cross stands in direct opposition to this posture of disinterest. Or as Soelle says, "'Take up your cross and follow me' means: join the battle. Give up your neutrality."[13] One cannot care *and* be protected from suffering at the same time. On the contrary, a theology of the cross means letting oneself be touched and take sides. This is consistent with Rollo May's understanding of empathy,

> Empathy means a much deeper state of identification of personalities in which one person so feels himself into the other as temporarily to lose his own identity.[14]

Such empathy experiences suffering. Again, this is an expression of "bearing witness" (again, *marturia*) to the suffering of another.

A political theology of the cross makes the "wounds" of historically imposed suffering visible. Soelle draws upon Simone Weil's description of affliction to remind us that suffering has these three essential dimensions: physical, psychological, and social.[15] Suffering does not reside in the psyche alone. Suffering is not physical pain alone. Suffering is not simply a private affair. Instead, suffering expresses an intense experience of pain endured

---

[13]Soelle, *Choosing Life* (Philadelphia: Fortress Press, 1981), 55.
[14]Hiltner, *The Counselor in Counseling: Case Notes in Pastoral Counseling* (New York & Nashville: Abingdon Press, 1941), 161.
[15]Soelle, *Suffering*, 13.

in the individual's embodied psyche and in the social and cultural world. Suffering is personal and political.

Because this is the case, a love that becomes biased is also a love that becomes political. It takes on flesh and unexpected meaning, as it becomes *just love* in the world. Such love finds that holiness, too, is a political moving force that engages the deep suffering of our day. The love that is bound and entwined in this political holiness becomes vulnerable as holiness becomes vulnerable. This is what the cross teaches us. How, then, does this vulnerable love understood as political holiness inform the traditional pastoral functions of guiding, healing, reconciling, and sustaining? How can these functions be reexamined from a political reading of the cross in order to address the deep wounds of historical suffering in our day?

Pastoral Functions Transformed by Love

Pastoral care has been seen as a set of functions, with healing the primary one. Almost without question healing has been seen as the lead function, with sustaining, guiding, and when recognized, reconciling acting to facilitate healing's aims.[16] Many would not see any conflict between the classical understanding of pastoral functions and Campbell's view that love is the aim of pastoral care. Although there need not be inherent opposition in these viewpoints, there is still potential misunderstanding for what they might entail in practice. We need to ask, Is the goal of healing from a functional point of view compatible with the aim of love, which takes justice seriously? If it is, we need to examine whether or not we are attending to the full range of issues people are facing. If it is not, we need to ask the harder question, Why not? As discussed in chapter 2, a functionalist approach promotes an almost exclusive focus on individuals and pragmatic results. If we understand the role of pastoral theology as interpreting the "functions" of pastoral care, we may bring unexamined assumptions into our current inquiry into the meaning of pastoral theology for today.

For example, while much of contemporary pastoral theology continues to focus on healing, broadly interpreted as restoring a person to wholeness, little critical analysis has been done to show what this actually means. When interpreted within a liberal theological reading of guiding, sustaining, and reconciling, restoring a person to wholeness can mean guiding, sustaining, and reconciling the person to the worldview of the dominant culture with which large portions of the church are identified.[17] We need to ask, Is our current understanding of restoring a person to wholeness introducing

---

[16]Some have added additional categories beyond healing, guiding, sustaining, and reconciling. Howard Clinebell, for example, talks about a nurturing function in his *Basic Types of Pastoral Care and Counseling: Resources for the Ministry of Healing and Growth,* rev. ed. (Nashville: Abingdon Press, 1984).

[17]Douglas John Hall, *Thinking the Faith: Christian Theology in a North American Context* (Minneapolis: Augsburg Press, 1984), 114.

something fresh, or are we primarily supporting "what is"—when "what is" is crumbling? Are we in truth *practicing* the arts of healing as they were understood in the past, even as we *think* about the person in new ways? In other words, is restoring a person to wholeness still understood as a function of pastoral care, and is this sufficient?

With the renewed interest in spirituality, I think our sensibilities are beginning to shift from merely a functionalist approach to care to one that is more open to symbol and ritual than it was in the past. But even as we begin to practice healing in new ways, another question needs to be asked: What happens when we view healing as the "goal" of pastoral care, even when healing is understood as wholeness? When we understand healing as a "goal," might we be communicating that healing is something we can "achieve"? When we do this, healing can easily become associated with the mastery and success ethics of contemporary North American culture.

If an identity confusion happens between the aims of healing and the cultural notions of success, healing risks becoming objectified as another thing among many to be consumed, acquired, or achieved by some means or another. This is a "commodification of healing" that comes dangerously close to identifying with a *theologia gloriae*. With this caution in mind, our examination of the pastoral functions will need to begin from a different place. The "thin tradition" of the cross we have been discussing invites us into this inquiry to examine the limits and possibilities of the traditional pastoral functions of guiding, healing, sustaining, and reconciling. In this way, the "thin tradition" begins to illumine some basic differences between liberal interpretations of care and the requirements of love.

When love is the aim of pastoral care, healing is not a goal to be accomplished; rather, it is a gift to be received. This reflects the tradition of *theologia crucis* as a theology of grace. This also suggests that, in light of the previous discussion, grace and justice have a very close affinity: Both rely on mercy. Mercy, however, is not a function—but it is the source of hope. Hoping is crucial for healing. But hope is not wishing and sighing for what is desired. Hope, from the perspective of the cross, is more closely tied to paying attention to what is really going on. It is dependent on becoming aware, learning to see what is difficult to see, and *learning to imagine alternatives*. This hope needs a particular kind of instruction, guidance, and encouragement from others.

Guiding has been seen as the pastoral function that helps people come to their own insights for the sake of self-transformation. Its aim is transformation toward personal wholeness. Guiding as a pastoral practice that involves the healing of historical wounds also honors self-awareness and wholeness, but it does so through the raising of critical consciousness that depends on the insights of others whose experiences say something to us we cannot know by ourselves. Hope depends on trusting other voices to guide us as well as our own, so we can learn to hope for healing together.

Guiding involves turning our attention outward as well as inward, so we learn to "wake up" completely. Guiding in this manner will lead to a corporate healing if there is to be any health or wholeness at all.

Wholeness will depend on reconciliation. It will involve restoring a just environment in which love can be known as something to give and be received. Reconciliation, then, cannot be forgotten or eliminated from our pastoral plans if love is the aim of pastoral care. If love involves justice, reconciliation becomes the practical goal of pastoral theology when exercised by a practice of care informed by the political cross of the "thin tradition." The unfinished agenda of reconciliation means there can be no separation of love from justice. There can be no separation of personal needs from public renewal. Reconciliation requires this unity and so affirms the centrality of just relationships.

Pastoral care does not begin in theory; it has always tended to flesh-and-blood relationships first, and only then turned to reflect on the meaning of an encounter. Relationship is the cradle of theory. Traditionally, the forming of pastoral relations starts when someone comforts another who is hurting or in some kind of crisis. This "being with" someone has been understood as a ministry of presence in the form of sustaining another during his time of need. Sustaining is what one person does for another during times when conditions cannot be changed or circumstances readily altered. But when we say that the starting place of a pastoral theology from a political reading of the cross is the cry of suffering people resulting from brokenness in the human community, this shifts the meaning of pastoral presence and the meaning of sustaining. Sustaining now means becoming present to this suffering that is a consequence of the rupture of the divine-human economy. This is where pastoral relationships take on new meaning. Sustaining still involves comfort, but it also means, first and foremost, becoming involved with those people who are vulnerable and most burdened with our historical reality, and not abandoning them.

From the political perspective of the cross, sustaining presence now becomes a pastoral practice of nonabandonment through solidarity. It becomes a way of sharing life with those who are enduring historical wounds. Sustaining as solidarity means being willing to stay beside people in their struggle to be free from unnecessary suffering, being willing to fight with them and not necessarily for them for their release. The meaning of sustaining as solidarity becomes the first movement of a pastoral theology whose aim is love. Solidarity is the primary action of pastoral care in a movement that hopes for healing.

The pastoral functions informed by a political theology of the cross will call for completely new interpretations. Healing, from this view, is not a function at all; rather, it is the gift that comes when the requirements of love are met. Reconciliation will need to be seen in light of the requirements of love, which means the demands of justice must be met. Guiding will need to involve consciousness raising in order to connect personal pain with public tyranny and devise strategies to alleviate both. Sustaining, as just stated, needs to be understood as solidarity, that place where people join together to repair every aspect of their lives. Solidarity will involve us in new forms of vulnerability, the recovery of historical memories, and the capacity to imagine a future radically different from the one we now know, because it will be radically just.

Solidarity is the first movement toward the aim of pastoral care as helping people to know love as something to give and as something to be received. This is a *just love,* a love that exhibits pastoral care through social responsibility. In the next chapter we take a closer look at solidarity as a foundational practice of pastoral care that seeks to help people know and practice socially responsible love.

CHAPTER
SEVEN

Pastoral Solidarity toward the Reconciliation of People

... my anger moves, a storm into the sunlight
where women and men fight alongside each other
in the battles against degradation, poverty, manipulation, fear
where anger is pure as the love I have for freedom
where desire is the catalyst for action
where the possibilities are rice and flowers and children
growing strong everywhere [1]

NELLIE WONG

In this chapter we will look at two functions of pastoral care, sustaining and reconciling, from the perspective of the political cross. From this angle these pastoral functions cease to be functions from the liberal theological point of view and instead become pastoral practices of solidarity and justice making, which cannot be separated from each other. As Cardinal Jaime Sin reminded us in the previous chapter, "Love without justice is baloney." [2] Any pastoral theology that does not recognize this at the center of its theory

---

[1]Nelllie Wong, "For an Asian Woman Who Says My Poetry Gives Her a Stomachache" in *The Forbidden Stitch: An Asian American Women's Anthology,* ed. Shirley Geoklin Lim, Mayumi Tsutakawa, Margarita Donnelly (Corvallis, Oreg.: Calyx Books, 1989), 86.

[2]Cardinal Jaime Sin, quoted in the *Seattle Times,* 9 May 1987.

125

is missing its calling and vocational aims. Yet the connections between love and justice have not always been clearly drawn, particularly when pastoral activities have been viewed as functions that mainly serve individuals.

Much of the pastoral care literature has identified sustaining as a function that involves ongoing care and support for someone during times of distress when the surrounding circumstances cannot be immediately altered or perhaps not ever changed at all.[3] According to William Clebsch and Charles Jaekle, the sustaining function has four movements, beginning with helping people preserve some *equilibrium* in the wake of a critical loss or devastating experience. The second involves *consolation,* helping relieve people of their sense of misery through comfort and support. The third is *consolidation,* attending to the resources people have access to in order to restore their lives. And finally *redemption,* in which someone is helped to move on with his or her life in a new and meaningful way.

The four movements of sustaining have been understood as supporting the vital pastoral function, healing. Hiltner in particular emphasized, "There must be a healing intent before there can be even a sustaining effect."[4] Healing has been seen as the primary pastoral function, even when it cannot be achieved in the foreseeable future. This has been interpreted to mean that even if the situation of a person cannot be changed at all or altered at a particular time, healing is still possible. Here, the fundamental understanding of healing is that a person can potentially be restored to wholeness whatever the circumstances may be. It follows, then, that healing as the goal of sustaining means that sustaining is aimed toward restoring a person to wholeness.

As this view of sustaining has evolved within the traditional liberal pastoral paradigm, it has placed strong emphasis on the value of aiding another to draw on his or her own inner strengths and resources.[5] While this is commendable in order to foster healthy self-confidence and self-worth, it has also put an accent on avoiding attitudes of dependence, on the part of the one seeking counsel as well as the caregiver. The one offering care is supposed to be nonjudgmental and able to keep clear professional boundaries between him- or herself and the one seeking help. A certain

---

[3]Seward Hiltner, *Preface to Pastoral Theology* (Nashville: Abingdon Press, 1958); William A. Clebsch and Charles R. Jaekle, *Pastoral Care in Historical Perspective* (Englewood Cliffs, N.J.: Prentice Hall, 1964); Howard J. Clinebell, *Basic Types of Pastoral Care and Counseling: Resources for the Ministry of Healing and Growth,* rev. ed. (Nashville: Abingdon Press, 1984); and Edward P. Wimberly, *Pastoral Care in the Black Church* (Nashville: Abingdon Press, 1979). The treatment of the pastoral functions by these authors have become reference points for many pastoral theologians.

[4]Hiltner, *Preface to Pastoral Theology,* 139.

[5]These and the following views can be found in the writings of Hiltner, which have influenced modern pastoral theology and care until the present day.

disinterest combined with acceptance of the one suffering is deemed absolutely necessary, so neither caregiver nor care receiver falls into discouragement in the face of painful circumstances. This kind of disinterest is supposedly unbiased and nonpartisan, leaving open avenues for sustaining to move someone toward wholeness.

One of the requirements necessary for functioning in the sustaining role as understood here is that caregivers guard against becoming involved in the problems of people who are suffering. In some ways this has served to protect caregivers from the hardships involved in caring for others. It has also functioned to protect the caregiver as well as the receiver from confusing their identities with each other. However, while it is important to respect differences and recognize alternative points of view and experiences, too strict a boundary can also render the caregiver distant and invulnerable, and in extreme cases, a spectator of another's suffering. A political interpretation of theology of the cross complicates this dynamic by eliminating the option of the observer–the disinterested observer, or even an interested observer–by insisting on the necessity of becoming involved, even if it poses certain ambiguities and risks. Rather than an observer, the cross requires a witness. This calls for pastoral maturity and discernment in order to adopt the faith requirement to "bear witness" *(marturia)*.

Someone who bears witness cannot look on from afar. Holy necessity requires the witness to bear the reality of the other within his or her very being. Witnessing is an embodied practice. The mystery of incarnation confirms this reality as a life-giving and death-defying expression of love. At the same time, this is not a risk-free enterprise. The witness is never free from the suffering to which she or he is exposed. This is the risk of becoming the organic intellectual mentioned earlier or an organic pastoral theologian.

The political theology of the cross is in contradistinction to any form of therapeutic rapport that calls for emotional distance. Dorothee Soelle condemns all such risk-free responses as apathetic avoidance and a denial of suffering:

> To meditate on the cross means to say good-bye to the narcissistic hope of being free of sickness, deformity, and death. Then all the energies wasted on such hopes could become free to answer the call for the battle against suffering.[6]

Sickness, deformity, and death are forms of suffering that affect individuals and whole communities. Doing battle against them means becoming "exposed" to them and risking carrying their "virus" in our own bodies.

People suffer in relationship to communities, not apart from them. Even when they are isolated from a particular community, it is still a

---

[6]Dorothee Soelle, *Suffering,* trans. Everett R. Kalin (Philadelphia: Fortress Press, 1975),131.

community from which they are estranged. The cross points to the depth of brokenness found in people in communities and stands as judgment and consolation. Sustaining that is present to this depth, then, is always a communal practice, even as it always pays attention to the very particular person who is crying out. To hear the cry and bear witness to it means sustaining will become committed and involved with those who suffer. It means we learn to *identify* with their suffering, which is an expression of solidarity.[7]

Sustaining as Solidarity

When sustaining becomes solidarity, it is no longer a pastoral function but a communal *practice* aimed at healing and restoring community life by responding to the holy presence in and for the life of the world. Here, I am using the term *practice* similarly to the way Craig Dykstra and Dorothy C. Bass do when they say, "Practices are things that Christian people do together over time in response to and in the light of God's active presence for the life of the world."[8] I am suggesting that sustaining is fundamentally a practice that a community does over time in order to shape, heal, and restore community life by becoming partners with all that is holy for the well-being, or wholeness, of its members. In fact, each historic *function* will be viewed in just this manner. Sustaining, reconciling, and guiding will be reconceived as communal pastoral *practices* open to the healing activity of the holy in our midst. When looked at this way, sustaining as pastoral solidarity will express the classical fourfold sustaining process of preservation, consolation, consolidation, and redemption as *promising, vulnerability, memory,* and *vision.*

Solidarity as Promising

In the beginning is solidarity. Not healing first! Solidarity is the starting place where people make a commitment and come together. It is where we learn "who is with me" and "where do I cast my lot" with others for mutual advocacy on behalf of justice and hope for healing. Solidarity is not something that just happens. It involves making a promise and keeping it. It means that risks are unavoidable; nonetheless, we will stay present with the people to whom we have made promises. This involves a great amount of courage and humility. As difficult as promise keeping is, as harrowing as

---

[7]Scott Hope writes about this when he says: "We identify with the suffering of others not by seeing the other in agony or by knowing about that pain but by translating it into our own experience (no matter how trivial our suffering might seem when compared to another's). My toothache has political implications. When I say that something experienced by another is like something I have experienced, then I have begun to own the other's experience." *Network Journal* (July 1985): 3.

[8]Dorothy C. Bass, ed., *Practicing our Faith: A Way of Life for a Searching People* (San Francisco: Jossey-Bass, 1997), 5.

risk taking might become, as awkward as humility suggests, this way of commitment is the only way to create the kind of environment that makes a future possible. Although our promises bind us, they also free us and orient us to move with a sense of purpose and responsibility. Our promises show us how we are most human, because they provide us the pathway to trustworthy relationships.

When we enter into solidarity with others who suffer, we promise and say yes to the possibility of weaving together a trustworthy communal tapestry through the power of God's love that draws us into just relationships in the first place. Promising invites solidarity, though it cannot determine the outcome. Those who dare to promise together give up all entitlements, all trappings of privilege—whether knowledge, skill, experience, or desire. Solidarity through promising means we can never determine or predict what is best for someone else, even while we desperately join in seeking it. When we make a promise, we become vulnerable.

Solidarity as Vulnerability

Solidarity at a most basic level involves our becoming vulnerable to others who are suffering. It means we become open to being transformed by those with whom we become united in resistance and struggle for wholeness. Solidarity that is created out of vulnerability is marked by a capacity for intimacy and not by a posture of distance.

Intimacy is central to our capacity for becoming more human. But intimacy is not confined to interpersonal warmth and comfort or even physical and emotional proximity. The intimacy of solidarity involves more than this, even while it begins with a fundamental posture of respect and goodwill.

Intimacy through solidarity is a public and shared confidence that depends on communal practices and a theological imagination. It is an intimacy that yearns to cultivate a kind of inner knowledge of another's situation or worldview through a trust in God's all-embracing love. I am not suggesting that one can "know" across differences so easily. One needs to be open, but one also needs to be offered an invitation. Honest desire and good intentions are not enough. In fact, how and when we come together is often the place in which we experience the pains and frustrations of solidarity. Solidarity must proceed with a kind of trust built on promises that are kept, even as it moves forward by invitation toward an uncertain outcome. Trust held in a cradle of uncertainty seems fragile and perhaps unlikely. It almost seems contradictory. Uncertainty, contradiction, and paradox are what make us extremely vulnerable. Yet to practice God's just love in circumstances of disarray is also what makes us able to become trustworthy. Where solidarity is practiced, we will find intimacy in spite of uncertainty, not cynicism; humility in the face of contradictions, not conceit; imagination where paradox confronts us, not rigid beliefs. It is a complex and wondrous arrangement when those who are used to positions of power and those who have received injuries as a result of abuses of power can come together in new ways and work together for just love in right societal relations. Such is the intimacy of solidarity.

A desire for intimacy reveals the heart of a pastoral theology that seeks to understand the relationship of the divine and human encounter. It views God as desiring some form of intimacy with all the created order. If God, who in the beginning declared the day and night good, desires a relationship with all of the diverse created order, such a relationship without intimacy would be sterile at best and demonic at worst. In truth, relationship without intimacy is the seedbed of hatred. Hatred starts in a situation where there is contact without companionship, or in the words of theologian Howard Thurman, contact without genuine "fellow-feeling."[9] A political reading of the cross refutes a distant deity and reveals instead the vulnerable God who is involved in the lives and destiny of people, indeed the whole created order.

The cross not only speaks about vulnerability, it is a vulnerable theology. In theory and in practice it risks everything, even ridicule, so that a new order might be established. It is never a last word theology. Because theology of the cross seeks to destabilize the contented and satisfied, it is always open to criticism and suspicion. If one is living comfortably, one might say it is a foolish theology. Why would anyone risk a well-off position? If one is suffering, one might still say it is a foolish theology because it promises intimacy where there is so much animosity. There is precious little evidence to warrant such an absurd risk! The cross must never be invoked to satisfy or embellish the power of the elite. On the contrary, the cross says, "Your comfort is really your downfall and ultimately the source of your own disease." Contentment and animosity live in opposition until they are resolved together.

As unpopular as it may be, solidarity involves risking ourselves in the hope of saving others. Like the taunt to Jesus on the cross, "He saved others; he cannot save himself" (Mk. 15:31), a pastoral theology that embraces the cross requires identification and solidarity with this tradition of vulnerability. In fact, it will be a pastoral theology that invites the kind of intimacy that will most definitely involve suffering. Although not drawing on a theology of the cross explicitly, Alastair Campbell alludes to this outcome when he talks about the courage of "loving leaders" as costly and dangerous: "We cannot lead without risking ourselves."[10] Stephen Pattison also points out our vulnerability when he talks about the risks of failure in pastoral care. He emphasizes that every stage of care involves risk when we become

---

[9]Howard Thurman, *Jesus and the Disinherited* (Nashville: Abingdon Press, 1949), 74.
[10]Alastair Campbell, *Rediscovering Pastoral Care* (Philadelphia: Westminster Press, 1981), 45.

involved with people, vulnerable to them, and trusting of them.[11] This is not a masochistic calling. Solidarity does not mean we ask to be beaten down or "crucified." But to save others means that we let go of the illusion that we can be free from involvement and still look after our own future. It means that we are more likely to suffer if we act to save ourselves apart from others. In the end, to save others means we learn to depend on one another, hope together, and knit our lives together for a different and better future.

Perhaps nothing makes us more aware of our vulnerability than loss. And for those who live through them, extreme circumstances and multiple losses make this even more evident. At different points in history, a theology of the cross has been articulated during just such extreme situations. Speaking from a Japanese perspective of the cross after the bombings of Hiroshima and Nagasaki, Kazoh Kitamori writes about the vulnerable God who risks intimacy and in the process becomes broken and wounded. On the cross God suffered because God "embraced those who should not be embraced."[12] For Kitamori, Hiroshima and Nagasaki represent crucifixion events. In the shadow of these images, the embracing God is a powerful image of vulnerability, intimacy, and solidarity. "Those who should not be embraced" are understood to mean all those who participated in the bombings and all that led to them, the innocent as well as the culpable. All who are not easy to embrace include those who, because of their extreme suffering, cry out for explanations that cannot be fully given; those who, because they followed orders without question, perpetrated one of the gravest atrocities of the twentieth century; those who were intoxicated with the wonders of new technology and could not refrain from using it; those who, because of ignorance, indifference, bigotry, or apathy, allowed it to go forth. On the cross God suffered because God "embraced those who should not be embraced" for whatever reason. This spectrum of "all" makes us realize how difficult it is to become vulnerable. It shows us how costly it is to really see and identify with the suffering of others, especially if we do not understand them, or want to distance ourselves from them.

Our willingness to be vulnerable becomes particularly problematic when we have in any way contributed to another's distress. Not understanding people can be painful enough. But when we do come to know our place in someone else's suffering, this new knowledge can be devastating, particularly as we begin to learn why it is that we are not to be trusted. We learn that we, too, are "those who should not be embraced." And yet, we are. This knowledge is the beginning of humility.

---

[11]Stephen Pattison, *A Critique of Pastoral Care* (London: SKM Press, 1988), 154–55.
[12]Kazoh Kitamori, *Theology of the Pain of God* (Richmond, Va.: John Knox Press, 1958), 22.

The process of coming to new awareness, or new knowledge, often involves us in something Antonio Gramsci calls a "self-inventory." For those of us who, to whatever extent, participate in the dominant culture and have access to privileges, self-inventory involves learning how these positions impact other people whose experiences are different from ours. Through genuine solidarity our impact on others becomes revealed to us through the eyes of others. This is a painful process if it is an honest process. Our safe place is shown to be our vulnerable place when we see how our privilege becomes played out in the lives of others. We begin to see the relationship between our comfort and another's animosity, and we grieve. When we learn to be in real solidarity with the suffering of others, our own suffering as a result of our privilege becomes revealed to us as well. This is one place where identification with the suffering of others takes place. It is where intimacy through shared pain informs solidarity. Kitamori hints that this identification is an aspect of the pain of God.[13] Solidarity really begins with the realization of God's solidarity with humankind through the intimate knowledge of shared pain. Here is where theology leaves abstraction and becomes vulnerable and truly historical.

The ultimate vulnerability is the experience of total abandonment. Soelle points out that all extreme suffering evokes the experience of being forsaken by God. In the depth of suffering, people see themselves as abandoned and forsaken by everyone.[14] This experience cannot be overlooked or explained away. A theology of the cross means to stay with and not abandon anyone who says "My God, why have you forsaken me?" To stay and not leave is to bear witness to the continuity between the historical cry from the cross and the pain of people today. To stay means to remain vulnerable to this cry as though it were emanating from our own depths. If we stay and do not abandon, we stand, as Soelle says, on the side of "the damned of this world."[15] Solidarity seeks to bring the silent suffering of the damned into public speech, to make personal forsakenness a public outcry.

Solidarity through Memory and Longing

Solidarity is only understood when it is practiced. Solidarity is a practice marked by memory and deep longing. Memory stretches back, and longing leans forward; these two movements together make a future possible. Through solidarity one learns to accompany another and to recall with him or her the circumstances of his or her pain as a way to counter the present reality. Memory is crucial for this journey.

---

[13]Ibid., 22.
[14]Soelle, *Choosing Life* (Philadelphia: Fortress Press, 1981), ix.
[15]Ibid., 53.

Like the solidarity of promise making and vulnerability, memory is always historical and specific. One does not remember "in general." Even vague memories are sketchy recollections about something identifiable and tangible. Memory's very power lies in its particularity. When a person or community is engaged in remembering, it is in the process of gaining new truths about life. When the Japanese American community sponsors a *Day of Remembrance,* as it does annually on February 19 (the date Executive Order 9066 was issued in 1942) in various locations across the country, Japanese Americans remember the internment experience and how those "years of infamy" adversely impacted their lives and those of their children. But over time, they not only recall the personal and very existential circumstances of their suffering, they also remember the unjust societal factors that contributed to their mistreatment. They celebrate those who exhibited courage, dignity, and moral excellence under cruel conditions. They remember those who, in spite of hardship and suspicion, resisted their unfair and illegal treatment. *Day of Remembrance* is the way one community remembers together and invites others to join with them in a form of solidarity through memory.

The presence of another person is often needed in order to remember and to remember truthfully. Soelle suggests that the verse from the gospel of John, "the truth will make you free" (Jn. 8:32), means we need one another in order to believe.[16] Sometimes this means that the people who are suffering need one another in order to believe that their historical injuries are real and they are not the cause. Some of the children of the Japanese Americans who where imprisoned have formed the "Sansei Legacy Project" to sort out the meaning and implications of their historical inheritance in just this manner. They have found that they carry a silent pain from their parents' experience that rarely finds expression. Through their sharing stories and experiences together and engaging in critical cultural and social analysis, they are coming to know and believe the truth about their own lives connected to the experiences of their parents. They are beginning to name this intergenerational pain as something shared and real, not an isolated symptom or personal idiosyncrasy.

Remembering is more than personal memory. Through solidarity, personal memory is linked to the memory of a community. Memory belongs to the history of a people and offers an alternative identity to the false one imposed by those who would dominate and control their destiny. Solidarity through memory offers an avenue for freeing people from the tyranny of history that defines the past as determinant. "It has always been this way" is a false reading of life. Johann Baptist Metz refers to uncovering alternative historical accounts as "dangerous memory" that loosens the grip of dominant claims about the way life is:

---

[16]Ibid., x.

Memory has a fundamental theological importance as what may be termed anamnetic solidarity or solidarity in memory with the dead and the conquered which breaks the grip of history as a history of triumph and conquest interpreted dialectically or as evolution.[17]

Memory can reveal the lie of injustice and open up a way to imagine a different future. The Day of Remembrance is the result of a long process of recovering the "dangerous memory" that imprisoning innocent American citizens is wrong. The reparations granted the survivors of the camps is one sign that this lie is revealed and that authentic citizenship, however belated, has been recognized and a new future is in the making. The Day of Remembrance is also an ongoing "dangerous memory" that reveals the sin of racism that contributed to this historical atrocity and is still not eradicated.

In contrast to the understanding of sustaining as helping someone to discover courage from within by drawing on his or her own resources, solidarity through memory understands courage to be bound up with those who have gone before. Though fragile at times, memory offers the particular experiences of hope and liberation through those who have struggled and resisted intolerable circumstances. These resisters are powerful agents providing courage in present situations. The examples of relief from suffering that they accomplished kindles hope and new imagination. Many Japanese American children of the camps have drawn tremendous strength and courage from their parents' and grandparents' examples of dignity and resistance during the internment. Their memories place them within a very specific history of human suffering; their experience is just as "normative" for understanding the truth about life as the experience of the "victors in historical struggles."[18] Out of this alternative position, however, new and painful insights are gained about what it means to be a citizen of the United States.

While "dangerous memories" can be painful memories, they also become powerful memories that evoke a sense of longing that things might and indeed can be different now and in the future. Memory offers an alternative reading of a current situation by saying, "This is not home! I will not stay here!" The suffering that has been endured need not be the final word. The Day of Remembrance communicates this clearly when people are called to resist the ongoing structures of injustice by engaging in programs and politics that promote an end to historical suffering. The longing for things to be different, evoked by the memory that "this is not

---

[17]Johann Baptist Metz, *Faith in History and Society: Toward a Practical Fundamental Theology* (New York: Seabury Press, 1980), 184.

[18]Sharon D. Welch, *Communities of Resistance and Solidarity: A Feminist Theology of Liberation* (Maryknoll, N.Y.: Orbis Books, 1985), 38.

home," becomes the seedbed of hope. The "normal" world turns out not to be normal after all. A different possibility for life emerges as the seemingly impossible becomes possible once more. Memory in this sense is congruent with a political theology of the cross that reveals the false reality that is imposed on the life of the sufferer.

Yet, sometimes alternative experiences or different interpretations of suffering may seem so dim as to not appear at all. While some understandings of sustaining have stressed a nonjudgmental listening to one who is in pain, solidarity under these circumstances goes further. Solidarity asks listeners to remember on behalf of someone who is overwhelmed, so that she or he may carry on and live. Solidarity asks listeners to give information, offer examples, and help name the experiences within their communal history of suffering that suggest alternative interpretations of pain and survival. It is a communal listening that aims to link the feelings of one with the identity and experience of the whole community. In this way the community's alternative memory of relief from suffering can become a source of hope by providing examples of incidents where people have been mobilized to resist and overcome suffering and its causes. The community's alternative identity becomes a viable pastoral resource in which human dignity is affirmed. Solidarity through memory and longing is not only about accepting or not accepting feelings, it concerns naming circumstances of injustice and resistance to them in order to restore the face-to-face relationships in a community. The shift from sustaining to solidarity is a shift from personal assessment to societal judgment. The aim is to live into the hope and promise of delivery from suffering and injustice. The object here is not how this is to be done, only that it be done.

Solidarity through New Vision

Solidarity is born in a cradle of vulnerability and dares to enter a world of memories, not necessarily our own. New vision emerges when memory is honored. The alternative experiences that are evoked by remembering incidents, examples, and stories in which human dignity is affirmed stirs the imagination toward the possibility of something different from current suffering. Memory says to us that what we experience now is not the final word. A vision of a new reality where people are released from the powers and principalities that crush and wound is a powerful force of resistance against the injustices that cause and perpetuate suffering. Solidarity becomes alive, invigorated, and captivated by a new vision where things are different. In traditional language this new vision prefigures the realm of God, the world of shalom, the time of jubilee, the heavenly banquet. It holds out the prospect of a good that transcends present reality, because there are hints and glimpses of it now where people join together to make it a reality. This vision feeds the political interpretation of the cross that fosters hope without falling victim to despair.

Jesus' acts of healing, particularly those depicted in Mark, were occasions that evoked new visions of possibility for the ones suffering as well as for those in the community witnessing what was going on. He sought to transform lives by demonstrating the emerging realm of God through his healing activity.[19] As signs of the new reality of God, the healing miracles he performed and the healing conversations he engaged in were aimed toward the restoration of right relationships between neighbors and faithfulness to God. In this way, sickness and its healing were not private matters but very much a part of the social reality of his day. The removal of illness was an occasion in which the whole community experienced the ability to imagine a new and restored future. Healing was intimately tied to vision, a vision caught up with the dawning reign of God.[20]

Pastoral care rooted in love with solidarity as its primary practice requires a theology that cannot be separated from the vision of the dawning reign of God if it seeks to be faithful to its origins. Solidarity, understood within this framework, is not simply an emotional and spiritual exercise, but a physical activity that sacrifices comfort, privilege, and the security of "being right" for this life-giving vision. Solidarity recognizes the wound in the corporate body as a physical wound requiring a physical response. In this way solidarity fulfills the root meaning of sustaining, to give material sustenance to another.

Historical injuries are emotional, spiritual, and physical. They re-present the cross-inflicted physical torture of one human body that radiates pain across history, throughout whole communities. Solidarity through vision, as it retains the meaning of sustenance, means "removing the body from the cross" and finding it shelter and protection. It means removing bodies from their crosses today! Solidarity with those who suffer today means actualizing the prayer for "the vision of the day when sharing by all will mean scarcity for none."[21] This means paying attention to the physical realities of suffering: lack of food, housing, medical attention, work, safety. Rosemary Ruether reminds us that the vision of the realm of God is about the prospect of something good beyond present reality. It is above all practical, material, and political in its implementation:

> The fulfillment of people's basic human physical and social needs: daily bread, remission of debts, which includes both the wrongs that we have done others, and also the financial indebtedness that holds the poor in bondage to the rich, avoidance of the temptations

[19]John T. McNeill, *A History of the Cure of Souls* (New York: Harper, 1951), 73.
[20]R. H. Fuller, *Interpreting the Miracles* (London: SCM Press, 1963), 40.
[21]United Church of Christ, *Book of Worship*.

that lead us to oppress one another, even in God's name, and finally deliverance from evil...human historical evil.[22]

The discrepancy between fulfilling the vision that Ruether outlines and the lived reality is the continuing material and political cause of suffering for many people today. But the longing to fulfill this vision is also cause for hope. When we begin to notice the material circumstances of people's lives as the spiritual conditions of their lives, we will begin to understand our lives bound up with theirs in a new way. Our material circumstances are tied to their material circumstances–and so is our spiritual condition. We belong to a unity called life, and it is for this reason we become compelled to offer resistance to all conditions that deprive people of well-being. Solidarity with people and sharing a vision and longing for restored life is another expression of suffering as bearing witness. Suffering struggles and strains to bear this vision into being.

Solidarity in Suffering

A constant theme we keep emphasizing is the need to resist and protest against suffering caused by injustice. Through solidarity, suffering is accepted in order to protest and name its causes, dismantle its "props," and resist its continuation. We have called this bearing witness *(marturia)*. It is this practice of suffering as bearing witness that makes transformation possible. It provides settings where mute pain can become cries of grievance, where forces can be activated to alter damaging environments. Soelle reminds us, "Christ made loving the other person the highest value; but that cannot be done without suffering."[23] When we honor those we love, we "stake our lives" on the promise of just and right relationships. "Staking our lives" means affirming life. Staking our lives by accepting suffering for this end is the meaning of "take up your cross."

Liberal Protestant pastoral theology fears that we will confuse our suffering with that of Christ's. Strangely, this has perpetuated a false need for an empathy that does not suffer. Soelle notes:

Good Friday sermons are full of the fear that someone could "mix up" Jesus' suffering and ours. But that means an end to the worth that human suffering had as an extension or completion of Christ's sufferings. The assertion that in Christ everything has been fulfilled remains in that case completely without content, an ideal of lordship that excludes us.[24]

---

[22]Rosemary Radford Ruether, *To Change the World: Christology and Cultural Criticism* (New York: Crossroad, 1983), 15.

[23]Soelle, *Choosing Life*, 16.

[24]Ibid., 133.

Jesus went to the cross not for the sake of suffering, but for the sake of justice. This offers a vision of human possibilities and a hope for humanizing even our suffering.[25] Solidarity with Christ's suffering strengthens those who suffer with courage.

As Soelle reminds us, life as we know it involves suffering. Suffering is finally inescapable. The only choices we have are, Which forces do we serve, and for whose sake do we suffer?[26] There is no such thing as neutrality. Solidarity means we recognize in those who suffer unjustly our opportunity to relate ourselves to them. Through our own willingness to suffer in solidarity with others, suffering becomes humane, not inhuman isolation. This practice of suffering, Robert Schreiter argues, "enables us to regain our humanity."[27] The suffering of Christ teaches the worth of this human suffering of bearing witness. This, too, is the meaning of "take up your cross."

Historically, this sort of suffering activity is found outside the centers of power. Jesus was crucified outside the city away from the temple and the palace. There is the place of the cross: a place without honor, power, or position. Yet this place is the very source of the activity of God. This is the place where the promises of God become known, where God's weakness is revealed to be stronger than human-made powers of dominance and oppression. The cross, a symbol of defeat and failure, is the powerful sign of love and justice, a place where new vision occurs. Vision for restored life always takes form through God's solidarity with the ones who suffer along the margins of society. This is a pastoral angle of vision from a political reading of the cross.

Suffering, then, is a description of "what is," not a prescription for hurting people. Suffering for the sake of and because of others is temporary and not an end in itself. The intent is to allow the full recognition of the experience of suffering that already exists and in this way "agree" to suffering, not deny it or explain it away. Again, this involves being a witness to and not a spectator of suffering. Identifying oneself with suffering in this way is necessary, for it is only those who are suffering themselves who will work to abolish conditions that produce suffering.[28] To actively accept this experience of suffering is a way to allow suffering to become visible, to be felt so its causes can be addressed. Bearing witness to suffering is practiced for its elimination where at all possible. It is always an activity with a focus

---

[25]Jürgen Moltmann points out that those who are oppressed find in the crucified Christ not a God who tortures them as their masters do, but a God who becomes their companion. They find their true identity "hidden and guaranteed in the Christ who suffers with them." *The Crucified God* (New York: Harper & Row, 1974), 49.

[26]Soelle, *Suffering*, 133.

[27]Robert J. Schreiter, *Reconciliation: Mission and Ministry in a Changing Social Order* (Maryknoll, N.Y.: Orbis Books, 1992), vii.

[28]Soelle, *Suffering*, 2.

on a greater cause, a just and loving cause. The focus on suffering is always toward a vision of wholeness, restored relationships, and a healed world.

Solidarity is the fundamental practice of pastoral care that takes the realities of historical injuries seriously. It sets the tone for the other pastoral practices. Its aim is the restoration of wholeness through glimpsing the in-breaking realm of God. Solidarity seeks to create a just environment where people who are suffering are recognized and the causes for their suffering are addressed and eliminated. Reconciliation, then, is an aim of pastoral care that practices solidarity.

Reconciling: The Work of Justice

The historic pastoral function of reconciling seeks to reestablish broken relationships between members of a community and the community with God. The marks of this activity include admonition, confession, restitution, and forgiveness.[29] However, the interpretation of this pastoral function in much of the modern pastoral literature has tended to emphasize conflict resolution and the role of harmony, or peaceful coexistence, as a goal and a sign that reconciliation has been established. Margaret Kornfeld talks about this as first-order change, in which people adjust to their present situation and learn to function better while their basic situation does not change.[30] While this can be an important strategy in order to establish safety and a sense of equilibrium in the midst of chaos, the danger in stopping here is that too often some people have harmony at the expense of the well-being of others. When this happens, as Harold Wells reminds us, "the message of reconciliation can be used ideologically to protect the privileges of the powerful."[31] Harmony and conflict resolution left to their utilitarian ends alone can reinforce an unfair status quo in which true reconciliation is not possible. But Kornfeld also talks about a second order of change, a paradigmatic shift in which "a whole constellation of beliefs, attitudes, and actions are altered because of a new perception of reality."[32] This shift involves a radical reversal of established ways of seeing, knowing, and behaving, one in which whole systems are changed.

Reconciliation as we are considering it from the perspective of the political cross involves more than first-order change. It is more than a process of conflict resolution that fosters compromise, so that respective parties can retain their own positions in an atmosphere of relative peace. It is more closely related to a second order of change, the place of radical

[29]William A. Clebsch and Charles R. Jaekle, *Pastoral Care in Historical Perspective* (New York: Harper & Row, 1964), 9.

[30]Margaret Kornfeld, *Cultivating Wholeness: A Guide to Care and Counseling in Faith Communities* (New York: Continuum, 1998), 7.

[31]Gregory Baum and Harold Wells, eds., *The Reconciliation of Peoples: Challenges to the Churches* (Maryknoll, N.Y.: Orbis Books; Geneva: WCC Publications, 1997), 189.

[32]Kornfeld, *Cultivating Wholeness,* 7.

reorientation, in which power relations are altered and reversed. Here, reconciliation is called on to address the deep wounds of injustice that prevent people from coming together. According to Catholic theologian Gregory Baum, reconciliation demands that people or groups at odds with one another examine their own history "and in a leap of faith redefine their path into the future."[33] This is about restoring wholeness in community and communion with God through the work of justice.

Within the history of pastoral care in the church, the claims of justice have been a continuing part of the task of reconciliation, often surfacing during times when people are enduring incredible hardships. This has been the case even as the needs for harmony and so-called first-order change were practiced.

Historical Glimpses of Reconciliation

Reconciliation in the early church had to do with restoring a lapsed member to the life of the community. After Jesus' death the small group of followers who met together regularly for worship were deeply impacted by the fall of Jerusalem to the Romans and the destruction of the temple in A.D. 70.[34] These early followers of Jesus found themselves in the unique situation of anticipating the second coming within their lifetime. This small worshiping community, known as the *koinonia,* became the locus of reconciliation as they practiced admonition of one another, public confession, and repentance during worship. Because they expected an immediate fulfillment of the reign of God, they were not particularly concerned about addressing the historical conditions within their social and political situation. More important was a member's adherence to his or her baptismal vows and their corporate faithfulness to God. They were concerned for the purity of the gathered community. Reconciliation addressed the purity of the community gathered for worship awaiting the return of their teacher and companion. You might say that they were engaged in reconciliation as first-order change so they could adjust to and function better in their present situation.

As time passed, "the end" did not appear. Reconciliation began to take on different forms as Christianity spread and developed. During the Constantinian church era it was used to further the aim of a church and state alliance. Here, harmony, or first-order change, again prevailed, as reconciliation became largely associated with administering and enforcing standard church policy. In fact, one of the tasks of the imperial church was to educate its new members in how to understand and follow these church policies in order to adjust their lives in harmony with them. To be a member

---

[33]Baum and Wells, *The Reconciliation of Peoples,* 189.
[34]Norman Perrin, *The New Testament: An Introduction: Proclamation and Parenesis, Myth and History* (New York: Harcourt Brace Jovanovich, 1974), 40.

of the state was to be a member of the church. Reconciliation functioned to help people address their personal problems as church members coterminous with being citizens of the empire.[35] It helped them harmonize their personal lives with their civic responsibilities.

With the rise of the episcopate, rites and rituals of the church were put under the control of the Christian bishop. The sacraments became central in the lives of the people and the main channel through which salvation was imparted to the souls of men and women. Salvation and reconciliation were closely identified. Ernst Troeltsch observed:

> Outside the Sacrament there is no salvation and, since—with negligible exception—there is no sacrament without a priest, so there is no salvation outside the Church. The Church possesses not merely the sole truth, but also and chiefly the sole power of imparting salvation through the sacraments which link the world of sense and the super-sensible world.[36]

In this way, reconciling gradually became subsumed within the sacraments and rituals through a particular historical understanding of the relationship between church and empire. In this situation the role of the church took precedence over the needs of individuals, while harmony between church and state eclipsed the need for a fair deal on behalf of the citizens. Personal grievances and corporate suffering began to seek expression in other places. Equilibrium or harmony cannot satisfy indefinitely, and those for whom it is least satisfactory are the first to look elsewhere. First-order change has within it a motivating thrust toward second-level change, radical reorientation.

Reconciliation as a call for justice began to take place along the margins and sometimes outside the sacramental system of the "official religion." During late antiquity, reconciliation was often effected through the roles of the holy men and women in Byzantine Christianity; in the Latin regions, through the activities around the graves of the martyrs. These activities of reconciliation and healing involved believers who were seeking relief from their social troubles and personal ailments. Often these were seen as related.

Holy Men and Women

The appearance of holy men and women in the region of Syria during the fourth and fifth centuries provided an alternative to the church-administered sacraments for people seeking relief from their troubles. Village life was in transition during this time. Violence and aggressive exploitation of one villager by the others was a common occurrence. The

---

[35]Clebsch and Jaekle, *Pastoral Care*, 20.
[36]Ernst Troeltsch, *The Social Teaching of the Christian Churches*, vol. 1 (New York: Macmillan, 1931), 95.

morale of the people was low, and their sense of community was weak if not absent. There was a marked crisis in leadership that contributed to the rise of holy men and women. Peter Brown writes:

> Caught between a bottomless God and an archaic system of public penance laymen flocked to the holy men [or women] to know whether there was anything at all they could do, in their small way.[37]

These holy men and women acted as arbitrators and mediators in village life and represented an alternative source of power to that of the bishop and other forms of secular power. In their own bodies these holy people represented "clean power" associated with the Divine. You could say that their bodies represented access to second-order change. Through them human corporeality was linked with the Divine, thus legitimizing the holy person's earthly power. To visit a holy person was to go where clean and just power was, and there find relief.[38] The rituals of healing and reconciliation functioned within this view of clean power. Here, purity is associated with a power for enacting justice.

Through ascetic ritual, holy men and women dissociated themselves from society, much like the prophets of old, and became the "holy strangers" within the community. It was a long and drawn-out ritual in which the holy person deliberately became the stranger who could stand outside the ties of family, community, and economic interest as one who owed no debt to society. In this manner, the holy person was able to present him- or herself as one who could draw on power from outside the strictly human sphere to create a liminal space for resolving tensions and violence in the human community.[39] This can be seen as another form of "bearing witness."

The holy person gained credibility in the community by establishing him- or herself as the stranger who could contain and focus the suffering and misfortune in the community. But even as a "holy stranger," the holy person was not seen as disinterested or remote. On the contrary, above everything else he or she was approachable. Through their accessibility, the holy persons carried the burden of making a distant God relevant to the particularity of human needs:

> In his [or her] person, the acute ambivalence of a Christian God was summed up in a manageable and approachable form: for the holy man [or woman] was both—easily moved to tears of

---

[37]Peter Brown, *Society and the Holy in Late Antiquity* (Berkeley & Los Angeles: University of California Press, 1982), 145.

[38]Ibid., 121.

[39]Ibid., 184. Here, Brown describes how power drawn from outside the power structure of society represented a role inversion. Paradoxically, this device was a means of inclusion rather than exclusion; the outsider was given position within the power structure of the society.

compassion and, at the same time, the heir of the Hebrew prophets.[40]

While the communal exercise of reconciliation was being de-emphasized through the rise of the authority of the bishop who alone could wield the *mysterium tremendum* of the eucharistic sacrifice, this was not the case where holy men and women provided alternative means to deal with misfortunes that arose amongst and between the people. Reconciliation included attention to communal satisfaction of wrongdoing and took place through ritual and communal activities as the holy person operated as both healer and confessor.[41] An example of how this took place is the case of the holy person's treatment of those believed to be "possessed."

Violence was a constant problem in Late Antiquity and often found expression in the form of demonic possession. But the experience of demon possession was not understood as an individual malady alone. Instead, possession was seen as both a personal and a communal phenomenon. The one possessed was viewed as someone who was giving expression to a layer of violence that was both evident and at the same time below the surface of community life. In this way possession was like a window into the core dynamics of the community. For this reason, the holy person paid particular attention to the relationship between the one perceived as being possessed and the nonpossessed, carefully orchestrating a ritual of reconciliation between the two. Possession and its ritual working through was a way in which the small community could both admit and control its disruptive experiences by playing them out.[42]

The ritual between the holy person, the possessed, and the community was one of reconciliation. Through the ritual of exorcism, pent-up violence as a result of grave injustices as well as festering frustration from other sources were allowed to be focused. They became expressed and expunged from the life of the community through the ritualized exercise of the power of the holy person over the power of the demonic:

> The demon in the possessed abuses, and even attacks the holy man: and the holy man shows his power, by being able to bring into the open and ride out so much pent-up rebellion and anger.[43]

The exorcism here was not seen as restricted to the "possessed" alone, but was understood to be an exorcism of the demonic in the life of the whole community. Not only the one possessed was changed; so was the community. Through the ritual of exorcism the possessed was reintegrated into the life of the community through the assertion of power over the

---

[40]Ibid., 144.
[41]Ibid., 140, 141.
[42]Ibid., 123.
[43]Ibid., 124.

demons on the part of the holy person.[44] Exorcism was a ritual of reconciliation performed by the holy person in the midst of the community for the community.

In rituals of exorcism, healing and reconciling were combined to redress the brokenness in the community and point its members to a new and more just way of living. Confession and restitution were very much a part of this as the holy person stressed that future misfortunes could only be averted through penance. Penance, here, meant quite specifically a "new deal" among the villagers of Byzantine Christianity.[45] The cult of the saints from the third through the sixth centuries of Latin Christianity provides another example of reconciliation, as it addressed issues of justice through the remains of the holy martyred ones.

Martyred Saints

Late Antiquity Christians were concerned with the location, the specific place or setting, of the holy as a source of power for remedying misfortune. While Byzantine Christianity identified this sacred place in the person of the "holy stranger," Latin Christians, through the cult of the saints, found heaven and Earth joined in the dead bodies of holy men and women, confessors and martyrs.[46] Here, the ecclesiastical hierarchy of Western Europe became joined to the tombs of these dead martyrs. The power of the bishop coalesced with the power of the shrine in these special locations, the cemeteries outside of cities, where the graves of the saints became centers of ecclesiastical life in the various regions.[47]

The power of the shrine came from the healing power of the saints who were martyred and later buried there. The martyrs were seen as having a special and intimate relationship with the deity through the suffering they endured during their life on earth and their faithful perseverance in spite of their circumstances. They were seen as those in whom integrity triumphed over disintegration. Their souls remained intact even in the face of all manner of torment, and this "survival of the untouched soul" was the very essence of their integrity.[48] The martyrs were thought to be still available to believers, as protectors and invisible companions to those who sought them out with hope and reverence.

---

[44]Ibid., 125.

[45]Ibid., 127.

[46]Peter Brown, *The Cult of the Saints: Its Rise and Function in Latin Christianity,* Haskell Lectures on History of Religions, new series 2 (Chicago: University of Chicago Press, 1981), 1. The theme of "the joining of tomb and altar" is discussed at length here. Brown shows the relationship between the role of the patron in Latin Christianity, the bishop, the "invisible companion" (invisible beings who were invested with features of beloved and powerful figures), and the saint along with his or her tomb, as well as relics of the martyrs.

[47]Ibid., 9.

[48]Ibid., 83.

The sufferings of the martyrs were understood as miracles in themselves. It was impossible for someone to withstand, let alone overcome, some of the mistreatments and torture that they had endured, yet they did. Furthermore, the martyr did not allow suffering to define his or her life and circumstances. This, too, was a miracle. At the root of every miracle of healing at a martyr's shrine there lay this miracle of pain.[49] Pain was powerful. Pain was real and crushing. But pain was not given the final word. Instead, it was the belief in God's promise of the resurrection, experienced in and through the power of the martyred saints, that accounted for the miracles around the shrines of the very special dead.[50] The shrines where the saints were buried were places where good, clean power was shown to exist on Earth by being played out in the form of miracles.[51] Those possessed with all manner of ailments and distress came with anticipation and trust that a miracle would be wrought in their lives.

Possession was a common phenomenon of Latin Christianity, as it was in the East. But the drama of exorcism was played out differently in the cult of the saints than it was in its Byzantine counterpart. Where the invisible power behind the human agent was pitted against the power of the "demon" in the possessed in the person of the holy stranger of the Syrian desert, a successful exorcism in Latin Christianity's cult of the saints had as its background the ordeal of the martyr:

> The original act of "unclean" power, by which the martyr had been tortured and condemned is transmuted into its reverse. Now the martyr is the judge;…and the demons, who had stood behind his persecutors, are the culprits under interrogation.[52]

The possessed who came to the tombs of the martyrs comprised one category of people along with beggars who regularly participated in the healing activities at the shrine. When they arrived, they were fed, blessed, and set to scrubbing the floor of the basilica.[53] Not all of these people were already possessed; some came in order to become possessed. Still others came so that they might place their particular situations before the saint rather than face the hard justice of their peers:

> Those who had been placed outside the human group by their sins or by their hard dealings, or who had been broken by the

---

[49]Ibid., 79.

[50]"The explicit image of the martyr was of a person who enjoyed the repose of Paradise and whose body was even now touched by the final rest of the resurrection. Yet behind the now-tranquil face of the martyr there lay potent memories of a process by which a body shattered by drawn-out pain had once been enabled by God's power to retain its integrity" (Peter Brown, *The Cult of the Saints*, 80).

[51]Brown, *Society and the Holy*, 18.

[52]Brown, *Cult of the Saints*, 109.

[53]Ibid., 111.

injustice of others, might, through the rhythm of cure played out in public, find their way back to that small face-to-face world which is the basic unit of Late Antiquity and early medieval religion.[54]

The cures at the tombs were always conceived of as acts of justice and amnesty. The drama of exorcism, while an exercise of healing, was an act of reconciliation between the possessed and the community. The ritual of exorcism included prayers and exhortations to the group gathered at the shrine and not just ministration to the one suffering. These prayers and demonstrations stressed the ordering of the universe at the beginning of creation, the position of the sufferer as a temple of God, and the reentry of God into God's temple. A call to reestablish the order of God's original creation helped the individual regain a rightful place amongst his or her contemporaries. Those possessed who made confession for wrongdoing were afforded the chance to make reparations. Those healed at the shrine often gained a change of social status: "Serfs [were] emancipated from their former owners, and [became] part of the *familia* of the saint."[55] The power of the saint through the drama of the exorcism served to reassure all the participants that the exercise of clean power was able to define, limit, and contain the destructive and divisive forces in their midst.

The healing effected through the power of the martyr, then, was not only the healing of personal ills. Healing involved restoring the integrity of the sufferer within his or her community, where unity was highly valued. It was the martyr who, through the humility of death, was the true servant of God and could bring human beings closer to God and back into harmony with their neighbors.[56] The graves of the martyrs became very special places where the intimate connection between healing and justice, healing and reconciliation took place.

Jürgen Moltmann has pointed out that "the closest form of following the crucified Christ was to be a martyr."[57] The martyr participates in the ongoing suffering of Christ, permitting a connection between the suffering of Christ and the suffering of a later time. The cult of the saints recognized this. The holy men and women of Byzantium evidenced this same continuity.[58] The martyred saints and the holy men and women of Late Antiquity embraced suffering and were willing to become "broken" in order

---

[54]Brown, *Society and the Holy*, 19.

[55]Brown, *Cult of the Saints*, 113.

[56]Ibid., 72. In Christian art, the martyr is often shown in the pose of the Crucified. "This identified him not only with the suffering of Christ, but also with the unmoved constancy of his election and the certainty of his triumph."

[57]Moltmann, *Crucified God*, 57.

[58]Sebastian P. Brock and Susan Ashbrook Harvey, Introduction and translation, *Holy Women of the Syrian Orient* (Berkeley and Los Angeles: University of California Press, 1987), 11. The authors describe Simeon the Stylite (389–459), who stood for forty years on the top of a pillar sixty feet high. As people watched him with his arms outstretched, they saw a living crucifix of Jesus and a symbolic fulfillment of the call to imitate Christ.

to serve justice and restore integrity for their people. They embodied "passionate" suffering in order to abolish unjust suffering.

Reconciling Today

Clebsch and Jaekle have noted the relative absence of references to reconciliation in modern pastoral literature and suggest this for a new focus in the life of the church. At the same time, they call attention to the close relationship between reconciliation and healing.[59] Fortunately, with a renewed interest in spirituality and healing along with works addressing social injustice, the pastoral terrain is beginning to shift, and reconciliation and healing are being looked at afresh. New passion and commitment are being expressed. Pastoral theologians and practitioners are beginning to participate in the waters of justice and streams of mercy to dress wounds and bind up deep scars. Through this practice of dressing and binding, new truths are being discovered about what it means to care at the beginning of this century.

What I have been suggesting all along is that reconciliation is not a pastoral function; rather, it is a practice that has a long history evidenced through activity around alternative sources of holy power and healing over time. In the examples from Late Antiquity, these practices of reconciliation are powerful examples of compassion for those who are suffering.

Where there is compassion, there is recourse to the passion of Christ. The impassioned, compassionate, and initiating God who is made known through the passion of the cross is the heart of a theology of reconciliation. Kosuke Koyama develops this theme to address the suffering of people today through the image of the "Broken Christ": "The Broken Christ embracing a broken world…is an image of reconciliation."[60] It is through the broken Christ that the justice of Christ embraces unjust humanity on the cross and in so doing creates a new possibility for justice in the world.[61] This understanding of reconciliation brings the relationship between pastoral care and social ethics to the foreground and keeps it there. It calls pastoral theology to take leadership in breaking the conspiracy of civilized injustice that makes victims invisible. Like the ones crying out on the steps of the basilica who were listened to and integrated into the life of the community, reconciliation means really hearing the cry "My God, my God, why have you forsaken me?" and taking it to heart. Breaking the conspiracy of silence about civilized injustice brings the cry of the forsaken into the life of the community and the heart of our theories. Then those who cry out can initiate a process of reconciliation in which we can participate. For reconciliation is a process initiated by the ones who are wronged: those

---

[59]Clebsch and Jaekle, *Pastoral Care*, 81.

[60]Kosuke Koyama, *Mount Fuji and Mount Sinai: A Pilgrimage in Theology* (London: SCM Press, 1984), 256.

[61]Ibid., 257.

whose human rights are violated, the tortured, the raped, the impoverished, the marginalized. As Robert Schreiter points out, "The proper subject of Reconciliation is the victim, not the oppressor."[62]

Reconciliation from a political interpretation of the cross means restoring wholeness not only to individuals but to communities. This will involve developing a more corporate sense of self, in which personal and social structures are interconnected for communal wholeness. In this understanding, reconciliation cannot be about reestablishing an old order, or first-order change. Reconciliation takes people to a new place where they discover their lives in a new way–the paradigmatic shift of second-order change.

Koyama suggests that from the perspective of the theology of the cross, the broken Christ speaks about creation, construction, integration, reconciliation, and healing. This is second-order change. Through the broken Christ, "holiness and brokenness come together for the sake of the salvation of others"; this is the meaning of Christian sacrament.[63] How does the broken Christ reconcile and heal? This is a stumbling block and a foolish announcement. But it is at least a historical process that is communal in character. As a historical process it refers to "someone through whose suffering history is renewed," someone who, by way of the cross, confronts and renews by an inner persuasion.[64] This inner persuasion is the persuasion born of passion and compassion and *practiced* in history in order to transform and renew history where people are forced to suffer. This means refusing to repeat the past atrocities while cooperating with new signs of life now and for the future. Inner persuasion and passion form the heart of reconciliation that practices restoring justice. This reconciliation will redress all forms of power in the life of a community, repair broken relationships and help redistribute goods, and restore a life of meaning and purpose for all its members.

For a pastoral theology informed by the political cross, reconciliation must be at the heart of our practices of care. It is the practical aim of our commitments to people who suffer historical injuries. It gives public expression to a solidarity that promises nonabandonment in personal and public spheres. In these ways reconciliation along with solidarity can be seen as practices that include activities, postures, and gestures to empower those who have been harmed and excluded by structures of oppression and injustice. Empowerment is also a critical feature of the historical activity of pastoral guiding, to which we turn next.

---

[62]Schreiter, *Reconciliation,* 45.
[63]Koyama, *Mount Fuji,* 243.
[64]Ibid., 250.

CHAPTER
EIGHT

Pastoral Guiding as Empowerment for the Healing of People

Hope gives us the ability to recognize that we must refuse to scale down our aspirations to the level of the facts in our present situation because God is always calling us to move beyond the present to shape and mold a better tomorrow.[1]

EMILIE M. TOWNES

Guiding, like sustaining, has as its aim the reconciliation of people. It seeks to involve people in practices that help establish a realm of justice where love as something to give and receive is known by everyone. This means guiding is about empowering people to accept reality and transform it. It generates an active form of love that serves to foster what the introductory quote says: "the ability to recognize that we must refuse to scale down our aspirations to the level of the facts in our present situation." Thus, guiding as a practice of empowerment seeks to participate in the process of reconciliation by helping to transform the powerlessness of people who are afflicted into actions toward a "better tomorrow." This means to recognize that those who are suffering are the primary agents of change and not simply victims of circumstance. The transformation of powerlessness

---

[1]Emilie M. Townes, *Breaking the Fine Rain of Death: African American Health Issues and a Womanist Ethic of Care* (New York: Continuum, 1998), 181.

into active suffering is the power of love that originates in the agents of reconciliation and healing.

Historically, guiding has been associated with teaching and with assisting people in their life choices involving issues of deep meaning and concern. Over time two forms of pastoral guiding have evolved that are designated in the literature as eductive and inductive guiding. Traditionally, eductive guiding draws on the seeker's own experience and values, whereas inductive guiding appeals to external authority, primarily that of the classical Christian tradition.[2] In recent times, more liberal pastoral practitioners have relied on eductive forms of guiding, rejecting inductive guidance with its twin functions, discipline and teaching. Much of this attraction to eductive forms of guiding stems from a time when fear of authoritarianism and external pressure on people were legitimate concerns.

Pastors who practice eductive guiding, particularly those trained in the Rogerian orientation to care, stress drawing someone out and guiding him or her toward something he or she can already identify with from inside him- or herself. This is viewed as a good thing in that what is internal is deemed most valid and authentic. Guiding people to their interior landscape is seen as providing them with access to their personal values and variables, which can help them make free and responsible decisions with a degree of confidence that they are making the right or best choice possible. Seward Hiltner, who set the standard for interpreting guiding in this way, said that it is essential that pastors get hold of "the best possible grasp of internals—that is, the inner frame of reference of the other person"[3] While guiding as empowerment has things in common with eduction, in other ways it is very different when interpreted from a political interpretation of the cross.

Guiding as empowerment draws out what is inside a person, because it is important to discover what someone's internal references are. But it is equally important to not simply stop with this discovery and proceed with decision making as though what is discovered is sufficient for wise discernment. Instead of wisdom, this form of guiding can promote what Paulo Freire calls "naive consciousness," which considers itself superior to and in control of facts, free to interpret and understand them as one pleases.[4] A guiding that empowers will not automatically encourage someone to own or identify with what is discovered in his or her interior landscape in a naive way. This distinction is especially important when the interior reality of someone who is suffering historical injuries is the internalized norms, stereotypes, values, and experiences of the dominant culture. Some people

---

[2]William A. Clebsch and Charles R. Jaekle, *Pastoral Care in Historical Perspective* (New York: Harper & Row, 1967), 69.

[3]Seward Hiltner, *Preface to Pastoral Theology* (Nashville: Abingdon Press), 154. Here, Hiltner is drawing from Carl R. Rogers' nondirective and client-centered approach to counseling.

[4]Paulo Freire, *Education for Critical Consciousness* (New York: Continuum, 1994), 44.

of color talk about this as "internalized racism"; some feminists call this "internalized sexism." Left unexamined, this kind of internalized framework devalues, inhibits, and disclaims the lived experience and deeper reality within a person or a people longing for new life. To identify with an imposed internal reality reinforces a kind of dull resignation and helplessness.

Helplessness on the part of those living with imposed suffering is in part rooted in a lack of consciousness about the historical conditions of their lives. Powerlessness is further entrenched by a lack of imagination that feeds feelings of impotence in the face of suffering. Helplessness tempts people to believe that they cannot understand their own history or the factors that make up their lives in the present. Reinforcing this myth by accommodating "naive consciousness" works to keep powerful people in the seats of control and oppressed people from challenging the arrangement. This means people who are suffering see struggle as futile. And people who are comfortable become incapable of understanding the significance of struggle at all. Dorothee Soelle is unsparing when she says that the so-called good people who are complacent and do nothing lack faith. They simply remain captive to the forces of "objective cynicism" instead of resisting them.[5] Guidance as empowerment involves becoming conscious. This applies to everyone. But for those used to introspection, it is not only about "self-consciousness"; becoming conscious means becoming aware and knowledgeable about what happens in our communities and our world, and our part in it.

Guiding as empowerment draws on eductive forms of guidance in order to move people out of an imposed worldview, what Edward Said has called the "colonized mind." As empowerment, guiding operates to cultivate a critical consciousness that can integrate external reality for effective action in the world. In this sense, it has much in common with consciousness raising, or what Freire calls the *conscientizacao*. Guiding empowers people to assume critical positions in relationship to the rest of the world as subjects involved in "the transformation of the world, which humanizes them."[6] Walter Brueggemann writes about the task of the prophet, which can also be seen as the model for the kind of pastoral empowerment being suggested here.

> The task of prophetic imagination and ministry is to bring to public expression those hopes and yearnings that have been denied so long and suppressed so deeply that we no longer know they are there...Hope is the refusal to accept the reading of reality which is the majority opinion.[7]

[5]Dorothee Soelle, *Choosing Life* (Philadelphia: Fortress Press, 1981), 94.
[6]Freire, *Education,* 110.
[7]Walter Brueggemann, *The Prophetic Imagination* (Philadelphia: Fortress Press, 1978), 67.

Guiding as empowering seeks to bring to public expression a deeper reality, which may at first appear strange and foreign even to the ones caught in the throes of suffering. In this sense education is very important to engender this process of engagement. In order to do this from a pastoral perspective, guiding or empowerment will need to retrieve the teaching and discipline aspects more closely associated with inductive guiding.

Pastoral theologians have not generally seen teaching as an effective way to guide hurting people. Religious educators, not pastoral caregivers, practice teaching. For Hiltner, teaching was not appropriate because it tended to introduce something external to the one seeking counsel, detracting from a person's ability to direct him- or herself–again, the anti-authoritarian motif in pastoral care. This deep concern for not "intruding," along with the Rogerian nondirective approach to counseling with people, has influenced pastoral care practitioners to stay away from any practices that might be interpreted as overly persuasive or outright coercive. From a political perspective of the cross, however, these concerns and criteria are not so clearly defined. Nor are they necessarily understood within a one-to-one interaction between someone seeking and someone offering care.

Indeed, coerciveness is an inappropriate way to empower those who are the recipients of historical injuries. But coerciveness may not be out of place when directed toward those who perpetuate the very conditions that make for victims. The word of the cross speaks a different word to those who suffer unjustly and to those who cruelly inflict their pain, whether knowingly or not. The word of the cross is always grounded in history, directionally pointed, aimed at specific circumstances and concrete realities. The cross "takes sides" and is never disinterested; it seeks to persuade and yields a form of coercive, but not cruel, power. Those in positions of power rarely relinquish their control of the reins voluntarily. In recent history, one could look at civil rights legislation in the United States as a form of nonviolent "coercion" in order to alter societal conditions of injustice. Such coercion through legal accountability imposed on those who misuse power and public privilege opens the way for empowering people who have been disfranchised and hurt by such abuses. Coercion is a strong form of persuasion and when used to promote justice is consistent with a political reading of the cross. The cross teaches through persuasion. Guiding as empowering involves at least a measure of persuasion and, at times, coercion.

Kosuke Koyama claims that the cross affects us, and because it does, it guides and empowers us by means of inner persuasion. This kind of empowering through inner persuasion is closely connected to the solidarity that one enters into when accompanying another in his or her experience in order to remember "truthfully," with a critical consciousness. This is not merely eductive, "drawing someone out," nor is it coercion in the sense of imposing a position or response. Yet inner persuasion is a form of external influence on someone else because of the historical truth and integrity it reveals. As mentioned earlier, critical consciousness, or truthful memory, is an alternative to the internalized framework that someone inherits. In fact, it resists the false meaning that has been imposed. Truthful memory can be persuasive in a powerful way, drawing people closer to a new vision still to be realized. Again, Brueggemann is helpful when he says,

> To express a future that none think imaginable...means to move back into the deepest memories of this community and activate those very symbols that have always been the basis for contradicting the regnant consciousness...One is to mine the memory of this people and educate them to use the tools of hope.[8]

In this sense, empowering through persuasion involves more than nondirective conversations or disinterested empathy. It means evoking and invoking an alternative reality, which may seem to be something external to the one suffering–yet dimly familiar. Herein lie the seeds for rekindling hope.

Guiding and solidarity are closely related, because they both look toward a vision of reconciliation rooted in the in-breaking realm of God. This vision involves all living creatures and all living matter. It is a realm of justice where people can indeed "know love, both as something to be received and as something to give" and all pulsing life can know respect and protection. Koyama talks about the posture required for realizing this kind of world as one where we must stand for creation, not destruction; an inhabited world, not a bombed wilderness; life, not death; hospitality, not hostility; mercy, not cruelty; and a life of commitment, not callousness.[9] Guiding means empowering people to choose life, "to be free from our captivity, to rediscover a sense of discontent which can take us beyond cynicism and apathy."[10]

One way that Luther's "Hiddenness of God," discussed earlier, can be understood within our explicit political reading of the cross is through our ability to choose life in the midst of everything that seems to deny life. According to Soelle, this presupposes our power to struggle. It affirms our capacity to love and make justice instead of getting along well at the cost of others. The cross does not protect us from reality; it reveals terror for what it is and challenges all social constructions of reality by pressing for the truth that lies concealed behind the function of any symbolic universe.[11]

---

[8]Ibid., 66.

[9]Kosuke Koyama, *Mount Fuji and Mount Sinai: A Pilgrimage in Theology* (London: SCM Press, 1984), 257.

[10]Soelle, *Choosing Life*, ix.

[11]Peter Burger and Thomas Luckman, *The Social Construction of Reality* (New York: Doubleday/Anchor, 1967).

This is guiding as empowerment–*conscientizacao*. In this way, the cross teaches us to perceive historical and social causes of suffering.[12]

Guiding as empowerment is a holistic practice. It will call us to remember the communal fabric out of which we grow and flourish, or languish and die. Guiding as empowerment will re-member our body, mind, and spirit as one, and teach us that any person's or peoples' suffering is inextricably tied to the body, mind, and spirit of the larger community. Empowering people to seek the transformation of suffering will need to take this into account. Praying, thinking, and acting are the ingredients that make up guiding as empowerment from a political reading of the cross. And praying, thinking, and acting begin when the first cry escapes into the air, revealing the depths of suffering in the heart of the community.

Soelle names three phases of suffering that are helpful for our thinking about guiding as empowerment. Phase 1 is muteness, isolation, and powerlessness. Phase 2 is lamenting, finding expression for the suffering, and accepting the reality of one's situation. Phase 3 involves change, solidarity with others, and organizing to change social structures that cause and perpetuate suffering.[13] These three phases of suffering are related to aspects of pastoral guiding as empowerment: the power of speech, the power of conversion, and the power of doxology. The first phase of guiding as empowerment begins, then, with bringing to speech that which has been silenced.

Empowering Speech: Muteness Becomes Voice through Telling the Truth

Silence is powerful. It can mean many things. Often it signals a level of experience too deep for words. For those who suffer in silence, silence can conceal the core of an unbearable experience. Robert Lifton has called this kind of silence "psychic numbing," a protection of the self against the destructive forces to which it has been exposed.[14] Those caught in its grip feel isolated, cut off from the rest of humankind, including their own history. Lifton tells us that the survivors of unbearable suffering and prolonged humiliation feel a special need for nurturance, yet at the same time a deep shame for needing and accepting it.[15] Dorothee Soelle discusses silence of this nature as part of the mute phase of suffering:

> There are forms of suffering that reduce one to a silence in which no discourse is possible any longer, in which a person ceases reacting as a human agent...This initial phase of pain, which we

---

[12]Soelle, *Choosing Life,* 41.
[13]Soelle, *Suffering,* trans. Everett R. Kalin (Philadelphia: Fortress Press, 1975), 73.
[14]Robert Jay Lifton, *The Broken Connection* (New York: Simon & Schuster, 1979), 173–76.
[15]Robert Jay Lifton, *Death in Life: Survivors of Hiroshima* (New York: Vintage Books, 1969), 193.

experience again and again (Phase One), leaves us numb and mute.[16]

Respect for those who suffer in this extreme sense impresses another kind of silence on those who listen. It is a necessary silence, you might say an *imposed silence,* that is required to counter the *imposed suffering* to which it is exposed. For those who may be privileged to listen, this obligatory silence has an affinity with the silence that Jesus requested of his disciples when he asked them to "watch" with him while he prayed (Mk. 14: 32). Only we are not to fall asleep! To "watch" and be silent is part of what it means to bear witness to suffering. Alastair Campbell has a similar view of the role that silence plays when he talks about pastoral care as integrity, "that presence of one person with another which precedes all words."[17] Silence in this instance is more powerful than words. Campbell notes:

> Words are often the enemy of care, for they seduce the carer and the cared for into playing verbal games, concealing still further the wholeness they might be able to seek together, if they did not fear the simplicity of silence.[18]

The silence that precedes words is a silence of respect, where those who are used to talking step back and make room for new speech. The power of this silence waits with corresponding anticipation as it bears witness to the power of the speech that is struggling to be born. When guiding is empowering, the first response to those who are suffering is to listen to them so they might find their "voice" and speak the pain at the heart of their suffering.

Perhaps there is no more poignant example of guiding as empowering speech than the illustration Nelle Morton gives in her now classic "Hearing into Speech." A young woman began to share her story with a small group of friends. Morton goes on to describe what happened next.

> "I hurt," she began. "I hurt all over." She touched herself in various places before she added, "but I don't know where to begin to cry. I don't know how to cry." Hesitatingly she began to talk. Then she talked more and more. Her story took on fantastic coherence. When she reached a point of the most excruciating pain, no one moved. No one interrupted her. No one rushed to comfort her. No one cut her experience short. We simply sat. We sat in a powerful silence. The women clustered about the weeping one went with her to the deepest part of her life as if something so sacred was

---

[16]Soelle, *Suffering,* 68–69.
[17]Alastair Campbell, *Rediscovering Pastoral Care* (Philadelphia: Westminster Press, 1981), 27.
[18]Ibid.

taking place they did not withdraw their presence or mar its visibility. Finally the woman, whose name I do not know, finished speaking. Tears flowed from her eyes in all directions. She spoke again: "You heard me. You heard me all the way." Her eyes narrowed then moved around the group again slowly as she said: "I have a strange feeling you heard me before I started. You heard me to my own story. *You heard me to my own speech*"[19]

Silence is powerful. "Hearing another to speech" is empowering. Guiding as empowerment becomes expressed through "hearing another to speech" and helps start the process of making the reality of historically imposed suffering public and communal. Suffering begins to take form in groans and tears and the halting stammering language of muteness breaking open. These new expressions begin to say what a situation really means. It says "Hear me!" "Believe me!" Alan Jones tells us, "'Holiness' is another name for this…uninterfering stance towards another human being."[20] Not interfering is different from not intruding. To not interfere means to take a noncynical stance that dares to receive something most painful. From the perspective of the cross, this requires relational knowledge, intimate knowledge, through which *believing is knowing*.[21] One believes first, even if one cannot understand. Perhaps understanding will come later. But in order for new speech to come into being, believing first is required. Believing is an expressing of receiving; it is an offer of hospitality.

Through this initial action of listening and hearing, guiding as empowering points to what Brueggemann has called the "prophetic imagination." Here, an alternative consciousness is evoked in people that can energize them toward a new future by mining their deep memories of hope.[22] Guiding as empowering also evokes what was referred to earlier, a "dangerous memory," a remembering that breaks the silence about the historical conditions that cause suffering. Listening and believing lead to the dawning realization of the sufferer's place within history—and our own. It is out of this memory that political consciousness arises.[23] "Dangerous memory" points us to our place in "humankind's passion history," the birthplace of critical consciousness, or *conscientizacao*. When we remember, become conscious, we learn to perceive social, political, and economic contradictions and to take action against these oppressive elements of

---

[19]Nelle Morton, *The Journey Is Home* (Boston: Beacon Press, 1985), 205.

[20]Alan Jones, *Soul Making: The Desert Way of Spirituality* (San Francisco: Harper and Row, 1985), 55.

[21]Knowledge as insight requires seeing or understanding in order to believe. Intimate knowledge is the knowledge of inner persuasion, of intuition, of the fundamental bonding of humankind.

[22]Brueggemann, *Prophetic Imagination*, 62–64.

[23]J. B. Metz, "Erinnerung des Leidens als Kritik eines teleologisch-technologischen Zukunftsbegriffs," *Ev. Theologie* 4 (1972): 343.

reality.[24] Soelle points out that this political awareness teaches a readiness to act for change.[25]

The first phase of suffering, then, is where muteness finds expression through various forms of speech. Those who suffer become empowered to speak with their own voices. The ones who speak and those who hear are active in this form of guiding in which historical suffering becomes shared suffering through a listening that bears witness to the lives of people. When those who are speaking and those who are hearing are totally engaged, Soelle refers to this mutually involved process as "carrying out the act of suffering."[26] Guiding as empowerment is a mutually involved process that moves suffering out of muteness into a speech that is initially a form of lament. Lament initiates a conversion process that transforms suffering into struggle.

Guiding as the Power of Conversion: Lament to Protest

The purpose of carrying out an act of suffering is not for the sake of suffering itself. Instead, it involves the decision to act rather than be acted upon. Carrying out the act of suffering is aimed at making those who are suffering visible and the causes of their suffering known. Carrying out the act of suffering means doing something to eliminate these causes of suffering and breaking the cycle of silence and deception. Carrying out the act of suffering means transforming historically imposed suffering into struggle; the struggle is to reestablish justice, which is dimly remembered and now worth fighting for. Struggle transforms suffering, and struggle transforms people. Struggle is the power of conversion.

Carrying out the act of suffering begins with the acceptance of suffering, which triggers the onset of grief. Grief is honest and necessary. It acknowledges the absence of love, the eclipse of justice, and the painful oppositional relationships we live with instead of reconciliation. Grief does not allow us to shrink from these painful truths. Brueggemann is clear on this matter as well when he says that it is the task of the prophet to help the community to grieve so that a new vision will be born in their midst.[27] This new vision that gives genuine hope only comes after the way of tears.

Soelle, too, recognizes the importance of grief in order to carry out the act of suffering. Her second phase of suffering is one of lamenting, of expressing suffering through grief. It is through the eyes of tears that people can begin to analyze their suffering in the context of existing social and

---

[24]Freire, *Pedagogy of the Oppressed,* trans. Myra Bergman Ramos (New York: Seabury Press, 1970), 19.

[25]Soelle, *Suffering,* 125.

[26]Ibid.

[27]Brueggemann, *Prophetic Imagination.*

political structures. Head and heart are joined in order to see clearly the whole landscape. Historical injuries are looked at carefully, analyzed, and put into words, so that those who are suffering because of them can be mobilized to act on what is going on. In this second phase the act of suffering is transformed into protest against conditions that perpetuate suffering. This is the political meaning of conversion. It is a pastoral interpretation of conversion as well, in which the power of struggle leads to personal and political transformation.

An understanding of guiding as the power of conversion evokes the "dangerous memory" of the holy person of an earlier era. Like the holy person of yesterday, those who empower today mediate between the ones who are suffering and the broader community. Sometimes they do this through public symbolic acts. They help bring to consciousness the connections between the particular suffering of people and the social structures that inflict their suffering. Some would say that the recent demonstrations surrounding the meetings of the World Trade Organization are illustrations of this mediation. Protestors draw attention to the relationship between global economics and human rights and environmental jeopardy and refuse to let business continue uninterrupted. Oppressive structures become exposed for the destructive powers they wield and the life-destroying practices they generate. Like the holy person of Late Antiquity, contemporary guides work to uncover the intricate fabric of human relationships in order to reintegrate those who have been isolated, broken through exploitation and disgrace, back into the human community. Like holy persons, guides seek to exercise clean power, not oppressive power. Clean power comes from relational knowledge gained through solidarity. It becomes shared power to exorcise the demonic in history so that all people can find their rightful place in a community of just relationships. The goal is total transformation of the community and the sufferer's place in that community. One thinks of the class action suits brought against major tobacco companies that have begun to shift our entire culture's relationship to advertising and cigarettes. This is an expression of conversion.

Accepting suffering means accepting what actually exists in order to touch the core of its transforming power. At the heart of carrying out the act of suffering is transformation. In the history of Christian thought, transformation has always been understood as *metanoia,* or conversion. Guiding in the early church reflected this view of conversion as the fledgling communities of believers were led to live their lives as those in whom "Christ has wrought an inner transformation."[28] This allowed them to live as people of dignity and to be involved in service to others. This inner

---

[28]John T. McNeill, *A History of the Cure of Souls* (New York: Harper & Brothers, 1951), 88.

transformation or conversion is similar to the "inner persuasion" of the theology of the cross.

Conversion, though, is multidimensional. Those who guide and those who suffer are both "converted" by the suffering they accept and the new vision that arises out of the deep resources of memory and solidarity that they experience together. It is a conversion that is multidimensional because it not only transforms the guides and sufferers, it seeks the conversion of those very social structures that try to maintain only one way of seeing reality. It is a conversion that moves passive suffering to the passionate and active suffering of protest. Soelle's phase two of suffering moves passive suffering to passionate suffering, activating hope through protest against existing intolerable situations. This passionate and active suffering helps produce an alternative reading of reality. Perceptions become converted.

The kind of acceptance that moves people from lament to protest is a most powerful form of love known as compassion. This is the meaning of "suffering love," or the practice of suffering. It is a love shown through people at work accepting reality and transforming it. Guiding as empowerment for conversion is an expression of this power of love that begins to take the form of doxology.

Guiding as the Power of Doxology: Suffering to Discipleship

The transformation of lament to protest continues the conversion of passive suffering to active and passionate suffering. This corresponds to Soelle's third phase of suffering, in which analysis is translated into behavior organized to change structures of oppression and our relationship to them. Rebecca Chopp calls this the "praxis of solidarity" for the transformation of human agency and social structures.[29] Here, a political strategy that is informed by social analysis and an appropriate faith and spirituality becomes central to ground suffering as an instrument for change. Robert Schreiter defines this constellation as absolutely necessary to engage "this-worldly realities."[30] In Soelle's phase three, speech, analysis, faith, and behavior come together in a practice of suffering in solidarity for change. This active suffering is always practiced in the company of others, with compassion for others, because as Soelle says, "the pressure of suffering produces solidarity"[31]

In this third phase the cross and political struggle most clearly come together.[32] The joining of cross and struggle produces tremendous energy and excitement as the old world begins to crumble and the contour of a

---

[29]Rebecca Chopp, *The Praxis of Suffering: An Interpretation of Liberation and Political Theologies* (Maryknoll, N.Y.: Orbis Books, 1986), 3–4.

[30]Robert J. Schreiter, *Reconciliation: Mission and Ministry in a Changing Social Order* (Maryknoll, N.Y.: Orbis Books, 1992), 65.

[31]Soelle, *Suffering*, 73.

[32]Ibid., 54.

new order begins to emerge. A sense of joy begins to well up in the lives of the people who once were dead and now begin to hope again. Brueggemann traces this phenomenon in Israel's history, in which God's freedom becomes revealed through the politics of justice and compassion, producing life where once there was despair: "The *dismantling* begins in the groans and laments of [the people]; the *energizing* begins in the doxologies of the new community."[33]

Doxology signals the truth of a new emerging world and the falseness of the old one; the pressure of suffering produces this alternative possibility. As Brueggemann notes, "It is the 'no other' that is a threat to all pretended worlds."[34] Once this is revealed as false, people sing songs of the world of justice, compassion, and peace–the real world of right relationships. But these doxologies of the new community can never be naive songs. Doxology sings of something glimpsed but not completely available in action. Nonetheless, the old world cracks and loses its hold. Another possible world is now available. Doxology points to the truth that all the time something holy has lain hidden but not lost. The "dangerous memory" reveals this hidden treasure. The songs of doxology are wise and critical proclamations reflecting a very strategic hope to deal with new worlds within "this-worldy realities."

From the perspective of the theology of the cross, what guides hope hidden in the midst of suffering is the promise of the indwelling presence of God in the world. God does not forsake the suffering world. God enters into the world and dwells in the midst of those suffering in exile; in prison; in sickness, confusion, and pain. Koyama sees this God as the one who goes to the "periphery," the place without honor, prestige, and power.[35] The periphery is the place of exile, confusion, and pain. The extreme periphery is the place of the cross. It is on the periphery that the full reality of God's indwelling is identified with human forsakenness. The periphery is where the identity of God and the identity of humankind are bound inseparably in the divine embrace of the cross. Soelle also sees this connection, and she reminds us that it is in discipleship with the man Jesus who was tortured to death that we learn to understand our own lives.[36] And it is in discipleship with this same person that we learn what it means to offer doxologies. The cross speaks the truth about who we are, where we have been, and the possibility of a different future. This makes doxology a form of bearing witness to the holy lain hidden but not lost.

Suffering through bearing witness to the suffering of others is what Kitamori calls "serving the pain of God." Serving the pain of God can be

---

[33]Brueggemann, *Prophetic Imagination,* 109.
[34]Walter Brueggemann, *Israel's Praise* (Philadelphia: Fortress Press, 1988), 52.
[35]Koyama, *Mount Fuji,* 251.
[36]Soelle, *Choosing Life,* 47.

understood as an expression of doxology from the perspective of the cross. Kitamori draws from Matthew 25:31–46 ("Truly I tell you, just as you did it to one of the least of these...you did it to me,"[v. 40]) as a basis for what he calls "loving historical reality" as the way to love God. Loving historical reality is bearing witness in the way we have been talking about it. Interpreting this passage, Kitamori writes:

> God expects us to love [God] not as an immediate object, but rather through our neighbors. That is, God becomes *immanent* in historical reality. Moreover the reality denoted here is reality in pain. Hungry, thirsty, a stranger, naked, sick, in prison–these are the realities of pain. God becomes *immanent* in these realities of pain:..."for I was hungry." Accordingly, service for the pain of God cannot be accomplished by itself, but only through service for the pain of reality.[37]

Kitamori makes an analogy between human pain and the pain of God. From the perspective of the cross, it is at the point of deepest pain that intimate knowledge is revealed between God and humankind. Through the grief of God and God's longing for the restoration of right relationships, the cry of God from the depths, *De Profundis,* is "God is love!"[38] This is "suffering love." This is passionate suffering. When we recognize our pain rooted in the pain of God, we serve the pain of God. When through our own suffering we bear witness to historical injuries and guide others to do the same, we practice suffering and bear witness even to the pain of God. This links private suffering to public human solidarity, which is an act of discipleship. Discipleship is doxology in action.

God invites people to complete the work of creation, and this involves accepting suffering. The carrying out of the act of suffering cannot deny the pain of anyone. But carrying out the act of suffering means that pain can be lifted. And this is cause for joy. Although the suffering of someone cannot be exchanged with that of another, it can be shared through discipleship.

If the aim of pastoral care is to know love, discipleship as doxology means to fall in love with God through one's neighbor and in this way to serve the pain of God. This is bearing witness to completion. This is carrying out the act of suffering as an activity of solidarity and strategy for reconciliation. This is discipleship as an action formed through doxology.

Yet one cannot rest lightly on this note of solidarity and change. Doxology never fully leaves the world of lament while historically imposed suffering lingers in our midst. Soelle reminds us of those who never see the

---

[37]Kazoh Kitamori, *Theology of the Pain of God* (Richmond, Va.: John Knox Press, 1958), 89–90.
  [38]Ibid.

fruits of solidarity, whose lives are destroyed and beaten down beyond recognition. Remembering a long history of ruined hopes and lives, she writes: "Nevertheless there remains the question about those who suffer senselessly and are destroyed."[39] This question about destroyed lives cannot be answered, only protested against by those who learn through suffering and are willing to stay and not leave or fall asleep. They, and hopefully we, will not give up the attempt for change. Nor will they, and hopefully we, stop at the boundaries of this attempt. "Where nothing can be done, they will join in the suffering."[40] Here, suffering as bearing witness is discipleship in a profound way, and doxology becomes truly a prayer from the depths.

Guiding as empowerment, whether of speech, conversion, or doxology, is not a once-and-for-all activity. The "stigmata" of pastoral care and theology is the wound in the heart of creation that is not healed. Lives have been and are still being destroyed. The realm of justice is not here, and love is not practiced in all its fullness. Doxology is prayer, and doxology is protest against this wound on behalf of all who are broken. It is protest as well as praise for the hope that is found in hints of an alternative reality already in our midst. Doxology can never be completely unambiguous. As a true reflection of a theology of the cross, it is praise of God even against God. Elie Wiesel, speaking from a Jewish perspective, captures this theme in his haunting poem "Ani Maamin" ("I Believe"):

Pray to God,
Against God,
For God.
Whether the Messiah comes,
Ani maamin.
Or is late in coming,
Ani maamin.
Whether God is silent
Or weeps,
Ani maamin.[41]

From a Christian point of view, as well as from the perspective of the political cross, nothing came to an end in Jesus' death. Everything only began, properly speaking. In truth and struggle we discover signs of the resurrection. Resurrection is both a spiritual and a political concept. *Ani maamin* ("I believe"), God is the unending capacity to struggle, to love. *Ani maamin* is doxology.

---

[39]Soelle, *Suffering,* 171.

[40]Ibid.

[41]Elie Wiesel, *Ani Maamin: A Song Lost and Found Again* (New York: Random House, 1973), 107. Ani Maamin is a song, a cantata, that Wiesel used to sing in his childhood. Roughly translated it says, "I believe in the coming of the Messiah. Even though late in coming. I believe that the Messiah will come...one day."

Doxology, while incomplete, still points to something real. Healing is possible, practical, and drenched in providential moments in which justice is practiced and people come together with new eyes and hearts beating with the promise of life.

The Gift of Healing

Clebsch and Jaekle and others have described healing as one of the historic functions of pastoral care and also the aim of the other pastoral functions. Healing is also generally understood as restoring people to wholeness. According to Hiltner and those who have followed his lead, the restoration of wholeness is still the goal of pastoral care today. From the perspective of a political theology of the cross, however, the meaning of wholeness shifts to include the practice of reconciliation as the work of justice. From this perspective healing comes through carrying out the acts of suffering. With reconciliation as a proper aim of pastoral care, healing now begins to take on a different character. Healing becomes the fulfillment of a promise and the basis for hope in history. It is a gift and a sign that the realm of justice is not just wishful thinking but something tangible and real.

Healing is not really a function at all. Nor is it a practice in the sense we have been talking about. While solidarity can be practiced, reconciliation can be rehearsed, and guiding can strategize for justice's sake; healing cannot be achieved through calculation, design, or therapeutic skill. The notion of healing as a function, even as a practice, implies human agency is its origin. This reflects the image of "man the master" referred to earlier in the discussion of Douglas Hall. Healing does not come from outside the individual like a kind of application, nor is it drawn up from the inner resources of an individual. The *individual* is the operative term here. When the individual is still the autonomous human being of liberal thought, he or she becomes the private and separated self who is the final referent. In distinction to this individualistic notion of personhood is the growing recognition of the social nature and construction of the self and its corporate dimension. In this view autonomy is not absent, it is contextualized; to be a person means to be part of a people. The contextual self that is formed, nurtured, and revealed in relationship finds its first and final referent in what we call God. This understanding does not disregard human agency, but it also considers men and women as receivers. In this view healing is a gift.

Healing is something to be received, not something to be grasped or engineered. From this perspective healing comes not from inner strength and self-understanding alone, but through just relationships that are hospitable to the healing presence of the holy. The reign of God, the realm of the holy, is the locus of healing; it is a realm not conceived of or executed by technology, not even psychological or spiritual technology. Healing that is the basis for hope in history, a gift and a sign that the realm of justice is present in our midst, needs to be understood within this intricate web of human/divine relationships. Restoring wholeness refers to repairing the whole web. The aim of pastoral care as reconciliation means creating justice for this entire cosmos.

Healing has always in some way been associated with the holy within the context of the Christian faith, yet the holy has consistently proven elusive. There is an element of indirectness related to holiness, hiddenness if you will, with an attending sense of surprise when the holy has been "brushed up against." Healing has these qualities too. From the perspective of the theology of the cross, healing and holiness can only be revealed indirectly, not held completely, and never "understood" totally. As stressed throughout this work, revelation is not a private unveiling of the holy; instead, revelation requires a public debut. The self is not formed or known in isolation; the self is revealed through social relationships. "I know as I am known" is perhaps more accurate than Descartes' "I think, therefore I am." This means that healing is not merely a private phenomenon but a public happening. It is not a matter of insight; rather, it known and received through acts of corporate suffering that bring forth the promised new day.

Hints of Shalom

The scriptural record points to the public nature of Jesus' healing in the early days of his ministry. By far the majority of the healing events were enacted in public for the benefit of the community as well as the one receiving the cure. Earlier it was pointed out that the healing acts were connected with the message of the dawning reign of God. They were seen as "acts of the spirit or finger of God, direct acts of God...foreshadowing the establishment of God's final Reign in the last days."[42] The healing events of Jesus' day were never intended as private events, nor were they a reference to an inner or private world as the location of the realm of God. They functioned instead to call those who witnessed them to participate in the realm of God that was revealed to them.[43]

As signs of the dawning realm of God, healings served as signs of what was to come and at the same time was already appearing. As signs they prompted that sense of "inner persuasion" that motivated the early believers to live toward the promises of wholeness as nearly as possible. Healing could still be viewed in this way today if our imaginations were rekindled to see the deeper dimensions of reality, in which our own well-being is connected to the well-being of others and to the state of our world.

Clebsch and Jaekle have suggested that healing has been the most difficult aspect of pastoral care to understand in terms of its historical function.[44] Perhaps this is because, as we have been saying, it never really

---

[42]R. H. Fuller, *Interpreting the Miracles* (London: SCM Press, 1963), 40.

[43]James Breech, *The Silence of Jesus: The Authentic Voice of the Historical Man* (Philadelphia: Fortress Press, 1983), 38.

[44]Clebsch and Jaekle, *Pastoral Care,* 42.

was a function, at least not in any utilitarian sense of "function." They point out that in the modern era, healing is viewed primarily through the practices of medical science, thus narrowing its meaning for pastoral healing. In this regard, I worry about some of the ways spirituality is being reconceived as a tool for promoting health in medical environments today. While valuable and laudable studies are being conducted that show a strong correlation between the effects of prayer and physical healing, when viewed only with this end in mind, healing can be understood in a very limited and self-serving way. This instrumental view of spirituality for healing fails to take into account who has access to medical services in the first place, and it circumvents the problematics of our national health care policies and delivery system in the United States.

Reestablishing the relationship between healing and reconciling today can open pastoral theology and the health care professions to new understandings of health and healing. This would involve all of us in a more comprehensive study of economic theory and public policy. A new appreciation of the relationship between healing and reconciliation could offer a new vision of life in which restored relationships point beyond achieving a *status quo ante* to a genuinely new creation. If we take this seriously, we will need to take a deeper look at what role forgiveness plays in helping something truly different to emerge.

Signs of Forgiveness

In this chapter a new vision of healed creation has been described as working for justice through solidarity. This new vision is really the old vision longed for again and again–the dawning realm of God. This vision of justice, however, is future oriented. It dreams a future in which there is not just an absence of conflict and injury, but one in which people are taken seriously and their sense of well-being is fostered. Such a vision requires the practice of forgiveness. Not in the sense of pretending that wrongs have never happened or that they are not as significant as we once thought. No, forgiveness from a political interpretation of the cross means we take seriously Jesus' words of forgiveness from the cross meant for everyone: "...Forgive them; for they do not know what they are doing" (Lk. 23:34). Jon Sobrino tells us that these last words of Jesus do not suggest expiatory sacrifice or vicarious death on his part for the sins of people. That would, as Sobrino says, haul "God into the court of human reason." Rather, they show the God who comes among us to save unconditionally. The last word is not damnation; rather, it is acceptance. At the point of consummate gravity of sin, God is absolutely near to human beings to the very last.[45]

---

[45] Jon Sobrino, *The Principle of Mercy: Taking the Crucified People from the Cross* (Maryknoll, N.Y.: Orbis Books, 1994), 91.

The last word of forgiveness tells us what is real. Here, the injustice in which we all participate, whether as perpetrators, victims, witnesses, bystanders, or resisters, confirms that we are indeed related. We are bound together in a world where injustice is real but need not have the last word. Forgiveness tells this truth. Injustice is named for what it is. Through truth telling and the incredible gift of learning that we are all human together, forgiveness becomes the invitation to carry out acts of suffering for the sake of justice and mercy. But this is more problematic than it sounds. Forgiveness is a gift that requires our attitude of gratitude to receive it. Sobrino tells us that those who live in the First World find gratitude particularly difficult because we believe that we have come to be who we are by our own efforts.[46] We believe we can generate our own forgiveness—one readily calls to mind easily the popular slogans "I need to forgive myself" or "You need to forgive yourself." The posture of *receiving* forgiveness from those who are offended *by us* is more difficult for us to acknowledge. But the ability and willingness to receive from others, especially forgiveness, is precisely what makes us human. This is where "life is a gift" becomes more than rhetoric, rather a deep-down knowing in every cell of our bodies. Forgiveness becomes the way in which we engage in the world for the sake of restoring human identity in the image of divine holiness. Forgiveness and solidarity go together.

It is clear that during the time of Jesus' ministry the healing miracles were intended as signs of the in-breaking of God's realm, signs of the future restoration of humankind to one another and their Creator. Healing was understood as an expression of this promise and the possibility of reconciliation. Clebsch and Jaekle claim that "fulfilled humankind" is the aim of all pastoral care.[47] As the "first fruits" of reconciliation, "fulfilled humankind" is the basis for hope for healing in the world and points to the promise of God's power to heal creation. "Fulfilled humankind" is people with the ability to know love as something to give *and* receive.

Sacramental Vision

When the aim of pastoral care is reciprocal love, and healing is a sign of this love, pastoral care is involved in sacramental practice. Healing is an "outward and visible signs of inward and spiritual grace"[48] Healing happens where love and justice meet. This sacramental dimension is present in the inner persuasion of guiding. It is this sacramental element that is found in the heart that longs for the realm of God. It is found in human pain that serves the pain of God through acts of compassion and justice. Pastoral care from the perspective of a political reading of the cross takes these

---

[46]Ibid., 86.

[47]Clebsch and Jaekle, *Pastoral Care,* xvi.

[48]The Episcopal Church, *The Book of Common Prayer* (New York: Seabury Press, 1977), 857.

sacramental aspects of life most seriously. This means that a political interpretation of the cross is fundamentally a sacramental theology. Koyama says it this way: "When holiness and brokenness come together for the sake of the salvation of others, we have Christian sacrament."[49] This is the heart of the eucharistic celebration. In this manner the cross can never be a cross of glory, but it is a cross of joy.

A pastoral theology that is a sacramental theology begins with the cry of anguish and waits with the tears of the brokenhearted. Where people strain under the burden of oppressive structures and practice protest, new energy and hope issue forth as people catch a glimpse of the freeing and healing power of God's suffering love. This underscores the importance of the category of the future as well as the present. Pastoral theology has given tremendous authority to the past, the causal nature of human experience and meaning. Sacramental reality remembers the past, takes the present with utmost seriousness, and points to the future and the power of the future, which becomes enlivened through the creative gifts of imagination. We ritualize this every time we break bread and share the cup. We dream afresh out of a present experience of a holy presence made known to us by eating together as "one body" gathered around "one table."

Healing and reconciliation by the broken Christ embracing the broken world is a mystery. It is a mystical feat that opens political possibilities. Where pastoral care and theology engages in this mysterious and sacramental process, it does so from the perspective of a political theology of the cross. From the foot of this cross, pastoral theology is invited to participate in the vision of a "fulfilled humanity." Every time pastoral care and theology finds its identity in the eucharistic act, it receives the "ones who are dying [and] hands on their own lives as a legacy, as a heritage entrusted to the survivors."[50] Here, the work of suffering finds its source and the promise of a healed creation.

Summary

Throughout the last two chapters we have been talking about pastoral theology as a new form of theological consciousness. The new consciousness means that authentic pastoral reflection cannot allow suffering as a result of historical injuries to continue. Unfortunately, much of Protestant socialization in North America has reinforced a feeling of impotence, helplessness, powerlessness, and the sense that there is nothing people can finally do to change their fate. This has inadvertently become deeply internalized in some humanistic schools of care that aim to accept and not change a person's values, feelings, or perceptions. The one providing care offers a supposedly neutral or "disinterested" presence to the one seeking

---

[49]Koyama, *Mount Fuji*, 243.
[50]Soelle, *Suffering*, 139.

counsel. While the legitimate desire here may be not to manipulate someone and to respect his or her autonomy, this posture can also help reinforce a sense of powerlessness both on the part of caregivers and the ones receiving care. This kind of unbiased presence in practice can result in simply being an "audience," thus serving the balance and harmony of current social arrangements. As we have stressed, presence through solidarity is proactive and involves being engaged in struggle with others precisely to initiate change in persons and communities.

From the perspective of the political cross, solidarity is seen as the originating pastoral practice that seeks change. Through solidarity, people who were invisible become strong, "disruptive," and dynamic as they find new self-assurance and a language with which to communicate. Pastoral theologians who are in solidarity with people seeking liberation break away from all forms of neutrality and our safe place as a viewer. Instead, we begin to explore ways that we are being complicit with injustice. Through this we become changed. Our cynicism becomes tempered, and so does our apathy, as our lives become new in relationship to others. In reality, solidarity is an expression of faith and the strongest sign of new life. As Soelle says, "Where there is solidarity there is resurrection."[51] We cannot talk about pastoral work in the name of theology until we become a part of historical movements of struggle to end suffering from injustice. We dare not talk about God, especially *imago Dei,* until we participate in this process of change.

If the aim of pastoral care is to help people know love as something to give and something to receive, it cannot be exercised apart from communities of faith that take the work of reconciliation in the world seriously. As H. Richard Neibuhr has said, the purpose of the church is to increase the love of God and neighbor. Pastoral theology and care needs to be done collectively and based in communities of faith because, as Soelle reminds us,

> We need a group of human beings who make it possible for us to begin afresh; accept who we are; have faith in our repentance and believe we are capable of conversion.[52]

The close relationship between reconciliation and healing, and the role forgiveness plays, teaches us the way of gratitude where we cannot learn by ourselves. Forgiveness is something we receive from others that changes us. Healing is something we receive not as a reward for our labors, but as a gift freely given. Healing shows us that we are changed. Healing vindicates suffering. For this we give thanks and learn the ways of worship again.

---

[51]Soelle, *Choosing Life*, 88–89.
[52]Soelle, *Suffering*, 104.

Finally, active suffering for the sake of wholeness is not simply the "duty" of justice. The requirement of justice is moral, yes, but more than that. The work of justice is holy and beautiful. Wholeness has an aesthetic claim as well as an ethical demand. Ethics and aesthetics come together through suffering solidarity. In solidarity we become *broken and yet beloved.* This means we become beautiful, as worship is beautiful, when holiness and brokenness come together for the sake of human sacrament. People are lovely when they become totally engaged in holy activity without divergence.

In the next chapter we will explore solidarity as the starting place of pastoral care, reconciliation as the work of justice, and guiding as empowerment as "practices" of the faith community. We will do this by looking at a particular community of faith that lives out of these practices, the San Francisco Network Ministries. But first, we will revisit the shepherd metaphor, which has captured the imagination of pastoral theologians for so long, and explore the possibility of the "suffering righteous one" as a viable alternative image to guide a political interpretation of the cross.

Our assumption is that the "suffering righteous one" cannot be interpreted today as an *individual* person who offers care. This would misread the corporate nature of "active suffering" and play into masochistic accounts of sacrifice. The "suffering righteous one" needs to be understood communally, just as communities of faith need to be seen as collectives that incarnate the body of Christ. This orientation, exemplified through the Network Ministries, holds promise and meaning for pastoral care and theology. It is also a way of living that is closely related to the meaning and "practice" of resurrection.

CHAPTER NINE

Signs of Hope

A Communal Way of the Cross

Consider the darkness of suffering, the mystery of suffering for which there is no answer, there is only response. Part of the mystery is this, when I allow you to enter my suffering or when you allow me to enter yours, the darkness is not lifted; indeed, it is often deepened. Our connectedness allows us both to move to a deeper darkness enveloping our individual suffering within the suffering of God and all God's creatures. It is here that the star of Bethlehem, the vulnerability of God, is seen most clearly.[1]

GLENDA HOPE

Pastoral theology has always been related to communities of faith. As we have noted in previous chapters, it has been the liberal church in North America that most influenced the development of pastoral care and theology for contemporary settings. It was this theological orientation that guided Seward Hiltner and his followers to adopt the shepherding perspective for their understanding of pastoral care and theology.[2] Drawing on the metaphor of Christ as the Good Shepherd, they affirmed the christological

---

[1]Glenda Hope, *The Network Journal* (January 1988): 19.

[2]James Luther Adams and Seward Hiltner, eds., *Pastoral Care in Liberal Churches* (Nashville: Abingdon Press, 1970). In this work Hiltner identifies himself within the liberal church tradition and highlights other authors of similar view.

center of faith as the key to pastoral care.[3] While this understanding is helpful and valuable, there are also some limitations to the shepherding perspective.

The activities of the shepherd developed by Hiltner and his supporters have focused primarily on the person offering care, for "the shepherding" perspective. Until very recently, the qualities, abilities, and skills of an individual caregiver have been highlighted in texts on pastoral care, at times to the neglect of the role of the community of faith as a whole. Furthermore, in spite of attempts to acknowledge lay ministry, the "shepherd" who offers care has too often been portrayed as someone who is a professional, a member of the clergy, often someone who specializes in pastoral counseling. This depiction of the shepherd role bears a striking resemblance to the secular culture's understanding of what it means to be a professional helper, part of this being a specialist with clear demarcations between the helper and the one being helped.[4] Hiltner's adoption of the term *client* from Carl Rogers' "client centered therapy" is a case in point, and it has been carried forward into much of our current pastoral literature. But this term also brings other assumptions about how relationships are organized and understood. Among other things, it suggests the contractual arrangements of the marketplace that professionals such as lawyers, brokers, social workers, and so forth, make with their "clients."

When someone, usually an individual, contracts for service, the principle of exchange places the client in a different social category from the one offering care. The one supplying the services has a certain advantage over the one in need who is searching them out. The one offering the services is more likely to be seen as an expert, while the one receiving them is viewed as a novice. The professional holds the power of position while the client may be in a vulnerable situation when he or she is seeking guidance. The professional usually has credentials, while the client may be, at best, an amateur. Although these distinctions are inevitable in a fee-for-service arrangement, and for monitoring appropriate professional ethical boundaries, they are still problematic. In a society that is still stratified in terms of race, gender, class, age, sexual orientation, and so forth, a contractual understanding of care can actually serve to accentuate power differences and social inequities that mitigate against projects of mutuality

---

[3]Daniel Day Williams, *Minister and the Care of Souls* (New York: Harper and Row, 1961), 13.

[4]James P. Wind, Russell Burck, Paul F. Camenisch, and Dennis P. McCann, eds., *Clergy Ethics in a Changing Society* (Louisville: Westminster/John Knox Press, 1991). Martin Marty talks about the professionalization of the clergy in America as a result of the disestablishment of the church. This resulted in a movement away from a "theologically-ecclesiastically sanctioned norm" to the "contractual- entrepreneurial norm," resulting in the subordination of religion to secular norms for credentialing the clergy. For pastoral counseling this has meant that the norms and standards for credentialing pastoral counseling as a specialty have largely been derived from the secular disciplines, such as social work and psychiatry.

and solidarity as we have been discussing them in this work. In other words, rather than alleviating sources of suffering rooted in domination, contractual arrangements can serve to support them. When pastoral care uncritically models itself on the social and ethical standards of the secular helping professions, the shepherd as construed in much of our literature fails to offer alternative norms and values from the practices of the dominant culture.

A political interpretation of the cross supports a christological center of faith for pastoral care and theology. But it evokes an alternative image to that of Jesus as the Good Shepherd. Based on the political cross, the guiding metaphor is Jesus as the righteous One who risked everything for a new world order, even suffering death on a cross. As we saw earlier, particularly in the gospel of Mark, Jesus is not only someone who offered "tender and solicitous care" to individuals (Hiltner's Shepherd), but one who also lived, spoke, and evoked a different order of life for the whole community. His was a tender care that was also a costly care. It originated with the cry of suffering and became known in Christ as the Suffering Righteous One.

Yet, reintroducing the image of the Suffering Righteous One in the predominantly individualistic and therapeutic culture of North America is still problematic and potentially limiting. It can lead caregivers who identify *personally* with this image to adopt grandiose styles of leadership or masochistic ways of relating. Too often we hear of the professional helper with either a "messiah complex" or a "martyr complex." These extremes diminish and dishonor the dignity of both the ones offering and those receiving help. They, too, perpetuate a false dichotomy between people in helping relationships, which accentuates power differences and prevents authentic expressions of mutuality.

But Jesus did not act alone. He carefully chose companions. The vocation of the Suffering Righteous One was not an individualistic calling; a community was summoned to establish justice and offer mercy. Adopting this metaphor for today means to retain this communal identification in order to obtain its transforming possibilities. It is a community that is called to incarnate the Suffering Righteous One, and it will do so by embracing its *imago Dei* through the *imitatio Christi*.[5] The *imitatio Christi* is the church's societal vocation.[6] Or in the words of Dietrich Bonhoeffer,

> "If we are to learn what God promises, and what [God] fulfills, we must persevere in quiet meditation on the life, sayings, deeds, sufferings, and death of Jesus.[7]

---

[5]Larry Rasmussen. "Clues from Dietrich Bonhoeffer: Toward an Ethic of the Cross for North Americans." Unpublished paper, 1. Here, Rasmussen claims, "The *imitatio Christi* is the most promising and most underdeveloped dimension of the *theologia crucis*."

[6]Ibid., 21.

[7]Dietrich Bonhoeffer, *Letters and Papers from Prison*, ed. Eberhard Bethge (New York: Macmillan, 1972), 391.

Bonhoeffer wrote this while in prison for resisting Adolf Hitler's Third Reich. This is the way of the Suffering Righteous One. This is the way of the political cross. Instead of contracts that are associated with market economy, it will involve people in covenant activity that reflects God's formation and liberation of people in history. We have called this covenantal work "practices of care" that empower people to come together in solidarity toward creating just and compassionate communities. Instead of security, this will involve risk. Instead of acquiring social prestige and powerful rewards, it will involve people in relinquishing all vestiges of privilege. Instead of profit, this will mean sacrifice. Covenant, risk, and relinquishment are marks of a community that practices *imitatio Christi*, as it seeks to follow the way of the Suffering Righteous One.

An Alternative Pastoral Metaphor: The Suffering Righteous One

Through the *imitatio Christi* as the Suffering Righteous One, a community of faith recognizes that suffering is the place where the compassionate God meets humankind's deepest need. This compassionate God is found on the cross with Jesus. And it is this God who keep us "pegged to the world."[8] Pegged to the world through the body of Christ in the world is the truest expression of what it means to be the church. This is the community of faith that represents the Suffering Righteous One within the tradition of the *imitatio Christi* by way of the political *theologia crucis*. In this way Christ takes form in the midst of people here and now. The starting place is where we simply participate in the sufferings of God in the life of the world so that communities of care and justice might be realized.[9]

This is the pastoral as well as the moral vocation of the church, which is to be-for-others. But it must be-for-others as a community of faith identified as *ecclesia crucis,* a political expression of *ecclesia crucis.* Such a community of faith will find that it has a renewed confidence, that goodness and truth will prevail, and it will find new meaning in Julian of Norwich's words "All shall be well, all manner of things shall be well." Such a community of faith will find hope in the promise of healing that will surely come at last. Such a community of faith is an *ecclesia crucis* that trusts not in the contemporary myths of knowledge and progress, but the passion of Jesus, the way and power of cross and resurrection. Pastoral theology can depend on this vision of faith for its identity and integrity.

A community of faith formed by the Suffering Righteous One will guide by empowering people who suffer to express their pain, so that their sorrow will be led into protest. Their protest is something that is born from and borne by memories of relieved suffering. It offers genuine hope for liberation from current afflictions and serves to remind the whole worshiping

---

[8]Rasmussen, "Clues from Dietrich Bonhoeffer," 14.
[9]Ibid., 24.

community of the subversive power of doxology. This is the way a community of faith becomes motivated to work toward alleviating historical injuries by transforming passive suffering into passionate suffering. This is the vocation of a community of faith that embraces its *imitatio Christi.* Such a community formed by the Suffering Righteous One is the body of Christ incarnate in the world, signifying the resurrected crucified one.

A community of the crucified and resurrected one goes the way of the cross, the way of messianic suffering, which is the passionate suffering of bearing witness.[10] It relates pastoral care to truth and power, the strange and paradoxical power exercised by the disfranchised who appear as the most unlikely ones to challenge existing social arrangements. It will be found at the periphery of society in the seemingly godforsaken places, where, for God's sake and for the sake of all who suffer because of injustice, a witness will be established and reconciliation required. Such a community will live the life it seeks to engender in the midst of the society it hopes to renew.

This idea of a community of faith open to those excluded by the dominant culture, including the church itself, is not a new idea. Jürgen Moltmann talks about this in *The Open Church: Invitation to a Messianic Life-Style;*[11] Rosemary Radford Ruether talks about it in *Women-Church: Theology and Practice of Feminist Liturgical Communities*[12] as a new expression of the "Christian Quest for Redemptive Community;"[13] Latin American liberation theologians describe Base Christian Communities as vital expressions of the church active in the world giving expression to alternative worlds of justice and care.[14] Dietrich Bonhoeffer prefigured this prototype in his *Life Together.*[15] Yet perhaps it is the African American Church in North America that has most consistently and persuasively given expression to this alternative way of being church in the United States. Larry Rasmussen points out:

> The "church" in American Protestantism, *with the notable exception of the Black Church* has been largely the individual and the nation,

---

[10]Ibid., 2. Here, Rasmussen talks about the way of the cross as the way of messianic suffering. He underscores that *theologia crucis* means that Christ exists as a community, as the church's societal vocation by way of the cross. This communal self-understanding is the foundation for the full range of human experience.

[11]Jürgen Moltmann, *The Open Church: Invitation to a Messianic Life-Style* (London: SCM Press, 1978).

[12]Rosemary Radford Ruether, *Women-Church: Theology and Practice of Feminist Liturgical Communities* (San Francisco: Harper and Row, 1985).

[13]Ruether, "Christian Quest for Redemptive Community" *Cross Currents* 28/1 (Spring 1988): 3–16.

[14]For example, Leonardo Boff, *Ecclesiogenesis: The Base Communities Reinvent the Church* (Maryknoll, N.Y.: Orbis, 1986).

[15]Dietrich Bonhoeffer, *Life Together,* trans. John W. Doberstein (New York and Evanston: Harper and Row, 1954).

with denominations supplying ecclesiastical structure. Both the stance of the Moral Majority and the opposition of liberal Protestants to it betray an acculturated Christianity markedly lacking any sense of "church" whose normative shape is over against its own wider world.[16]

Although not identical with one another, these various communities of faith all critique the dominant culture as well as the liberal church when it is unreflective about its complicity in oppressive structures. Each holds a vision of an alternative reality and a willingness to work to create that reality, even though that effort may be costly. They offer expressions of what it means to be a faithful community in our time and are important contexts for pastoral theology. They offer significant alternative perspectives to the liberal tradition with which pastoral care and theology has been most closely identified.They represent the covenant-oriented, risk-taking, and sacrificial orientation of the Suffering Righteous One.

At this point we can ask, What might the contours of pastoral theology and care look like in the life of a community of faith that takes our deep historical connections seriously? First of all, a community of faith that goes the way of the cross will be found with those located at the periphery of society in places without honor, prestige, and power. There, the *imitatio Christi* as the Suffering Righteous One will be practiced as the resurrection faith of the crucified one. There, at the periphery, it will live as an *ecclesia crucis,* offering a future-leaning hope in which "God will wipe every tear from their eyes.Death will be no more; mourning and crying and pain will be no more, for the first things have passed away" (Rev. 21:4). Pastoral care and theology practiced on the periphery, within this posture of faith, will shed many of its professional trappings and move out of the office and into the streets. Conceived as practices of faith communities, it will be about the work of reconciliation as it goes to the "widows, orphans, and aliens" instead of waiting for them to come to the office.

In order to examine more closely how pastoral practices consistent with a political interpretation of theology of the cross might be exercised, we will look to the Network Ministries in San Francisco. Here, we will find pastoral offerings to the "widows, orphans, and aliens" and other disfranchised people. Here, we will find an example of people in ministry moving out into the streets in order to take our common life seriously and provide alternative places of meaning for people who are suffering. Yet all this is done with a clear recognition that what is at stake is the survival of our shared fabric of life through the shared ministry of all:

> We go into lobbies and tiny community kitchens
> which the people transform into sacred space.

---

[16]Rasmussen, "Clues from Dietrich Bonhoeffer," 31. Italics mine.

We pray. We read Scriptures. We make space for
their testimonies, until that time when they come
to know it is they, who support the weak and tend
the dying, it is they who are the real priests here.
We who, for now, wear the symbols of connection,
the stole and cross, are merely their acolytes.[17]

This is the way of the political cross of the Suffering Righteous One. Here, sustaining is practiced as solidarity with people in this community. Guiding is offered as empowerment, and reconciling is demonstrated as people come together to work for justice. When all participants engage these practices, healing begins to be experienced in and between people and communities. Implicit in the life of the Network Ministries is an interpretation of the cross that informs and gives rise to these pastoral and political practices. But first, it is important to understand a little of the history and context that gave rise to this ministry in San Francisco.

The San Francisco Network Ministries

The Reverend Glenda Hope of the San Francisco Network Ministries says, "The real thing is the Servant–the Servant people–whose bearing towards one another arises out of the life in Christ."[18] This is an understanding of people who embrace their vocation as the *imitatio Christi*. It is a corporate vision of the *imitatio Christi* as the body of the Suffering Righteous One in the world. The Network Ministries has attempted to live out of this commitment since it began nearly thirty years ago.

The idea for the San Francisco Network Ministries began to form in 1972 with a small group of people who met regularly for worship in the living room of Glenda and Scott Hope. From the beginning they shared a common concern for the growing number of young people who were flocking to San Francisco without means or resources to support themselves. Soon they formed what they called the San Francisco Young Adult Network as a way to address the physical, spiritual, and emotional needs of these young folks. This grassroots effort began as a collection of resources, meeting places, groups, and other services for people aged twenty to forty throughout the San Francisco Bay Area. They created house churches in various locations in the city, including San Francisco State College where Scott Hope was a professor. They began visiting people in the downtown resident hotels and started Bible study classes over the lunch hour with women working in the business district. Early on they established and opened the Network Coffee House on Bush Street.

---

[17]Scott Hope, *The Network Journal* (July 1989): 17.
[18]Glenda Hope, *The Network Journal* (June 1982): 5.

The Network Coffee House soon became the gathering place and central hub of activities for local residents and many young people new to the city. It was open seven nights a week, providing a different program each evening. Personal growth was the focus one night, on another intellectual development. Meaningful lifestyles and spiritual quests were favorite topics. There was always one evening devoted to issues of social justice and the politics of the city, many of which ended up generating political action for social change. Every Wednesday evening Network staff and volunteers led simple and inclusive worship services that were always well attended. The over-arching goal of the San Francisco Young Adult Network was "to work with young adults for their empowerment: mental, spiritual, emotional, political, and economic."[19]

From its inception the San Francisco Young Adult Network was committed to social justice. Its founders and leaders understood social justice and personal renewal as equally emphasized in the message of the gospel and made this their focus of ministry with the young people of San Francisco as well. They saw these twin concerns as the central role of the church in the world.

During its early years, the San Francisco Young Adult Network associated with the Third World Fund, an organization that provided seed money to community organizations involved in social change. These two organizations together formed the Genesis Church and Ecumenical Center, which helped groups and organizations whose constituencies had been systematically denied the right of self-determination. The projects funded encompassed groups committed to struggling against racial and cultural chauvinism, class privilege, and economic exploitation.[20]

In 1978 the Young Adult Network took on another challenge. It expanded its ministry to include the Seventh Avenue Presbyterian Church located near the University of California Medical Center in San Francisco. At the time, this stately old church was in the process of becoming a faltering community of faith struggling to keep its doors open. After conversations with the Presbytery, the Network staff moved from its location on Market Street to Seventh Avenue Church and became its ministerial leadership. The cooperation between the church and the Network broadened the scope and vision of both. Through mutually developing ministries in San Francisco the church gradually began to be revitalized as its members became involved in areas of the city beyond their immediate neighborhood. The Network Ministries found a new home and a closer tie to the outlying neighborhoods.

It was around the same time that the Network ministries moved to Seventh Avenue Presbyterian Church that the coffee house lost its lease on Bush Street. Not knowing where to turn, the Network approached the

---

[19] *San Francisco Network News Letter* (May 1976).
[20] Ibid.

congregation. After lengthy conversations with church officers and numerous meetings with church members, the coffee house was relocated to the church facility. With this unexpected change, new people began to show up at the church and new horizons began to open up for this cooperative adventure between the church and the Network, not the least of which was the congregation's deeper involvement in many of the Network's projects.

Besides Sunday worship in the sanctuary, the joint ministry with Seventh Avenue eventually included additional house churches in homes and other locations; retreats and "Pilgrim Days"; a senior citizens center; "Extended Family" groups for discussing world issues; Sunday concerts; tutoring (Indochinese); a Wednesday night gathering called "The Art of Conversation," where topics were discussed that ranged from philosophy, psychology, literature, political issues, educational issues, and so on; and the publication of *The Network Journal.* The goals of the Network blended with the activities of the church, and something new was created that enhanced the original visions of both.

By the fall of 1982, the Young Adult Network along with the Seventh Avenue Presbyterian Church added another focus to their already comprehensive ministry. They initiated an innovative approach to theological education and called it the Network Center for the Study of Christian Ministry. It offered a year-long program of study for students from the Graduate Theological Union in Berkeley, California, located across the bay from San Francisco. Students earned full academic credit for an integrated program that included core seminary course work, vocational discernment, spiritual direction, psychological understanding, and field work. Disciplined growth and formation in all these areas of ministry were addressed. Students engaged in theological reflection and social analysis of the Christian communities in which they served. They developed skills to critically probe the personal, institutional, and political realities of their ministerial contexts. And they took their basic academic courses in these settings as well.

After the new program with the seminaries became established, the Young Adult Network's name was changed to The San Francisco Network Ministries in December of 1982. To more accurately reflect the growing and changing direction of the Network, the goals were also refocused to read:

> ...to work with people for their empowerment, to preach good news to the poor, to proclaim release to the captives, to recover the sight of the blind, to set at liberty those who are oppressed, to proclaim the acceptable year of the Lord.[21]

---

[21] *San Francisco Network News Letter* (December 1982).

The scripture reference (to Jesus' words in Luke 4:18–19 and to Isaiah's prophecy in Isaiah 61:1–2) was not only to indicate the Network's new educational mission, but to express a growing recognition of the plight of the poor and homeless throughout the country, especially in San Francisco. While young adults remained a central focus, the new goals reflected the additional centers of ministry and concerns of the Network. As stated in an article called "Street People" in the newly named *Network Journal*:

> The original Young Adult emphasis of the Network is carried over into the Tenderloin; we work together toward mental, spiritual, emotional, political and economic self-improvement.[22]

In 1982 the homeless and the poor of San Francisco became the newest constituency of the Network Ministries. The Network Ministries soon joined with the Central City Shelter Network to provide short- and long-term measures for alleviating the deplorable conditions of people living on the streets.

Today the Network no longer provides the professional leadership for Seventh Avenue Church. The church is doing well with new leadership and is no longer debating whether or not it will be able to continue to offer meaningful ministry in the city. They are strong and active once more. In the meantime, the Network Ministries moved its offices into the Tenderloin area of San Francisco, where they began to reach out in new ways into this ravaged part of the city named for Saint Francis.

The Tenderloin district in San Francisco is a densely populated part of the city that has apartment hotels for the elderly as well as temporary lodging for those who prosper from various forms of business that thrive in the night. It provides housing in the form of run-down apartments and resident hotels for the elderly and for people who are ill and addicted. It has low-income housing for the unemployed and recent immigrants who crowd into cramped and often filthy places to survive. More than five thousand children live here in these sub-standard facilities—sometimes in a one-bedroom or studio apartment with an extended family of eight or more. The Tenderloin is an area where a large number of the city's homeless people congregate. It is also the section of the city that features luxury hotels and fine department stores. In the Tenderloin district there is a stark contrast between the affluent and the destitute. Those living on the streets, or seeking profit on the street, clearly stand out against the new structures of wealth. Some are there to try to feed from the leftovers of vacation shoppers. Others present themselves for the occasional "recreation" that some tourists crave.

---

[22]Betsy Lamb, "Street People," *The Network Journal* (December 1982): 6.

Since moving to this part of the city, the Network Ministries has expanded and deepened its commitment to the people struggling to survive in a harsh environment. A "listening post" ministry offers people who live in crowded and public spaces a place to drop in for quiet conversation. The Tenderloin Community Church, a storefront operation, provides a welcoming worship space to any and all who come through its doors. Finally, in 1995, a dream long in the making became a reality. In cooperation with the Asian Neighborhood Design housing developers, San Francisco Network Ministries opened the Ellis Street family apartments, a true alternative living space for people surviving on low incomes. It features large community rooms and beautiful décor as well as spacious gardens and an outdoor play area for children. There is even a separate meditation garden that provides a serene place for much-needed respite in a confusing, fast-paced urban setting.

About the same time that the Ellis Street housing facility opened, the Network Ministries opened a computer training center. New residents of the apartment complex as well as other neighborhood residents are now offered computer classes and other job training skills to help them gain access to employment opportunities previously not open to them.

But even with the development of these new facilities and programs, there was still one group of people that had not been reached, women who worked in the prostitution industry. In 1997, the Network staff and volunteers began to address the needs of these women in order to help them find ways to create new lives for themselves. Then together with the Sisters of Presentation they conceived and organized a structured residential facility for homeless women who want to leave the life of prostitution. By 1998, SafeHouse became a reality and opened its doors to such women, who can live there for up to two years while they participate in personal and vocational programs designed to help them to make critical life changes. Even during its short history of operation, women's lives are being dramatically changed at SafeHouse. One woman said, "SafeHouse taught me what self-esteem was and then helped me see that I am a person—I shouldn't have to sell my body."[23] Another said, "SafeHouse saved my life. I was dying out there on the streets and I didn't even care. Now I care. I am learning about myself and I have a safe place, a real home to come back to each afternoon."[24] Glenda Hope has said that this ministry with prostituted women is the culmination of her vocational life and work.

The Network Ministries is now composed of The San Francisco Network Ministries, the Housing Corporation, the Tenderloin Community Church, the Homeless Persons Ministry, the Ambassador Hotel Chaplaincy,

---

[23]Quoted in "SafeHouse," a brochure produced by The San Francisco Foundation.
[24]Ibid.

the Ellis Street Apartments, the Computer Training Center, and the recently established SafeHouse for women. Throughout these various expressions of ministry, pastoral care is understood and expressed in fresh and creative ways. Sustaining is practiced as solidarity as the Network participants become involved in the institutional policies and social structures that impact their lives. Guiding is exercised as empowering people for change. Reconciling is practiced as the work of justice as people engage in political action for communal well-being. The hope for healing as the restoration of wholeness for all creation is the vision that inspires and leads this ministry in its ecology of care.

The staff, the volunteers, and the participants from the neighborhood together provide ministry through their strong sense and communal understanding of service. They have an understanding of themselves as a corporate body, a communal agent of compassion and justice, active and involved in the wider community. Their self-understanding as a collective entity of justice and mercy can be seen as embodying the Suffering Righteous One, an alternative metaphor to the traditional shepherd perspective that offers mainly "tender and solicitous care."

Historical Suffering as the Starting Point

This work began with Robert McAfee Brown's quote "When we hear the cry, 'I'm hurting,' we must take it seriously." The claim that the starting point for pastoral theology today must acknowledge the cry of those suffering historical injuries has been stressed. Throughout these pages a political reading of the cross has been featured as the faith paradigm that can effectively illumine this outcry. From its very beginning the San Francisco Network Ministries has responded to the cries of the outcast and despised, the least and the lost, those hurt by circumstances and systems that deny their dignity and worth. The cross has figured prominently in their work in the community, offering a starting place for theological reflection and practices of care.

San Francisco has always drawn young people seeking self-fulfillment. Beginning with the early Gold Rush days, down through the flower children and anti-war protesters of the 1960s, to the "dot com" entrepreneurs of late, San Francisco has been a city of dreams and the promised land of satisfied desires. However, it also becomes a city of nightmares for those whose star falls to the ground. It becomes a city of smoke and mirrors for those who barely scratch out a living existence. And it represents a city of broken dreams for those who fall down and out and never rise up again.

There is much suffering that is historically shaped and too many needs that are chronically left unmet in the city of the Golden Gate. Glenda Hope says, "Sometimes when I am walking down Market Street I feel as though I am walking hip deep in misery."[25] However, the ministry of the

---

[25]Glenda Hope, personal conversation, San Francisco, January 1990.

San Francisco Network Ministries begins right here, where the cries of misery and suffering are uttered. Its understanding of itself as a community of faith is formed by this starting place.

The San Francisco Network Ministries steps into the margins of society, seeking out those who are ignored by many of the mainline churches and sidestepped by the upwardly mobile and seemingly successful pilgrims to San Francisco. Why does it do so? Perhaps a clue is given in one of the reflections by co-founder Scott Hope when he reflects on what optimism means in a city that promises more than it can deliver:

> Optimism begins with the belief that we cannot change the nameless, encounter a faceless enemy, solve a mystery without clues, find substance in illusion, and so on. We press forward by keeping rendezvous with reality, and if those rendezvous occur in dark places, then we can either flee or we can try to throw some light against the darkness.[26]

"To throw some light against the darkness," to participate in an optimism that dares to "rendezvous with reality" wherever that may lead, is a vision of ministry that sounds curiously close to a theology of the cross as we have been discussing it.

The optimism that characterizes a "rendezvous with reality" is not what Hall names as the "official optimism" of dominant American culture; rather, it is the fierce hope that begins where any reason for hope seems absent. Again, it is the hope reflected in a theology of the cross; it is a hope that comes from accepting reality as it is in order to transform it to what it is meant to be. This kind of hope leads to an optimism that allows people to know love, both as something to be received and as something to give, the goal of pastoral care named earlier. Again, this is not a sentimental notion of love. This is a hard-won love, a seasoned and persevering kind of love that passionately pursues justice. Admittedly, this is a faith statement, *fides quaerens intellectum,* a faith that reflects a political reading of the cross. And like the faith of the political cross, the "rendezvous with reality" takes the face and cry of suffering seriously.

Reverend Glenda Hope recently described one of these rendezvous that occurred in a "dark place." She spoke of one time in particular when she was walking past a group of six or seven men and women clustered together on the sidewalk. There was a woman who was quite agitated and speaking to first one and then another of the men, when all of a sudden she drew her head back and focused her gaze directly on Glenda. Flinging her arms wide in the air she cried out, "You must have some word for me!" Glenda said, "I felt that cry rip right through my own skin."[27]

---

[26]Scott Hope, "Cerebrations," *The Network Newsletter/Journal* (May 1979): 2.
[27]Glenda Hope, conversation.

Perhaps the woman was expressing a yearning to "know love"; maybe she was expressing something else; regardless, her cry was one voice representing the suffering on the streets in the city. Her cry is what makes it more and more difficult for us to avert our eyes from those who appeal to us for any word that will address their plight. Encounters like this prompt and inspire Glenda Hope's preaching:

> "It is never the will of your Father in Heaven that even one of these little ones should be lost." Was this the view from the cross? Not numbers printed in the paper but these suffering masses with separate and distinct human faces, drawing from Jesus those last few words, fully identified as he was with the Body of Humanity. His voice, drawn from deep within his own tortured body, gives expression to the pain and the longing of that Great Corporate Body of Humanity.[28]

Glenda Hope was not "safe" from the woman she met on the street. Emotional distance did not protect her from the pain of the one who cried out. She was touched by the stark reality and core truth of the woman's life, and she bore witness to that with her own being. The witness was not free from the suffering to which she was exposed. The vulnerability expressed in this example is an illustration of one of the risks of solidarity as a practice of pastoral care from a political reading of the theology of the cross.

Solidarity: A Promise of Nonabandonment

Solidarity begins with the ones who are suffering and involves a kind of listening until we hear, a kind of seeing until we see, a kind of searching until we know. Solidarity means beginning where people are, staying with them and not abandoning them, and recognizing that we might even come to understand ourselves in new ways and be changed. The Network Ministries embodies this through its ministry with the poor.

> In this way, we come among the poor. We come less in the sense of opting for them than of praying that they may accept us, inviting us into their lives. We who previously came merely to organize, come now to serve. We come to see and see, to hear and hear, until finally we may receive grace to perceive and understand life from the perspective of the poor, rather than observing–and managing–the poor from the perspective of our life. We come without plans, not insisting on nor even wishing to give them what we believe is best for them, but wanting to hear their lives into speech and praying for the God-given humility to allow the poor

---

[28]Glenda Hope, "A Glenda Sermon," *The Network Newsletter/Journal* (November 1979): 6.

to hear us into speech. We come affirming their strength, dignity and wisdom; to be political with them, not charitable to them; to be in solidarity with their struggle for justice, not merely helping them do a little better in an oppressive system...We come, trembling, *hoping we may allow Christ to contemplate us, see us, through their eyes.*[29]

No one is impervious to the suffering of another. We cannot so easily separate and protect ourselves. This means that we recognize in each other similar needs, fears, desires, and dreams. It means that in order to meet these needs and realize these dreams, mutual respect and cooperation with one another is absolutely necessary. A vision for this mutuality is found in contemplative people who allow God's burning to melt them into solidarity with all of life. The way of the contemplative reveals our connections with those who cry out in life. As Glenda Hope says,

> The contemplative may no longer distance self from the oppressed—the poor, the tortured, the addicted, the dying, the other animals, the earth, the bodies broken and spirits crushed by human sin and evil, for these now wail from within, crying from the contemplative's own mouth.[30]

The participants of the Network Ministries live this contemplative perspective in community. They live in the midst of the people they serve. As they share a certain level of corporate life together, they share suffering as well. But as they design and implement various programs, they also provide ways for suffering to be channeled into public forums and platforms. In this way they act on the challenge of Dorothee Soelle, "to make personal forsakenness a public outcry."[31]

Solidarity through Providing a Public Forum

One of the places where personal forsakenness gains a public forum is through the *Network Journal.* When the *Network Journal* was first published, it opened with professor Scott Hope's social commentary. His monthly reflection named the reality of the people in the Tenderloin. He quoted the local residents and provided space for their stories and viewpoints. Over time, this column became a regular forum for the Tenderloin population. This discussion in the *Journal* was usually followed by a sermon written by Reverend Glenda Hope or another Network staff member. The sermons gave another place for the people they worked with to become known beyond their geographical locale. By sharing their experiences and offering

---

[29]Glenda Hope, "Reflections by Glenda Hope," *The Network Journal* (August 1989): 12–13.

[30]Glenda Hope, *The Network Journal* (July 1989): 16.

[31]Dorothee Soelle, *Christ the Representative* (London: SCM Press, 1967), 108–9.

illustrations that related to the biblical message, the plight of marginalized people in San Francisco became a matter of open communication and moral outrage. Although the *Journal* has changed in form over the years, it has kept a focus on the needs of the people living in the Tenderloin.

Scott Hope died in 1997, and his astute social analysis is missed. But the *Journal* continues today, still offering reflections about the lives of people in the city, posting announcements regarding current events, and providing information about upcoming issues on the ballots in local and national elections. It continues to reflect the concerns and conditions of those who have little access to public voice, giving a place for their concerns to be heard in printed form. In this way, the *Journal* continues to provide a kind of "public record" for the conditions and concerns of those whose lives could otherwise go unnoticed and unrecognized.

Solidarity through Cultivating Memory

Memory is a powerful means to bring people together for solidarity and transformation. *The Network Journal* also provides space to highlight this important function for a community that is too often forced to forget its past as well as its dreams. On one occasion Scott Hope wrote, "Through metaphor and memory we discover reference points for commonality and unity...The memory's primary function...is to create a certain kind of continuum between the past and the present."[32] He reminded his readers that memory is like a metaphor through which we imagine the life of another and in turn we are understood: "Through metaphor, the past has the capacity to imagine us, and we it."[33]

Solidarity engages people in recovering their corporate memory of when life was different. The recovery of that "different vision of life" has the power to reimagine our current circumstances and us. This process of retrieval stimulates our very desires and our longings for an alternative to what we are experiencing now. It leads us to actively seek release from all forms of imposed suffering. The Network Ministries, through its worship services and opportunities for study, places the harsh and unjust circumstances of its participants within a Judeo-Christian history that remembers other times and places of oppression and celebrates release from suffering. The memory of release brings visions of possible worlds of care and justice.

Glenda Hope has commented on this powerful storehouse of memories to address the pain in the world: "If suffering is to be given meaning and transformed into power, connections must be forged with history and with other people and places and movements."[34] Her point is that these memories

---

[32]Scott Hope, *The Network Journal* (June 1989): 3.
[33]Ibid.
[34]Glenda Hope, *The Network Journal* (August 1989): 17–18.

should be mined and cultivated in our communities of faith. Our churches are or could be places of public memory, especially because "their task is to struggle against public amnesia."[35] One way that the Network has acted to combat public forgetting and apathy is through its attempt to bring to public awareness the grief that people experience that might otherwise be ignored or forgotten.

Solidarity through Sharing Grief

Grief has long been understood within the province of pastoral care and theology. However, grief has seldom been associated with the processing of public pain. Grief is private, lonely, an individual's pain. Grief is internal and is felt in the pit of one's stomach, the tightness of one's chest, the pounding in one's ears, and the scream welling up from one's throat. But grief is more than this. Its tentacles intertwine the very fabric of our lives together. Grief has a public face as well as a private ache. The Network Ministries recognizes this link between private grief and public pain and provides expression for this human experience.

Every Advent Season, the Network Ministries holds a memorial service on the streets of San Francisco, commemorating those places where the homeless have died during the year. The deaths of these people are seldom noted, and they are frequently ignored. But during the season of Advent something different happens. The homeless community gathers along with other local residents, business folks, and shop owners as they move from place to place where people have died. It is a simple service. Songs are sung. Scriptures are read from the different faith traditions: Judaism, Christianity, Islam, and Buddhism. And at each place where someone has died, his or her name is read out loud by one of the participants in the memorial service. Each person's name is read separately at each place where a man, woman, or child has died. It is not a group memorial. "Each name is read separately, because we die one by one."[36] This public act of remembering and mourning has become a powerful avenue for expressing the grief that a whole community experiences but does not always name.

This public act of mourning has helped make the relationship between personal suffering and the social conditions that cause it visible. It has helped make the social order of suffering clear, because it places those who are most affected by it in front of those who may prefer not to see them. The members of the homeless community and the housed and salaried come to recognize and even know one another. In a small way this annual service provides a way for different people from different places in life to recognize their human ties. It offers a time and a place for people to acknowledge the ways they have shared common space. And perhaps not so surprisingly,

---

[35]Glenda Hope, *The Network Journal* (June 7, 1976): 3.
[36]Glenda Hope, conversation.

this public memorial service that recognizes a community's shared grief leads to new social awareness, *conscientizacao*. It is a motivating force for joining in actions of solidarity with those who are suffering. This has led to further actions of solidarity within the Tenderloin community.

Every year at the close of the memorial service the people from all the different communities march together to City Hall, where they present petitions asking for legal and political responses to the plight of those whose lives are at stake on the streets of the city. Sometimes those who help organize the memorial service are asked why they have them at all: "Wouldn't it just make more sense to gather and march for better conditions and changes in city policy regarding the homeless situation?" Glenda Hope's response is always "No! First we grieve and then we march." The energy and motivation that gets released through the public memorial service fuels public action. Grief publicly expressed initiates that action. The public expression of grief becomes the occasion for disturbing the old order so that something new can break in.

At the moment when City Hall and city streets meet and begin to recognize each other, brokenness and compassion start to come together in a powerful way. To be moved is to see the structure of the cross in the order of suffering, which calls for the dismantling of unjust social structures. Grief expressed through the processing of public pain creates solidarity between members of a community, calling for alternative worlds of care and meaning.

In addition to the memorial service for the homeless who die on the streets, the Network Ministries is also asked to conduct more traditional funeral services for other poor people who live in the Tenderloin district. Glenda Hope says, "And in part those services are a crying out against muteness. Over the last couple of years we have conducted more than 30 services. Not one of those people who died appeared in the obituary columns. Not one."[37]

The public ceremony and funeral services for the poor who lived and died on the streets of San Francisco are ways of recognizing those who could have remained silent "nameless ones." Through these community rituals they are once again included within the face-to-face community. And perhaps even in a small way solidarity between the living and the dead is created through these rituals of memory.

Solidarity with People Living with HIV and AIDS

Solidarity has taken on additional meaning in San Francisco's Tenderloin district, which has attracted many people living with AIDS. But it is not only the Network staff who offer care; community members

---

[37]Glenda Hope, *The Network Journal* (February 1990): 18–19.

have also been moved to become involved. For example, there was a man dying of AIDS who moved into a Tenderloin hotel and was befriended by a woman who also lived there:

> His greatest fear was that he'd die alone. She took this man into her room, gave him her bed, slept on the floor, organized a 24-hour vigil so there'd always be someone there. He died there, in that room, "with sight of a loving face," as Mother Theresa likes to say. It was right out of Matthew 25–"I was a stranger and you took me in." How many people do you know who would do that?[38]

Since the early 1980s the Network has been developing a special ministry with these people who have often been rejected and isolated. By 1990 it established the Tenderloin AIDS Network, a coalition working for a coordinated, comprehensive approach to AIDS education and prevention. They raised funds for a "needs assessment" in the Tenderloin and monitored its progress. Then, because they received no support from city agencies, they held a press conference on the steps of the Public Health Department, pointing to the report's data-based conclusions that the Tenderloin community was severely under-served by public and private agencies. Since that time the Network has worked with City Hall to raise money to establish a Tenderloin AIDS Resource Center, where they offer support to people who are ill with the AIDS virus and their relatives and friends. Here, the compassionate personal care and political action for community response became clearly joined once again.

Living into the vision of a new reality does at some point involve sacrifice. It is part of what it means to be in solidarity with others. In a word, one links his or her own suffering with that of others out of a profound recognition of our mutual dependency on one another. Through their own lifestyle of simple living and their willingness to "rendezvous" with people in the dark places of their lives, the staff and volunteers with the Network "identify" their lives with those they seek to serve and are willing to sacrifice to do so. Sacrifice can only be sustained through the vision of a new reality in which people are released from the powers and principalities that crush and wound. It is a sacrifice that reflects a political interpretation of the cross that holds the promise for something different and something good that transcends the current harsh reality. A community is willing to sacrifice because it trusts the new reality *hidden* in the midst of the unjust life circumstances. This reflects Luther's *theologia crucis,* the hiddenness of God in what appears most opposed to God. Discerning what is hidden, yet not irretrievably lost, is central to what is involved in guiding as empowerment.

---

[38]Dexter Waugh, "Hope in the Tenderloin," *San Francisco Examiner,* 1 April 1990, Image section, 12–13.

Guiding: The Empowering of People

A political perspective of the cross sees guiding as empowering. This involves releasing the power of speech so that "mute" people who have been silenced by the crushing events in their lives can find their voices. This involves liberating the memory of a people and, through the power of imagination, discovering visions of other possibilities. As stated earlier, the process of empowerment is an expression of the "power of conversion," the transformation of lament to protest, which culminates in doxology. This empowerment process lies at the heart of addressing historical suffering.

As an alternative to guiding as a function that leads someone to identify with something already inside themselves in order to gain personal insight, empowerment as it is practiced by the San Francisco Network Ministries extends outward, so that a person can gain a clearer sense of his or her social reality. Because "rendezvous" occurs in dark places with marginalized people, self-knowledge has much to do with learning what one's life situation really means. When Network participants attempt to "throw some light against the darkness," this is not an expression of faith in human potential and progress. It reflects instead the yearning and the commitment of the cross bearers who accept harsh reality in all its complexity in order to transform it, or as John Douglas Hall has said, "to lighten our darkness." The relationship that developed between Reverend Hope and the woman who called out to her "You must have some word for me!" can serve to illustrate guiding as empowerment. We will call this woman "Mary."

The "Speaking" of Mary

Following Mary's initial outburst, she gradually began to exercise her voice in new ways. Beginning with her very first utterances, the transformation of Mary and the community that came to know her began to occur. This is how it happened.

It became obvious to those who saw her walking on the streets that Mary was "crazy." One Sunday she was out on the street corner cursing all four corners of the world, her face set in the concrete ache of anger and aging. Reverend Glenda Hope saw her and invited her into one of the Network "house churches" that meets in the lobby of the Cadillac Hotel. As Mary walked through the doors of that makeshift church, she was still railing and hurling her words to everyone and to no one in particular. She entered the room and took a chair, along with a dozen or so others, around a small table that had nothing on it but a single candle and a stole that was passed from person to person as each reflected on something during the course of the service. She was still restless, trying to find the right position in her chair, when the worship leader said, "Shall we pray?" At that moment Mary became quiet and attentive.

As the service progressed, Mary remained still and alert. When those around the circle were invited to reflect on the meaning of the scriptures for their own lives, Mary was still quiet. When at last she did say something, she spoke to the point and demonstrated a real knowledge of the Bible. She talked without using profanity. More importantly, she made sense. When she had said what she wanted to say, she stopped. No one had ever heard Mary speak in that way before. She appeared to have entered into the service as though easing into something familiar and safe. For a closing she led everyone in a simple but powerful prayer.

Now when Mary left that small service of worship, she resumed her diatribe against the world as soon as she hit the street corner again. But the next week, and the week after that, each time she entered the worship space the same transformation would occur. Mary would "come to herself" as she "came home to her God" in the midst of her newfound friends.

When Mary came into the house church, she began to find a new way to speak. Interpreting the scripture for her life and saying so in her own words started something new for her, and this new way of knowing did not end with the close of the worship service or even with her familiar forays back to the corner of Market and Ellis streets. Over time, a short time really, her words began to take a stronger form and became a means for communicating that eventually moved into new behavior. This is an example of empowering speech, where previously her voice had been silenced.

The hearing of Mary into speech has elements that are different from the clinical approach to pastoral guiding. Whereas the compassionate caregiver of the clinical paradigm might invite Mary for a conversation and utter supportive responses that her feelings are valid, that same pastoral caregiver very possibly would be scanning theories that explain strange or extreme behavior in terms of diagnostic categories. The clinically oriented caregiver might try to guide Mary to draw on her inner resources and encourage her to explore what options are hers so that she can make choices and assume responsibility for herself and her situation. Although these are widely practiced pastoral responses and appropriate in many circumstances, they will have difficulty touching Mary at her deepest need. Why is this the case? There is no one answer, but there are clues as to why some of our pastoral theories and responses are inadequate in situations like the one involving Mary.

One limitation has been called the YAVIS syndrome.[39] This means that those most amenable to our practices are (Y) young, (A) attractive, (V) verbal, (I) intelligent, (S) sophisticated, and by implication, financially able. These qualities are usually attributed to those who already have some knowledge and means to make use of the language and symbols of the dominant cultural system, which reflects mainly white, middle-class values.

---

[39]Derald W. Sue, *Counseling the Culturally Different* (New York: John Wiley & Sons, 1981), 28.

This means having the ability to use the language of popular psychology to talk about things such as "self-fulfillment," struggles with "self-esteem," and other related matters. Mary fails all of these "tests." The criteria of being young, attractive, verbal, and sophisticated doesn't fit her.

A pastoral approach that relies heavily on a clinical model and psychological categories will have difficulty hearing and responding to the cry of Mary and understanding the social and historical circumstances of her suffering. It fails to take into account the effects of poverty, violence, and abuse, which can make one old before her time, silent before unsparing suffering, and ill-equipped to argue her case. There are no clinical diagnostic categories that include the debilitating effects of poverty and homelessness. Through clinical standards alone Mary is rendered both speechless and homeless, outside the dominant systems of care. Mary's cry, "You must have some word for me!" shouts what displacement means not only in our cities and neighborhoods but also in many of our own theories and practices of care.

Primary methods of pastoral theology seek to correlate the insights of theology with insights of the social sciences, particularly psychology. But the ability to meet Mary goes beyond the capacity to employ methods of correlation, including critical correlation, as important as these are. What is urgently needed is the willingness to make a commitment. Commitment here means to make an "option for the poor," as liberation theologians say; "to put ourselves on the side of the damned," as feminist political theologian Dorothee Soelle says;[40] to stand with "those whose backs are against the wall," as the mystic African American theologian Howard Thurman claims.[41] Mary does fit these descriptions.

The caregiver who is able to respond to Mary will need to rethink what is needed for her situation. He or she will need to draw from theories and theologies that go beyond explaining strange or extreme behavior in terms of the familiar clinical diagnostic categories. Mary's voice alerts us to the need to find new ways of grounding our pastoral practice of guiding in order to empower those who are displaced and dispirited to find their voices once more.

The Speaking of Many Voices

When Mary came into the church and found her voice, no one attempted to translate the language of faith she spoke in worship into any other form in order to understand her. Instead, her voice was translated into communal action. In the weeks that followed Mary's first worship service in the Cadillac Hotel, she and the others who gathered there joined

---

[40]Soelle, *Choosing Life* (Philadelphia: Fortress Press, 1981), 53.
[41]Howard Thurman, *Jesus and the Disinherited* (Richmond, Ind.: Friends United Press, 1981), 13.

with the Network staff to collect signatures to petition the city to make their lives on the streets more bearable. When they had enough, they marched as a group to present their petitions to the mayor of San Francisco. To their surprise they were received, and in a short time their efforts resulted in new public facilities as well as new services. This action in which Mary participated grew out of her new ability to interpret her life and speak about it. She formed communication bonds with others who shared her plight, and out of their collective experience in that small worship space they began to act together. Mary's suffering finally found a public voice that took the form of political action in the wider community. The group moved beyond therapeutic forms of conversation as they began to act the language of passionate suffering through protest and advocacy.

The gathered community of faith was the context for Mary and her friends to experience the care that made it possible for them to begin once more. Through the exploration of scripture, Mary and the others found that their lives were connected to an extended community of faith over time, one that had known and experienced deliverance from unjust suffering. Their "dangerous memory" was evoked and helped stimulate their imaginations, leading them to an emerging awareness of their own place in history. Through the power of ritual, language, and shared images, they began to experience the raising of their political consciousness, and they acted on it.

Guiding as a shared practice of the gathered community empowered them to act for change. They discovered that through cooperative action they could begin to create new ways to forge alternative worlds of care and justice. In this way they became agents of change and subjects of a new way of living. The practice of guiding as empowerment has become one of the strongest aspects of the Network Ministries as it seeks to reconcile people through works of social justice.

Reconciling the Broken

In an earlier chapter, we noted that Clebsch and Jaekle argued as early as 1964 that the pastoral function of reconciliation needs to be restored to modern-day practices of care and given a central place. Reconciliation is clearly a central focus for the San Francisco Network, and its practice is evident in every aspect of its ministry. The historical aim of reconciliation, the reestablishment of broken relationships between members of a community and the community's relationship with God, reinforces the view that care and justice cannot be separated.

Kosuke Koyama's notion of "inner persuasion" is helpful for understanding the process of reconciliation as practiced by the Network participants. Inner persuasion is born of the joining of passion and compassion. This joining is found at the heart of reconciliation and is an expression of a political interpretation of the cross. Koyama makes this connection when he speaks about the inner persuasion of the "broken Christ" who reconciles and heals. When the San Francisco Network Ministries holds its public memorial services for those who die on the street, it is this "inner persuasion" that gets tapped by the heart-breaking truths revealed during the ceremony. Inner persuasion moves people, and change is initiated through its power. In fact, the inner persuasion that is evoked by the public processing of pain helps create the motivation for change. Reverend Hope has commented, "Suffering is not simply internal; pain is the fuel for action."[42] Where pain is a "fuel for action," impotent suffering is becoming passionate suffering. Soelle calls this "phase three" in the transformation of suffering. This is where people join together in solidarity and organize for liberation. It is a process of sustained hard work toward transforming and overcoming historically imposed suffering.[43]

During the yearly public memorial services a recovering of community begins to happen when people are open to being transformed by the sorrow that becomes expressed through public grief. This opening up and becoming willing to be transformed is a new way of knowing in which we receive the reality of another into our hearts. We have called this inner persuasion, the birth of compassion at the center of any reconciling gesture. The heart of this way of knowing is a kind of compassion that means involvement, not management; believing, not telling; sacrifice, not safety. This way of knowing leads to an understanding of reconciliation that accents the grassroots nature of political involvement, providing the linkage between pastoral care and social ethics. It becomes a practice of pastoral care informed by the cross, exemplified when the San Francisco Network stays with the people in the Tenderloin as they struggle to regain their lives and does not "manage" their progress or their failures.

It is important to note here that the compassion that becomes kindled through the face-to-face process of learning people's lives is a compassion that takes public form. Inner persuasion becomes public advocacy, not a private feeling. In this way it breaks the silent conspiracy of what can appear as "civilized" injustice, which makes its victims invisible, which is what happens when compassion is limited to a private or personal virtue. Public compassion means that the cries of the street become heard in City Hall. The message of reconciliation formed by compassion is released by a grief that is expressed publicly. It becomes an expression of hope revealed by the way of the cross, as Reverend Glenda Hope expresses it: "The message of the cross is to grieve and not be paralyzed by it."[44]

The Network Ministries has been very successful in starting a movement toward reconciliation between people living in poverty in the Tenderloin

---

[42]Glenda Hope, conversation.
[43]Dorothee Soelle, *Suffering* (Philadelphia: Fortress Press, 1975), 72–73.
[44]Glenda Hope, conversation.

and other residents and shop owners in the area. They have even been successful in gaining a response from City Hall. But they have been less effective in impacting the mainline churches through their ministries with the marginalized in the city. Mainline churches are hard to reach. On this issue, a "safe" distance remains between established religious organizations and the emerging urban faith communities.

Clebsch and Jaekle called pastors to reclaim reconciliation while they also talked about the neglected arts of healing. Although they did not explicitly link reconciliation with the work of social justice, they did see reconciliation as closely related to healing.[45] A political reading of the cross claims that the work of justice and the hope for healing are inseparable. One does not occur apart from the other. Healing depends on reconciliation. Reconciliation is a precondition for healing. And there is no such thing as true reconciliation without justice.

Healing as Signs of a Future Wholeness

A political interpretation of the cross is about the inseparability of love and justice; in fact, it is about "love in pursuit of justice."[46] This inseparability of love and justice defines wholeness. Wholeness is a sign of the coming of healing, when all relationships will be mutual, respectful, and just. Wholeness begins to take shape when long-time community members and newly created street people find something in common. Healing becomes a gift to people who strive for justice here on Earth and trust that love is possible even in an unjust world. Or as Glenda Hope says:

> Perhaps God would be in heaven if all were right with the world, but we know it isn't. God is not in heaven (wherever that is). S/he is in the midst of the world wherever people are struggling for human dignity and freedom, wherever that collective consciousness is forming. Where Christ is taking form in a band of persons in the midst of the world, there is where loneliness is coped with and joy (joy does not mean the absence of pain but the presence of God) surprises us.[47]

Joy is what we experience when genuine healing occurs. This healing that occasions joy has always been associated with the holy. Healing is a holy sign of hope, a promise; fundamentally, it is a gift. Always associated with the in-breaking realm of God, signs of healing signify that the landscape of justice is not just a mirage or simply wishful thinking.

---

[45]William A. Clebsch and Charles R. Jaekle, *Pastoral Care in Historical Perspective* (Englewood Cliffs, N.J.: Prentice Hall, 1964), 81.

[46]Rasmussen, "Clues from Dietrich Bonhoeffer," 36. Rasmussen is talking about an unfinished aspect of the Reformation, societal reform.

[47]Glenda Hope, *The Network Journal* (September 1976): 4.

The movement from muteness to lament-as-protest is a movement within suffering toward healing. Glenda Hope reminds us that the direction of this movement is critical: "It is *toward* healing and restoration. But they have not happened yet, and will not, until all wounds end."[48]

Complete wholeness, or total healing, is still a future-leaning concept, for we know too well that all is not right with people or with the world. The paradox of healing is that wholeness is glimpsed, even if only here and there and only occasionally, where people become empowered and reconciliation begins to takes place. Such signs are occasions for joy and provide specific and historical locations for hope.

We are told that Jesus came to offer people wholeness, to proclaim and to set in motion the process of healing for the whole people of God. His acts of healing were public works, within the hearing and presence of other people. Here is where the vision of wholeness began to arise. These acts were the creative activity of the word of God mobilizing the process of healing in a broken world. As such, they compel us to take seriously the prophetic role of pastoral care as it is practiced within the community of faith, where we are called to take stock of what is wrong and why. We can call this an emancipatory practice that requires us to repent and make amends through active involvement with God and one another in moving people toward wholeness:

> To this extent, we want to be healed, prophetic religion [pastoral care] plunges us into the life of the world where God is—knowing the poor and weak, confronting the rich and powerful, and by God's grace loving them all, as God does, willing to invest whatever of self and time love requires for our *corporate healing.*[49]

Such emancipatory pastoral practice takes place where the Christian community of faith goes the way of the cross. Its members sacrifice together as they bear witness to the suffering in their midst. Then, in solidarity with others, they work to repair injustice—and begin to miraculously experience healing.

The Paradox of Healing and Wounds

The wounds of suffering have been a powerful image in the biblical tradition. They are recalled in our liturgy and hymns: "O sacred Head, now wounded, with grief and shame weighed down; now scornfully surrounded with thorns, thine only crown."[50] Yet the wounds in the biblical tradition have also been strangely and inseparably tied to the notions of

---

[48]Glenda Hope, *The Network Journal* (February 1990): 20.
[49]Glenda Hope, *The Network Journal* (November 1984): 17.
[50]Words attributed to Bernard of Clairvaux (12th century), "O Sacred Head, Now Wounded," *Chalice Hymnal* (St. Louis: Chalice Press, 1995), #202.

hope and of healing, even the wound that pierced the heart of the one named Jesus, whom we call Christ. There is something about the authority of suffering that signifies entering the depths and finding hope again. On a subtle and profound level the expression of wounds reveals where the barrier between the world and us breaks down. There is where we become truly vulnerable. And where this barrier between us breaks down, there, too, is the possibility for healing.

The liturgy of the Lord's supper involves us in a profoundly meaningful event in which barriers become lowered and sometimes removed. When we recall "This is my body broken for you," it suggests to us that all human wounds can be brought to this particular wound in order to be healed. The very breaking of the bread symbolizes that holy space held open for healing. It prepares a place where we can meet each other in new ways. It offers the possibility of recognizing one another in the embrace of the holy God. When bread is broken, it opens that space where brokenness and compassion come together. This is where brokenness becomes blessed. This is holy space held open to us for healing. As Glenda Hope writes:

> Communion both heals and keeps the wound open. It keeps the wound open even as it heals. On the night he was betrayed...Jesus gave thanks. This is my body broken for you, my blood poured out for you...for the forgiveness of sins and as a sign of a new covenant of hope. At this table we confess the sources of our wounding and name the source of our hope.[51]

The healing effect of someone's wound on "my" wound is a phenomenon with which we do not really know how to deal. But we experience that our own ability to hope can be awakened when we meet someone who has come through woundedness and has been opened to healing. The Network Ministries attests to this hope that emerges among people who publicly express their pain and act on it. When people tell the truth about their lives, and their suffering finds a "reliable witness" in people of faith, holiness and brokenness do come together and become "blessed" as a true expression of the heart of the sacrament.

The community of faith that bears witness through suffering and resistance becomes "the outward and visible sign of an inward and spiritual grace." This is not sacramentalism, nor is it an escape into "another world." This is a feet-on-the-ground—"holy ground"—spirituality, a spirituality committed to another world that is a true alternative within history. Again, Reverend Glenda Hope notes: "God's healing does not leave us blissed out; rather, the giving of work to do is an essential part of that healing."[52]

---

[51]Glenda Hope, *The Network Journal* (November 1984): 20.
[52]Ibid.

The rigors of God's healing involves seeing our own brokenness more clearly than ever before and, nevertheless, feeling impelled to speak about what wholeness is, even while we know we are not yet there. Recognizing how far we are from being in union with God and all creation is part of the dailiness of the cross. And bearing those incongruities in our own selves and our life together is a communal self-definition.[53]

---

[53]Glenda Hope, *The Network Journal* (April 1985): 28–29.

CHAPTER
TEN

Broken yet Beloved
The Way of the Cross

If you remove the yoke from among you,
the pointing of the finger, the speaking of evil,
if you offer your food to the hungry
and satisfy the needs of the afflicted,
then your light shall rise in the darkness
and your gloom be like the noonday.

ISAIAH 58:9B–10

The San Francisco Network Ministries provides an alternative model of care to that of the shepherding perspective. It offers one example of how a community of faith can respond to the historical injuries of people through living out the vocation of the Suffering Righteous One. This alternative metaphor draws on the skills of active listening but does not focus on them extensively, nor does it rely on the clinical diagnostic paradigm. Instead, Mary, from the previous chapter, was "heard" within a theological framework of meaning when a small community received her into its midst and the members listened together to the familiar, yet always new, words of faith. Listening is still central, but understood differently. While the "tender and solicitous care" of the Good Shepherd is evident, the community of the Righteous One exercises this care in ways that reflect a political interpretation of the cross.

The practice of pastoral care by a community living the vocation of the Suffering Righteous One takes on six dimensions. Each is evident in the approach to pastoral care practiced by the San Francisco Network Ministries in some of the examples cited. These six dimensions are really theological practices rather than pastoral skills. Skills are usually learned and exercised by an individual. Practices do not refer to someone doing something. Rather, they are something that people are doing together over time.[1] Practices are something that people participate in. They are theological in that they lead all parties into a critically engaged response from a faith perspective to a particular situation requiring change. Taken together, practices can offer a framework for pastoral theology and an approach for pastoral care to engage the need for healing in our broken communities. These practices include listening, believing, beholding, advocacy, restoration, and interpretation. They are expressions of Solidarity, Empowerment, and Reconciliation toward just and humane communities.

Communal Practices of Care: Listening

Listening is central for pastoral theology. Normally it is seen as the empathetic posture of an individual caregiver toward someone seeking counsel. For the most part, it involves listening for feelings in order to gain insight into the personal circumstances of the one in need. It assumes that insight is a trustworthy source, sufficient for understanding the nature of whatever is causing the problem that brought the client to seek help in the first place. Many pastoral practitioners believe that empathetic listening is capable of eliciting the kind of wisdom that can eventually lead to healing. And there are recipients of this style of listening that confirm its worth. Yet although this method of listening has proven effective for many people, it is limiting for others, as in the case of Mary from the previous chapter. She required more; she needed a community of solidarity in order to speak and to discern the possibility of new directions in her life with others.

Although empathetic listening can be valuable, it can fool us into thinking that we understand more than we actually do. From the perspective of the political cross, listening means we need to recognize that there are many things that we do not know and perhaps can never know. In fact, it is precisely our "not knowing," our "not understanding," that leads us to an honest way of encountering others. Anthropologist Ruth Behar, speaking within the context of cultural differences, says that the best we can do when we are faced with what we cannot know is to attempt a "translation," not a false understanding.[2] Without this humble posture, understanding risks becoming presumptuous, or worse imperialistic, but in any event, dangerous. Therefore, listening needs to take a different form.

---

[1]Craig Dykstra, "Reconceiving Practice," unpublished paper, 11.

[2]Ruth Behar, *Translated Woman: Crossing the Border with Esperanza's Story* (Boston: Beacon Press, 1993), 297–302.

Listening from the perspective of the political cross means first of all listening with absolute respect. This may seem obvious, but in practice it is not always easy. Listening with absolute respect does not stop with acceptance. Absolute respect is more than the Rogerian notion of unconditional positive regard. Absolute respect is proactive and involves the willingness to make a commitment to the deep humanness of others. Here is where listening participates in covenant making that is prior to all contracts of care.

Listening from the posture of a political reading of the cross also means listening with a special kind of silence. Reverend Glenda Hope talks about the "life-stance of thankfulness" that waits for God's guidance in silence.[3] We could call this contemplative listening. It is a disciplined kind of listening in which we attempt to discard any of our preconceived notions, theories, and hunches about someone and their experiences. It begins in a silence that invites someone like Mary to express herself on her own terms. It means privileging and listening for her frame of reference. It involves listening even when we cannot empathize or understand her. This is why listening must be grounded in absolute and unequivocal respect. Listening to someone in this way means, in addition to empathy, to listen with an open imagination.

Imagination is more helpful here than empathy, because empathy still supposes the possibility of understanding the other, which may not be the case. Imagination draws on different sources of wisdom that do not necessarily entail understanding. It opens us to new possibilities not contained by given conventions or common definitions of how our world operates. It is what becomes released through "inner persuasion" when we allow ourselves to be unguardedly grasped by the reality of another. This is what solidarity is about. Imagination clothed in solidarity is part of the compassion that involves a theological commitment, which dares to entertain alternative social realities within the concrete pastoral situation.

Listening with imagination means bracketing empathy with a "hermeneutic of suspicion" and becoming willing to co-imagine a future of restored dignity, freedom, and hope–one in which we are not the chief architects. In this way listening with imagination involves a kind of listening that is not just listening, but *just* listening–a listening that participates in justice.[4] This involves the theological vision of a restored realm of God. It means listening to the experience of someone like Mary and refusing to stand above or behind her–standing alongside her instead as an expression

---

[3]Glenda Hope, *The Network Journal* (November 1981): 4.

[4]*Just* listening is a term that Nancy Eiesland used when she was delivering the Earl Lectures at Pacific School of Religion, 1999. She used it to signal that listening is not just a neutral activity. Listening itself can be a practice that fosters justice, or it may not.

of radical mutuality. It finally means something akin to being willing to look into each other's eyes and urge each other on to new beginnings.[5]

This first movement of listening with imagination is critical for responding to someone, like Mary, who is suffering from social and historical injuries. It is crucial for change in ourselves as well. It involves hearing the larger cultural and social context, because whatever it is that one person or group is suffering is symptomatic of the disease of estrangement that affects each one of us. We are ever so much more connected to one another in ways more fundamental than we usually acknowledge. Yet to listen with imagination offers a way to counter life-denying forces. As Maxine Greene suggests, "Imagining things being otherwise may be a first step toward acting on the belief that they can be changed."[6] This is a faith stance that claims that historical suffering need not remain the defining characteristic of life. Imagination, then, helps create space for a shift to occur that may foster levels of connection between listener and hearer in unpredictable ways, offering new possibilities for both. Listening means to respect people completely, and to believe them. Believing involves another practice that takes seriously people who are suffering.

Communal Practices of Care: Believing

Believing is not an entirely separate practice, because it involves a deepening of what it means to really listen. However, believing does not mean that we are naive. When Reverend Glenda Hope "believed" Mary, she did not simply render herself gullible; but she did believe that Mary's plea to her was authentic. When Mary cried out, "You must have some word for me!" Glenda didn't fully understand what this meant, but she was willing to enter into a relationship with Mary. Believing is an unguarded theological overture. It is a receptive attitude that is necessary for the kind of struggle that it takes to enter into the framework of those before you in a way that takes their cry of pain seriously, even if you don't understand them. It builds on the ability to trust the wisdom of the imagination—your own and the other's. Perhaps this is a variation of "faith seeking understanding" and can be further interpreted as "faith seeking expression." This shifts the accent away from insight, from "seeing is believing" to "believing is seeing." To believe is to make a commitment, to become deeply involved. This is the form that faith seeking expression takes, and it is where covenant becomes deepened as people begin to enter a relationship of trust.

But to listen in this manner and really believe is a risky business. It is where the safety nets of given theories and agreed-on pastoral strategies

---

[5]Maxine Greene, *Releasing the Imagination: Essays on Education, the Arts, and Social Change* (San Francisco: Jossey-Bass, 1995), 43.
[6]Ibid., 22.

are suspended. You could be fooled. You could fail. You could fall. In any event you will be changed! Scott Hope talked about the risky business of "believing":

> I've had four people, in whom I've placed most of my hope, come crashing down in the last few days. The four had been homeless at one time, had gotten their lives together, found jobs. Suddenly, they all "lost it," and now all four were either in jail or institutionalized. I know a number of people have written off one of the guys. My standpoint is, "No, you can't do that."[7]

"Foolishly," Professor Hope believed that redemption is always possible. This made a difference to those he met. It certainly proved the case for Glenda Hope. A woman who had known her some ten years earlier drove eighteen hours roundtrip to participate in a conference she was leading in order to tell her, "You were the first people who ever believed in me–ever thought I was somebody. Everything has been different since."[8]

Perhaps "believing" in this manner is a bit like trying to become a trapeze artist. As you let go of the familiar bar that you cling to for your life, you fly at first unaided, suspended in midair, and you wait, trusting that you will be caught and not plunge to your death. To put yourself out there and believe someone, not believe in the abstract but believe another flesh-and-blood human being without reservation, means that you are far less than the expert by yourself. Because of this you will need the arms of a community of listeners to "catch you," because they have a claim on you and you on them. No person alone can discern the contours of a new horizon. And you will need the arms of those you are in solidarity with, because these tellers of tales hold the keys to new knowledge and new visions of restored community.[9] Believing in such a committed way holds the promise of fostering more just relationships necessary for new ways of reading the world. It does so precisely because it risks our own ways of knowing and living as well. Here we begin to see the deepening implications of close and interdependent relationships with people who provide new sources of knowledge necessary for forging new forms of community life that can inform pastoral theology. Here we will find security removed from

---

[7]Scott Hope, *San Francisco Examiner,* 1 April 1990, Image section, 14.

[8]Glenda Hope, *The Network Journal* (June 1984): 7.

[9]Marjorie Bard, *Shadow Women: Homeless Women's Survival Stories* (Kansas City: Sheed and Ward, 1990), xii. Bard uses the personal narratives of homeless women to record the oral history of how they became homeless and what solutions they discovered for their situation. She notes that as they describe their process of becoming marginal members of society, they also offer solutions that exist in the public and private sectors that may be unnoticed, not taken seriously, or misunderstood and mismanaged. In addition to Bard's argument, I am suggesting that listening to and believing the stories and the meanings they have for those who tell them becomes a theological practice.

our theories and practices as we become more vulnerable and at risk in every way, in every setting.

Communal Practices of Care: Beholding

When you listen and believe, in that moment of silent recognition of the one before you, you stand on holy ground. It is a kind of null moment when all professional trappings are stripped from your grasp and something new holds the possibility of coming into view. At such a moment you are entering into a third pastoral practice, which is the act of beholding the other before you.

To behold also reveals the need to be held. Like Glenda, who felt the misery in Mary's cry "rip right through her," your heart too will be broken, for we are not left untouched by what we behold. If I behold someone, some scene, or some situation, I do not just look and see what is in front of me. If I truly behold someone or something, I am moved, involved, touched, even to the point of becoming "heartsick" when it involves tragedy, suffering, or a great loss. I, too, will "feel it rip right through me!" Pastoral theology from the perspective of the cross reclaims this null moment as a part of our practice–to be moved, touched, involved to the point of being "heartsick," by what we behold.

The act of beholding participates in the sacramental aspect of pastoral care in which something so ordinary becomes holy and transformative. It suggests the giving and receiving of the bread that is broken in the offering of new life. When the bread is broken, it makes an open and holy space into which we enter and take part. It is that place where we come to God and where God can come to us; a space where we can come to each other and learn about who we really are. Then, like Mary's experience in the Cadillac Hotel worship service, we, too, will learn to speak our lives and offer prayers. In the moment of sacramental renewal we behold one another and God while we are beheld by one another and our God. This is an expression of radical mutuality that illumines what it means to be in relationship in the first place. At this moment we glimpse a vision of what our healed world might look like. Where the holy space is created, conversation takes on deeper meaning, and new understanding is called forth as hope for restoration is kindled.

The act of beholding is the theological as well as the pastoral place of holy silence. It offers the beginning place, which is the givenness of the other with whom I am related. It is this givenness that precedes any description or explanation. It is the poetry that comes before prose. Perhaps Howard Thurman says it best when he talks about the woman brought before Jesus who was caught in the act of adultery:

> Jesus raised his eyes and beheld the woman. He met the woman where she was, and treated her as if she were already where she

now willed to be. In dealing with her he "believed" her into the fulfillment of her possibilities. He stirred her confidence into activity.[10]

To behold someone is about having absolute respect for another living being and not about forsaking appropriate boundaries. Boundaries are important, because they help us recognize our differences. However, to behold someone means to recognize that in our difference is our inescapable relatedness. Dorothee Soelle talks about this kind of attentiveness as something that can restrain our prejudices, expectations, and preconceived notions so that we can become clear to what another person is expressing.[11] To behold is really to practice love.

> Love is the active permeating and penetrating of another person whereby the desire for knowledge is satisfied by union...In union I know you, I know myself, I know everyone—and I "know" nothing...The only thing that leads us to complete understanding is an act of love that goes beyond thought and words.[12]

To behold honors the complete subjectivity of people. From this holy center new speech becomes possible for re-creating our lives.

Communal Practices of Care: Advocacy

Advocacy is about honoring the voices of people like Mary in their diffuse protests as well as their strong communications of resistance to urban tyranny. It is about joining with them in their own self-determined restorative behavior. This involves our personal commitment, communal identification, and public action to transform the circumstances that impact the lives of people who are suffering and our own lives. Advocacy stays close to the original context of the people who are speaking out. If we are asked for a word, like Mary who called, "You must have some word for me!" the "word" that is required is not an explanation, not even an answer, but a call to co-resist life-denying forces. Resistance honors the speech of those who cry out by accompanying them and not abandoning them in their new words and actions. Advocacy, then, aims to cooperate with people who suffer historical injuries. Advocacy seeks to restore the lives of suffering people by engaging their crises of survival and well-being with them and linking them to systems of power and public policy. Pastoral involvement in public life helps break forms of silence that have been galvanized by false beliefs

---

[10]Howard Thurman, *Jesus and the Disinherited* (Richmond, Ind.: Friends United Press, 1981), 105–6.

[11]Dorothee Soelle, *The Strength of the Weak: Toward a Christian Feminist Identity* (Philadelphia: Westminster Press, 1984), 34.

[12]Ibid., 178.

in "neutrality" that comply with injustice. Advocacy finally means that people who are suffering are not abandoned or left alone. It also means that pastoral theology is a political and communal practice through and through.

Pastoral advocacy is a form of solidarity that seeks to participate in what some theologians are calling "emancipatory praxis," a way of doing theology that takes seriously the reforming of our academic, communal, and political life together.[13] It reflects the theological implications of *just* listening. However, the term *emancipatory practice* is a more appropriate term for our purpose here, because it accents the role of faith communities committed to addressing cultural and structural issues that cause harm. These communities incarnate the *imago Dei* revealed in scripture as the God who advocates on behalf of those who suffer by sending the Suffering Righteous One.

Communal Practices of Care: Restoration

Advocacy aims at restoring lived expressions of justice and mutual respect. Restoration means that people like Mary who are suffering are heard, believed, and held and are no longer displaced outside the face-to-face community. In this sense restoration is a kind of "homecoming" that offers the possibility of reunion, the reestablishment of wholeness in community life. This vision of homecoming is totally contrary to displays of cynicism or official optimism that keep people who are suffering in our midst invisible. It is contrary to any sentimental notion of easy reunion. Restoration, like reconciliation, can only be approached through resistance to all forms of injustice, even those perpetuated through theories of care that distort human community by imposing unexamined and biased standards of "normalcy" that are harmful.

Restoration can be a pain-filled embrace borne by histories of misunderstanding, mistrust, and betrayals. Therefore, it can never be jettisoned or trivialized. At the same time, while restoration cannot be forced whole, it can be rehearsed in part, practiced in brave kinds of ways that offer glimpses to help keep hope for healing alive. Hope for restoration is woven deep into a people's longing for wholeness. Restoration can be understood as the theological implication of listening in which radical mutuality is risked for deep visions of healing. This theological reading of listening says something to us about what it means to be faithful in our calling to work together for the restoration of God's good creation. Only from this involved practice is it possible to begin a process of pastoral interpretation in which meaning can become an authentic representation of people's lives.

---

[13]Rebecca S. Chopp and Mark Lewis Taylor, *Reconstructing Christian Theology* (Minneapolis: Fortress Press, 1994), 21–22.

Communal Practices of Care: Interpretation

Perhaps through actions that oppose injustice, the pastoral theologian can earn the right to begin a process of interpretation with the people she or he relates with. I say "perhaps" because we cannot take this for granted. Interpretation is always confessional in nature, provisional in form, and a gift in fact. And it is always partial. It is also hazardous.

Even when a theological practice of interpretation seeks to be just and freeing, it involves a degree of representation that reduces the full expression of an event, and the people who are part of it, to something different from the original experience. The mere attempt at interpretation involves a measure of decontextualization, a diminishing of the subjects, and some change in meaning. This involves a level of violence toward those being represented through any interpretation.[14] Interpretation will never be innocent.

Furthermore, interpretation cannot be one-way. A style of interpretation that means one person interprets another (the diagnostic model) will not work for a pastoral theology from the perspective of the cross. The cross requires that theology and care become contextually engaged in projects of emancipation. Something more than one-directional interpretation is required. Ruth Behar describes this dilemma for anthropology:

> At this juncture in the politics of feminism, it is gratuitous to think that an ethnographer "gets" a less-privileged woman's "experience" by taking down her life story; and it is even more gratuitous to think that her work is done when she has framed the other woman's "own words" with a few comfortable generalizations that make no connections to her own position as the one who brings the story back across the border.[15]

To paraphrase her observations for pastoral theology from the perspective of the cross:

> At this juncture in the *politics of the cross,* it is gratuitous to think that *a pastoral theologian* "gets" *the experience of someone who is suffering historical injuries* by taking down *his or her* story; and it is even more gratuitous to think that *the pastoral theologian's* work is done *when the other person's story is* framed *in his or her* "own words" with a few attempts at generalizations... *What remains is to make stronger* connections to *our* own position*s* as those who bring the story back. (author's emphasis)

What is being suggested here is that we cannot stop with simply making a connection between another's suffering and the context of his or her

---

[14]Behar, *Translated Woman,* 271.
[15]Ibid., 272.

living, or even with our advocating with him or her to change the social structures that perpetuate alienation and harm. What remains is to make the connection to our own position as one who brings back the story. Through this kind of connection the pastoral theologian also becomes interpreted. Our own knowledge and position becomes revealed along the borders and in the shadows of our relationship with someone like Mary who is suffering. Through relationships of mutuality and solidarity with people who are suffering, a clearer understanding of who we are and what we are practicing begins to emerge. Radical mutuality through solidarity places "us" in a situation of being "other." If we take empowerment seriously, it begins at the point were "we" become "other." As a Chicana character in a story by Sandra Cisneros says, "Making the world look at you from my eyes. And if that's not power, what is?"[16]

Becoming seen through the eyes of those who are suffering might make us feel uncomfortable. As Behar learned through her own experience of mutual interpretation, we will come to an awareness of the "privilege" of our pens, how we have gained the authority to speak, conduct research, and write texts.[17] Yet just such an awareness of this privilege is critical so that we can come to a more complete knowledge of ourselves and the work we are called to be a part of. It is a knowledge that allows people like Mary to shake or radically alter the given canons of our field that keep some people invisible and others overly noticed. Here, interpretation reveals the painfully relational character of meaning.

Interpretation, then, is completely interdependent. Through solidarity we become vulnerable and mirrored through the eyes of one another. However, this makes pastoral theology paradoxical and a hopeful enterprise. Each of us confronts our inability to comprehend the experience of another, and yet we recognize the absolute necessity of continuing the effort to do so.[18]

Interpretation, then, not only includes the voices of people like Mary, but depends on them for our own self-understanding. Understanding ourselves through another's eyes helps all of us discover more fully what it means to address brokenness in our common life. And through our encounters that lead us to participate in projects of justice and reconciliation, our mutual "translation" becomes a means to reimagine and transform pastoral theology.

Interpretation from the perspective of the political cross works from the bottom up. It includes physical, bodily, historical, political action that

[16]Sandra Cisneros, "Never Marry a Mexican," in *Woman Hollering Creek* (New York: Random House, 1991), 75.

[17]Behar, *Translated Woman*, 338.

[18]Linda Brodkey, "Writing Critical Ethnographic Narratives," *Anthropology and Education* 18 (1987): 74.

leans into what might be called a "resurrection movement." The "dead ones" become "alive" and assume their rightful places. Mary found this in the small community that gathered to worship in a makeshift sanctuary in a run-down hotel. As Soelle says, "The only possible proof of Christ's resurrection and our own would be a changed world, a world a little closer to the kingdom of God."[19]

Communal Practices: The Way of the Cross

An alternative pastoral paradigm begins to emerge through the "thin tradition" of the cross. The six practices of pastoral care reflect a political interpretation of the cross that reframes the classical pastoral functions as solidarity, empowerment, and working for justice. They prepare an environment for receiving healing. Within this interpretation the myths of the reigning pastoral paradigm begin to shift as individual autonomy encounters models of interdependence. Here, self-realization becomes joined to projects of liberation, and personal insight broadens to historical consciousness. Diagnosis becomes tied to social analysis, and hyper-rationalism is tempered by the mystic's vision. Finally, functionalism gives way to a practice of suffering in which hope is vindicated through transformed and reconciled lives and communities. Through these processes, the suggested practices of care can be seen as explicating the three steps Soelle outlined for transforming passive and debilitating suffering into active and passionate suffering.

Soelle's first phase of suffering, the movement of inarticulate pain into an expression of grief and lament, involves listening, believing, and beholding in the way described here. Her second phase seeks to understand suffering within its social and historical context; this involves restoring people in community for the ongoing interpretation process as we have discussed it. Her third phase involves people joining together to oppose the forces that perpetuate unnecessary suffering, entailing the work of advocacy, which is really a part of every pastoral practice.

The six practices of listening, believing, beholding, advocating, restoring, and interpreting suggest ways that the three steps of suffering can be implemented. They are practices that can address the shattered myths of modernity that signal our days of loss and the eclipse of the holy that many are experiencing today. They are practices that can acknowledge a longing that sometimes goes unnamed yet still plagues us when the night becomes disturbingly still. These alternative ways of practicing pastoral care are reflected in the Network Ministries as people stop and turn to hear one another into speech, process pain and grief publicly, and act in solidarity with one another in order to create alternative worlds of care and meaning.

---

[19]Soelle, *Choosing Life* (Philadelphia: Fortress Press, 1981), 88.

A Pastoral Theology Broken Open by Tears

Where, then, does a pastoral theology begin that practices emancipatory care? Precisely with Mary, who cries out, "You must have some word for me!" As suggested from the beginning of this work, her cry makes historical suffering the necessary starting place of our theory and practice. This starting place means that everything we do originates with her cry and others like it.

At the same time, a pastoral theology that practices emancipatory care means that Mary's voice is not simply "added" to what we already know, or "included" in our theories and theologies in order to support what we think we know. However, this does not mean that the pastoral theologian's wisdom is ignored. On the contrary, it is brought into the foreground as a critical dimension of the relationship with "Mary." In this way the significant and critical intersection between all the subjects who figure in the situation is given recognition. This is important because it allows for all the questions, the unspoken longings and meanings embedded in every gesture, to participate in constructing pastoral theology through the shared commitment of all the participants. These usually "hidden" dimensions of pastoral practices then become ways that open us to see more than our own opinions, offering us the possibility of multiple ways of knowing our world and the people in it.

Through this alternative method of constructing pastoral theology we can learn to listen for what we do not know so that we can find ways to hear Mary and all the other "Marys" for their sakes and for our own. As we learn to know from another's point of view, it is hoped that we will not keep perpetuating theories and practices that unknowingly recreate harmful situations for people like Mary–or for ourselves with our own particular "impairments" such as privilege.

A pastoral theology broken open by the tears of compassion and remorse will occupy itself with how to recognize the various forces shaping the world and our communities and how we will win, defeat, or neutralize them. It will foster a deep desire for reconciliation and wholeness in the fabric of our lives. It will be dedicated to a vision of the full flourishing of all people. A pastoral theology broken open by tears will listen, believe, behold, and advocate for people to be restored to life. In this way it will participate in movements of resurrection, in which people are "being sent back into the life of the world with new exposure to its brokenness and a concern for its mending."[20] This brings us to the brokenness that faith wants to make whole and away from the false wholeness that faith wants to

---

[20]Douglas John Hall, "*Ecclesia Crucis:* The Disciple Community and the Future of the Church in North America" in *Theology and the Practice of Responsibility: Essays on Dietrich Bonhoeffer,* ed. Wayne Whitson Floyd, Jr., and Charles Marsh (Valley Forge, Pa.: Trinity Press International, 1994), 59–73.

break open.[21] This is the meaning of suffering for discipleship, the power of doxology in the work of love.

Broken and yet Beloved

It is a complex and stimulating time for pastoral care and theology. We are at a time of reckoning in which the ills and evils in our culture and our world need all the wisdom and resources that can be brought to bear. Individual suffering does have political meaning and is a symptom of our communal disease. Our neglect of this reality has in large measure contributed to the eclipse of the holy in our midst and a frantic pursuit of illusionary selves. A pastoral theology informed by the theology of the cross can honor this reality by reuniting the personal and political toward more authentic living. As the San Francisco Network Ministries demonstrates:

> The personal and the political are yin and yang of all pastoral work, calling for different risks and developing different gifts...Both must be carried on in the context of community in which each person is supported and held accountable. Both inevitably confront us with larger issues.[22]

A pastoral theology informed by a political theology of the cross begins at the crossroad where the personal and political meet. It informs our practices of care so we can embrace people who are experiencing the effects of dehumanizing forces in their lives. It offers us a way to cooperatively live out the way of the cross that starts with listening to people in a way that attends to the larger context in which we all live. This way of paying attention is more than an intense form of listening. It is an acute kind of hearing that evokes new speech that has never been spoken before. It invites speech that not only reflects the particular situation of someone but also refracts it in such a way that we can see and understand it in all of its depths. These depths, which often remain hidden, sound beneath and around us all. They announce the possibility for a renewed depth of life. They signal the way to the retrieval of the holy.

When Mary cries, "You must have some word for me!" she calls from the depths and echoes the cry "Why have you forsaken me?" from the cross of Jesus. She joins in a chorus of "Why have you forsaken me?" with others who suffer from unjust circumstances–who now turn to us for a response. When we hear her cry and believe her, we see her anguish and desolation as a symptom of her personal pain and the social and political "dis-ease" that affects each one of us. When we allow our hearts to be

---

[21]Gary Gunderson, *Deeply Woven Roots: Improving the Quality of Life in Your Community* (Minneapolis: Fortress Press, 1997), 123.

[22]*The Network Journal* (January 1990): 21.

broken open by this cry, we will find that her question and defiance have a place in our research and practices, because they arise in the context of our solidarity with her for a more just and humane place to live. Her cry will become our cry until there is no need to cry anymore. Pastoral theology originates in this pain and is oriented by a promise—the promise of a restored life.

The political cross offers a framework for pastoral practices that can address the task of reconciliation required in our world. It does so not primarily through providing skills of correlation, but through new arts of communal conversation. Instead of the synthesis between science and religion, it offers a language of promise and practices of involvement. It is important to recognize how the dominant culture restricts our language and our capacity for speech, and how we can counter this through alternative cooperative agendas that generate trust and build new communities of meaning. But new language and programs will not be sufficient if they are too laden with our own ways of thinking.

One of the reasons we know so little about the dreams and visions of people like Mary is because pastoral theology has been written largely from the perspective of the successful. We need to listen to those who stumble and stutter or merely groan as they seek an expression of the experience that is theirs. When we do, we will learn to understand the world quite differently from the way we ordinarily perceive it. We may even hear their strong criticism of the way we go about our business and become changed. Then, as we really hear these voices, we will have the chance to discover together the true meaning of historical suffering and begin to address its causes and hope for healing.

We hope for healing, because healing is still to be realized. We do not yet know how to attain the wholeness that we seek. There is no direct theology of healing, just as there is no direct theology of hope. The political cross means there is no way to hope except through Christ's image, the image of the "broken Christ," as Koyama says. Therefore, "brokenness" is the essential mark of pastoral theology informed by the political cross. Why? Because it is an inefficient theology encumbered by the demands for inner persuasion and communal participation in projects of reconciliation. It is a "limping" theology, because its place of origin is within history, where suffering is real and pain is relentless. It is a theology broken by historical contingencies and interrupted schemes of life. Because it is not a last-word theology, it must remain an open and self-critical theology, confessing that there is more to understanding this world where people and communities still bear the marks of brokenness.

And what about those who suffer in vain and without respite? They depend on those of us who are willing to bear witness and actively suffer in accordance with justice.[23] This is the way of the cross of the one who died

---

[23]Dorothee Soelle, *Suffering* (Philadelphia: Fortress Press, 1975), 150.

outside the city forsaken and abandoned, yet who also was raised from the dead and took the form of a community struggling to be faithful to the vision entrusted to it. Jesus' indirect way of healing and hope gives direction for what it means to express pastoral care via *theologia crucis:*

> It is true that Jesus was raised from the dead and lives not to counsel peace but to give it. But it is his own peace, the peace he had with the cross looming over him. Jesus does not philosophize or rhapsodize about resurrection; he embodies it, and his way there is known to us. It is the way of the Cross. Our hope lies in an Easter illumining but never negating Good Friday; a resurrection which does not obliterate or somehow correct the crucifixion but catches it up, transforming it into the power of self-giving love.[24]

The San Francisco Network Ministries illustrate pastoral care from the perspective of a political interpretation of the cross that does not obliterate historical suffering but somehow "catches it up, transforming it into the power of self-giving love." Its practices have historical roots, beginning with the ministry and crucifixion of Jesus. They reflect the theology of the cross articulated by Luther to address the church of his day, reinterpreted by Dorothee Soelle to reclaim a prophetic vision for her day, and spoken again by Douglas John Hall to address the current context in North America. These interpretations of the cross have always been pastoral theologies that address the eclipse of the holy in their respective times and places and are valuable perspectives for pastoral theology today.

Broken yet Beloved is inspired by the Network Ministries and stands with others who believe that pastoral theology can take more seriously the issues of culture by reclaiming our faith heritage. But pastoral theology cannot indiscriminately reclaim every tenet of faith. A theology of glory will never address the needs of our time. Today, pastoral theology needs to recognize our corporate failure, our awareness of life's spinning out of control, the abuses of life, and our too often unwillingness to do anything about them. In short, we need to reclaim our "mother tongue," spoken by the brokenhearted, so that we can more authentically work to create just and caring communities. Such is a political theology of the cross. As pastoral theology allows itself to become de-centered by the cross, it will find itself participating in projects of emancipation and liberation. Its method will be participatory and inductive and will rely heavily on a narrative approach.

A political theology of the cross is really a hopeful theology. It longs for the day when "God will wipe every tear from their eyes. Death will be no more; mourning and crying and pain will be no more, for the first things have passed away."[25] Such a faith yearns for resurrection and is

---

[24] *The Network Journal* (May 1983): 4.
[25] Revelation 21:4.

willing to work for this new reality. Resurrection means that the cross is not a last-word pronouncement on life. Resurrection means that the work of justice is ongoing and that everything is possible. Resurrection means that on the cross the life of struggle did not end. Struggle and sacrifice are imprinted on the lives of those who are willing to live into the eucharistic vision in which "sharing by all means scarcity for none." This is not a risk-free venture, and it requires our total commitment where we will become broken. Yet we are also promised something in advance. Perhaps these words of a former SafeHouse resident express it best:

> It will be hard and people will try to knock you off the path you are on and they'll try to get you to use again and you'll feel so alone and you'll cry and your tears will fill a bucket and that bucket will become your wishing well and then if you pray that bucket will become your mirror and you'll see the face of God.[26]

To see the face of God is a resurrection promise, a future-leaning hope gleaned from a political interpretation of the cross. Pastoral theology within this tradition means people will be brought down from the cross, and their tears, and then ours, will become beloved mirrors of the face of God.

---

[26] *San Francisco Network Ministries Newsletter,* December 1998, 4.

1442

Printed in the United States
76549LV00007B/351

9 780827 202320

DATE DUE

NOV 28 2015			
MAY 15 2018			